The New Deal

& American Youth

The University of Georgia Press   Athens & London

The New Deal
& American Youth

IDEAS & IDEALS IN A
DEPRESSION DECADE

Richard A. Reiman

The University of Georgia Press   Athens & London

© 1992 by the University of Georgia Press
Athens, Georgia 30602

Designed by Kathi L. Dailey
Set in Caledonia by Tseng Information Systems, Inc.
Printed and bound by Thomson-Shore, Inc.
The paper in this book meets the guidelines for permanence
and durability of the Committee on Production Guidelines for
Book Longevity of the Council on Library Resources.

Printed in the United States of America

96   95   94   93   92   C   5   4   3   2   1

Library of Congress Cataloging in Publication Data

Reiman, Richard A.
    The New Deal and American youth : ideas and
ideals in a depression decade / Richard A. Reiman.
        p.   cm.
    Includes bibliographical references and index.
    ISBN 0-8203-1407-2 (acid-free paper)
    1. United States. National Youth Administration—
History.   2. United States—Social conditions—
1933–1945.   3. Youth—United States—History.
4. New Deal, 1933–1939.
HV1431. R44   1992
362.7′0973—dc20   91-22124
                                         CIP

British Library Cataloging in Publication Data available

Contents

Acknowledgments

U nhappily, no attempt at a written appreciation can do justice to the many people who helped me see this book through to completion. As is usual, the scholars who mined the National Youth Administration (NYA) story before me are credited in the notes and bibliography. The same is true of the staffs of the Franklin D. Roosevelt Library and the National Archives. Unfailingly energetic and helpful without exception, these professionals left their imprint on every page.

Frank Freidel was one of seven scholars who read and critiqued the manuscript, always to good effect. While most readers were anonymous to me, and all recommended dramatic additions or redirection in focus, I often found their advice too wise not to adopt. Accordingly, each successive draft became not so much a revision of the old as a brand-new history of the NYA. Many of the substantive improvements achieved along the way must be credited in significant degree to these readers. I thank them for the suggestions they made that resulted in a better book.

The very earliest drafts of the manuscript were placed under the critical eyes of graduate students in Zane L. Miller's Urban Frontiers seminar at the University of Cincinnati. Their comments helped me gain a much better understanding of the intellectual thrust of the 1930s. I thank Professor Miller for his own numerous and always trenchant comments. When this project was still a dissertation, I was able to devote full time to the NYA as a result of financial assistance in the form of a Charles Phelps Taft Fellowship for 1982–83 and 1983–84. Subsequently, teaching positions at the University of Alabama, the University of Missouri at St. Louis, and especially Georgia Southern University provided the stimulating academic environment vital for any scholarly pursuit. Pat Tolzmann typed the initial drafts, always with speed, accuracy, and patience. With her enthusiasm and hard work, my teaching assistant, Tina M. Taylor, furnished me additional time to complete the revisions during the manuscript's final phases.

My editor, Karen Orchard, has been extraordinarily helpful in patiently guiding a first-time author through the labyrinths of scholarly book publishing. I thank Karen and the entire staff of the University of Georgia Press for their keen editorial judgment and careful assistance.

Of those who are indispensable to a book's existence, few are so important as the individuals who suggest the topic in the first place and who keep it alive at critical moments with their unfailing interest, gentle prodding, and inspiring scholarly example. It is a measure of the debt I owe to him that all these roles were played by one person, my dissertation director and friend, Roger Daniels. Whatever contributions to knowledge this book may lay claim to resulted principally from the concepts and concerns offered by Professor Daniels and those mentioned above. The errors that remain are, of course, mine alone.

Finally, I owe an inestimable debt to my family, who never faltered in the encouragement they offered to a project that must have sometimes seemed without end. Had it not been for the love and example of my mother and father, there would have been much less love of learning in my life and much less appreciation for the influence that principles can have on a flawed world. I hope that this book is, in some small way, a reflection of these things.

Introduction

The National Youth Administration appears in historical literature in two dramatically different guises. In writings about New Deal efforts to conserve human resources, the NYA is frequently dismissed as a "junior WPA" that occupied young people with jobs of more value to society than to the young themselves. To those tracing the depression-era origins of the civil rights movement, on the other hand, the NYA represents a liberal conscience seldom seen in New Deal actions. For the first group of historians, the NYA reflects the conservative vision of an administration seeking pragmatically to rescue rather than reform an educational establishment drained of students and funds in the depression.[1] For others, it appears as a harbinger of the course that liberals took on the issue of civil rights under the Johnson administration, as a foe of Jim Crow in an administration that usually tolerated racial injustice.[2] The NYA symbolizes to some what the rest of the New Deal might have been had all the alphabet agencies been so bold in their commitment to liberal reform. But for nearly all, it represents a Roosevelt agency that possessed few links or ties to the New Deal as a whole.

Yet the effects of the NYA, apart from its symbolism, were frankly conservative. Most of those young people whose parents had never been able to afford to assist them in acquiring a college education were no more likely to attend college after 1935 than before. The NYA saved rather than spread the dream of a college education, preserving rather than creating a century-old trend in which a greater percentage of the American people were attending institutes of higher education. Unquestionably, respect for the existing structure of American education would have suffered a greater depreciation in young minds had it not been for the NYA. By heading off a more serious movement to overhaul that structure, the New Deal retarded change in the schoolrooms of the nation.[3]

To read into the distant past the concerns of more recent times is to misunderstand the full scope of the NYA's plans for youth. Remembering the agency primarily for its famous alumni (playwright Arthur Miller, Peace Corps director Sargent Shriver, presidents Lyndon Johnson and Richard Nixon, among others) invites amnesia as to its raison d'être. Such a reading of the NYA implies that the NYA was designed primarily to assist those who had enjoyed access to America's educational opportunities before the depression and who might have lost possession of this American dream without the NYA. The NYA's brush with issues central to the nascent civil rights movement has fascinated historians as much as its rendezvous with future playwrights and presidents. The NYA initiated the first federal affirmative action program in history, an aid program for black graduate students. In 1938 the agency also convened the first federal conference on the plight of American blacks, a conference on the needs of black youth. The unofficial head of Roosevelt's black cabinet of advisers was Mary McLeod Bethune, director of the NYA's Division of Negro Affairs (the first intraagency bureaucracy within the federal government devoted to black problems). Within the New Deal, no one urged FDR to battle the poll tax or topple the pillars of southern economic feudalism and poverty as much as the NYA's Alabama-born executive director, Aubrey Willis Williams.[4]

Ironically, the NYA's very egalitarian moments indirectly drew attention to its liberal failings. The NYA's achievements invited comparison in the 1960s to Great Society accomplishments against which it could not possibly measure up. An agency very much of its times, the NYA could not fail to have had its conservative side, for the 1930s was a time when all the old verities were under siege and in transition. The NYA sometimes seemed designed more to rescue those with existing educational skills than to contribute to education reform and a more democratic social structure. No more than 37 percent of the jobless and out-of-school youth at any one time received NYA jobs between 1935 and 1943. For the educators who taught middle-class youth but failed to address the needs of low-income youth for varied forms of job training, the NYA represented both a threat to local control and an opportunity to continue teaching those whom they

had long taught.[5] The NYA provided a forum for discussion of black problems and outraged southern conservatives with some of its symbolic acts,
but it posed no threat to segregation (the NYA predeceased the poll tax
and Jim Crow by many years). Partly as a result, the NYA has usually been
regarded as an agency that possessed colorful personalities and a potential unrealized by its own administrators. "Prosaic" and "conservative" are
words used to describe its objectives and results.

Any description of the NYA as two-sided suggests that one is looking at
the parts of the NYA in isolation from the whole. In common with most of
the New Deal relief agencies, the NYA did have a conservative intent. Yet
it is also true that individual leaders of the NYA discouraged race discrimination wherever they encountered it and sought to modify an educational
structure they believed had broken faith with the American promise of
equal educational opportunity for all. But what Anthony J. Badger has described as the New Deal's self-limiting pragmatism ensured that the NYA's
first substantive assault on Jim Crow would also be its last.[6] NYA leaders
were frequently too willing to defer to the rigid segregationist climate of
their times in hopes that they might plan today for an assault against Jim
Crow tomorrow. Their sincerity cannot alter the fact that the more pro-
pitious moment for reform for which they were planning never came, at
least not during the New Deal.

From the perspective of later generations, however, the NYA was *both*
conservative and reformist in the sense that its administrators believed
that the conservation of some existing American ideals, in education and
citizenship training, required the reformation of a school system that had
long paid these cherished ideals only lip service. The NYA's real significance lies not in the degree to which it compares favorably with the Great
Society but in how it combined and brought to resolution the separate
strands of ideas about American youth as old as Horace Mann and the New
England transcendentalists and as recent as progressivism and the Great
Depression.

This book is about the intellectual origins of the NYA, the planning behind the creation, and the changing focus of the NYA between 1933 and
1943. I make no promise to treat comprehensively the story of what the
NYA achieved, although scholarship is just as needful of such a story.[7] The
premise of this book is that the nature of the New Deal and the American
mind in the Great Depression are more clearly illuminated by a chronicle
of what the planners of the NYA hoped to achieve than what the acci-

dents of politics, economic upturns and downturns, and war forced them to accept. I devote little attention here to the politics by which appropriations were pried from Congress or the extent to which student jobs were vocationally meaningful, interesting and important though these issues are.[8] Nor is this an administrative history of the NYA. Rather it is a story of the New Deal's intent to assist, enlist, and make use of youth in an effort to realize for the first time an old American dream of equal educational opportunity.

I contend that the NYA did not emerge directly as a response to the numbers of youth out of school and out of work in 1935. Instead it was a product of a curious alchemy between ideas about youth fashionable during the interwar years and fears for democracy in a decade of worldwide economic collapse and totalitarianism. To view the NYA in its planning stage and early evolution is to experience a surprise. The NYA between 1933 and 1938 was not what it subsequently seemed to be. The NYA possessed three purposes, not one. Moreover, the traditionally accepted notion of the NYA's cardinal objective—conserving existing educational patterns by rescuing existing students—turns the actual purpose for which the NYA was founded on its head.

First, the NYA's creators within the New Deal relief wing wanted to shock an American educational establishment perceived as elitist into accepting a halfway revolution of the nation's educational curriculum. New Dealers wanted the schools to serve a wider spectrum of the nation's youth. Certain that the depression had created a permanent economy of scarcity, the Roosevelt administration believed educators must supplement their middle-class-oriented curriculum (aimed at dispensing a traditional, humanist liberal arts education) with job-training courses. Only in this way would the millions of unemployed youth clogging the job lines in 1935 voluntarily reenter the schools. Only in this way would the millions more projected to matriculate into the breadlines of the future avoid that fate.

Yet educators between 1933 and 1935 were divided between conservatives resisting any change and radicals who saw hope only in a revamping of the whole political-social system.[9] The NYA planners perceived school officials as people possessed of an almost medieval hostility to reform, conservatives anxious to protect, guildlike, their prerogatives as deliverers of American education. Believing this, New Dealers designed the NYA to give existing educational professionals the choice of dispensing NYA "on-the-job training" (in hopes that such activities would become habit-forming) or watching the New Dealers undertake the work.

The NYA was thus designed in part to democratize the delivery of American education. It would extend the promise of equal educational opportunity to low-income youth but only temporarily alter the personnel doing the delivering. A temporary federal program along the lines of the NYA was necessary to prod the schools down a path whose destination was equal opportunity, but the program would be administered at the local level. New Deal planners hoped to exploit educators' enormous fears of the specter of federal control. They reasoned that even a federal program locally controlled (the NYA) would raise educators' hackles, prompting a demand for private control. The NYA, having established the principle of "learning by doing," would happily cede such control, having never desired it in the first place. After achieving their objectives—to change not the personnel delivering education but the curriculum and population receiving it—NYA officials would terminate their work. The NYA educational policy failed,[10] but it offers an intriguing glimpse into New Deal plans to promote a halfway revolution, a revolution to be completed not so much from above as from below.

Second, NYA planners, with the full knowledge and support of Franklin D. Roosevelt, desired to superintend and guide the minds of young people in the interests of both national security and the young people themselves. With the sole and special exception of the army, the NYA was the first federal agency concerned exclusively with youth to teach political education or citizenship training.[11] Passing in opposite directions during the 1930s, one falling and one rising, were two ideas that achieved their greatest influence at altogether different moments in the twentieth century. The waning idea was the notion born in America's first modern decade, the 1890s, that youth required physical conditioning and group organization under adult supervision and guidance for their successful integration into adulthood. Reflected in the creation of the Boy Scout movement in Britain in 1908 and the *Wandervogel* movement in Germany in 1901, this idea slowly declined after World War I. By the early 1930s, with so many young people entering colleges or aspiring to a college education, the notion that youth were more physical in activity than thoughtful had waned, but the notion lingered that youth still required organization under adult guidance, if not of their bodies then of their minds.[12] The problem of morale began to take precedence over the problem of morality.

The rising idea was the popular notion that the nation was in a permanent state of crisis, with the mind of youth the battleground between those seeking the nation's preservation and those thought to be seeking its destruction. This concern for the patriotism and plasticity of young minds waxed most dramatically in the American imagination between the depression and the end of the Vietnam conflict.[13] A rising anxiety about youthful anomie dovetailed in the Great Depression with an older conviction that young people required supervision in groups. The melding of these two views rendered a national youth organization attractive in the 1930s. It was then that a national program seemed necessary not merely to appeal to young people's patriotism but to organize and supervise them on behalf of that ideal thought to be most gravely threatened—democracy.

No federal agency in history had presumed to target the minds of a portion of its citizens for ideological maintenance. Yet, at the darkest of moments and with the best intention—the preservation of democracy— the NYA hoped to teach young people by example the "ropes" of self-government; that is, the practice, responsibilities, and rewards of citizenship. Although the NYA's concerns for organizing young people on behalf of the nation's dominant ideology may seem eerily reminiscent of fascist youth movements abroad, two factors reveal an unbridgeable chasm between them. The NYA objectives were varied, not monolithic, and were designed to assist young people as well as the interests of the larger society. Moreover, preservation of the status quo in all its features was not part of the NYA agenda.

When one examines the ideological intentions of NYA planners, a design familiar to those who have recently studied such agencies as the Civil Works Administration (CWA) and National Recovery Administration (NRA) emerges. Bonnie Fox Schwartz and Theda Skocpol, analyzing respectively these two agencies, argued that they represented no New Deal effort to "control" the "forgotten man" in the interests of conserving the power of large-scale corporate capitalism. Rather each was an effort to offer the forgotten man temporary means of support until such time as a modestly modified capitalism could, for the first time, live up to the old promise of offering equality of opportunity for all. The New Deal's attempt to make real the promise of capitalism, widening opportunities for "the forgotten man" within the existing free enterprise system, satisfied neither "corporate liberals" nor radicals on the left. Both "the economic royalists" and the Communists attacked the New Deal as the ally of their enemies, while in reality the Roosevelt reforms represented a holding operation for the old dream of a capitalism that would work for all. If the New Deal really intended to control youth's behavior and mold their minds (which it did not), it selected in the NYA an instrument singularly ill-equipped for that task. The NYA operated through a procedure whereby young people would learn self-government and a skill by working at jobs they or their neighbors selected themselves. If they were college students they would learn these things by working under supervisors of their own choice. The fact that the NYA's administrative structure was remarkably decentralized and locally controlled reveals how ideological instruction in America was altogether different from instruction in Germany during the same dark decade. The ideological approach to youth was as open and benign when mapped out in Washington as it was deceitful and malevolent in Berlin.[14]

This concern for the thoughts of youth and the future of democracy helped give rise to the NYA. But ironically, the intellectual climate that produced the NYA was almost completely snuffed out within five years of its creation. By 1940, radio broadcasts and newspaper headlines communicated to every American the threat to democracy. With conscription a reality and public opinion shifting toward the support of a limited form of collective security, the necessity for the NYA as a schoolhouse for citizenship responsibilities was no longer so apparent as before. Well aware that they had secured approval for their program as a result of national security fears, the NYA's original planners sought to save it by arguing that it remained as essential to that objective as ever. Congress could not accept an argument so increasingly difficult to sustain, and denied the agency further funding and life in 1943.

In a sense, however, time had not passed the New Dealers by between 1935 and 1943, though it certainly seemed that way to those aware of the NYA's public objectives. The Roosevelt administration had a *third* objective, one that was not publicized. Ultimately, the survival test that the NYA had to pass, year after year, was a continuing popularity and utility to Roosevelt's political strategies. At least until 1942, officials of the agency were able to demonstrate the requisite flexibility to tack with the political winds and remain aligned with the president's often inconsistent course. Roosevelt expected the NYA to fulfill not only his policy objectives but also the political needs of the presidential wing of the Democratic party. From the 1936 campaign through the 1938 effort at achieving party realignment, the NYA moved in a leftward direction along with the president. It thus helped Roosevelt retain the support of leftist elements within the Democratic coalition, which was no doubt one of his objectives. When Roosevelt shelved realignment as a political goal after the congressional elections of 1938, he called on the NYA as a minor aid in his effort to achieve a diminution of isolationism at home and a strengthening of collective security ties abroad. Politics continuously reshaped the NYA, an agency designed to advance Roosevelt's grander policies, whatever those were at any given moment.

The legacy and direction of the New Deal's plans for youth were always primarily a result of the ideas of the time. The NYA's post-1935 shifts in policy and its effect on future federal education programs emerged partly as a result of the clash between its intellectual origins and changing ideas on the domestic and international scene. For example, in 1933 college presidents and professional educators, fearing for the financial standing of their *institutions*, spoke of student enrollments and teachers' jobs as the heart of the education problem in the depression. The president, the First Lady, and Aubrey Williams, on the other hand, voiced deeper fears for the attitudes and educational destinies of *young people* themselves. Williams spoke of school leaders as the enemy, and Mrs. Roosevelt voiced her concern that "we may be losing this generation." [15] In word and deed the president seemed equally concerned with relieving the political pressure on behalf of youth and designing a program that would speak to the climate of ideas on the subject of youth. In 1935 that climate was suffused with fears for the future of the democratic way of life. As the climate of ideas changed, so changed the NYA. In 1938, as Roosevelt veered left domestically but toward collective security in foreign relations, the NYA embarked in a similar direction by abandoning some of its ideological training programs (the famous resident training centers) in favor of efforts to test public support for closer international relations (a refugee assistance program). In 1939 this trend continued as the NYA was retooled to train youth to work in industries vital to national defense. Riding piggyback on the war effort, the NYA expired in the very midst of the fighting.

Even though the NYA was disbanded in 1943, it is still remembered, although not without considerable amnesia regarding the agency's original intent. Subsequent generations, even as they have transposed an imaginary NYA for the one the New Deal made, have dismissed the NYA as an agency irrelevant to contemporary concerns. Few remember that the NYA assaulted educational problems that continued to endure after the war. As long as the NYA existed, it was possible to plan educational programs for the postwar era that would express the same educational concerns and procedures pioneered by the New Deal. The administrative provisions of the college student aid section of the GI Bill of Rights, for example, were redolent of the NYA. But soon the agency became a battleground for old New Dealers, politicians, and writers influenced by agendas the NYA's creators never knew.

As the NYA's ideological origins were forgotten, it appeared more and more as something it had never been: a "junior WPA" or a repository for "reds" of integrationist proclivities. A depression-era agency struck few observers as appropriate to a postwar America flushed with prosperity, especially since it was not understood that only one of the NYA's objects was to relieve unemployment. Had the NYA's ideological origins as an answer to totalitarianism been recalled in the late 1940s and early 1950s, it might even have been praised (especially in that anticommunist decade). In addition, it might have provided ideas to assist a nation wondering how to aid the impoverished "other America" blocked by poverty from access to education. But instead, the NYA was wrongly recollected as a response to an economic depression that seemed likely never to recur. The example of the NYA thus had a curiously negative impact on Great Society planners of federal student aid, who praised New Deal precedents while studiously avoiding student work in favor of loans (which remain the favorite method of providing college student assistance).

In a sense, of course, the collapse of communism in much of the world and the talk of a new world order have perhaps diminished the anxiety for democracy which so galvanized Americans of the 1930s. Therefore the ideological NYA described in this book may seem at first glance as irrelevant for Americans of the 1990s as the mythical NYA—the "junior WPA"—appeared to Americans of the 1950s. On the other hand, if as a result of the collapse of communism, the American penchant for crusading turns homeward, a national consensus may again identify a symbiosis between the welfare of the whole society and youth unemployment, as it did in the 1930s. The persistence of poverty among the members of the black underclass may be but one of the spurs to such action. Indeed, such a concern may be nearer than one might think, given America's recent experience in war. Just as the mere presence of American Indians among the doughboys of World War I sped the conferral of full citizenship rights on all native Americans in 1924, the "Double V" campaign by American blacks in World War II played no little role in generating the momentum behind the triumphs of the civil rights movement to come. The Persian Gulf War and the collapse of communism may contribute to the same sense

of national responsibility toward those who, in common with the past casu-
alties of ageism and racism, were its disproportionate victims: the young,
the poor, and the black.

Last but not least, the record of the "ideological NYA" should remind
Americans that not so long ago, the federal government thought that a
good way to preserve democracy was to employ and teach those too young
to know from experience the blessings of democracy. And in that quest
to shield the "American way of life," the agency taught democracy not
through faith, rote, or drill, but through the characteristically American
method that became the NYA's motto: "learning by doing."

CHAPTER ONE

The Old Deal
Defines the New

I n August 1933, President Franklin D. Roosevelt spoke to the press for the first time on a question of mounting public interest: the relationship between the New Deal and American students. In that season of mushrooming federal action, Roosevelt's cautionary words must have seemed to some like the strictures of a nineteenth-century Whig president, not the exhortations of a New Dealer. He insisted that his administration would do all it could to stay out of the business of channeling direct federal aid to high school graduates or their teachers. "If we start taking care of teachers," he explained, "we are beginning to give special consideration to a class, and if we do it for teachers, why shouldn't we do it for boilermakers?" Federal aid to students, too, raised "pretty serious" objections, Roosevelt added, "and the chances are ten to one that we won't do anything in the way of sending boys and girls to college."

Yet even as he delivered these self-abnegating words, the new president was fully aware of an intellectual ferment within his administration that was just then supplying the ingredients for a new deal on behalf of youth. Inside the Roosevelt administration and out, the concept of providing part-time jobs to students had been the focus of increasingly impassioned discussion. But the reasons for such a program also gave the Roosevelt administration a desire to hide from public view the broader ideological and reform objectives that lay behind it. Roosevelt's press performance provided a hint of the public relations problem involved in announcing even an idea whose time had arrived.[1]

The New Dealers had little immediate desire to publicize in advance the strands of ideas, both old and new, that were woven together to create the fabric of the NYA. No one disputed youth's need for some sort of federal assistance in 1933, but labor leaders, businessmen, and conservative educators worried publicly about the form that federal assistance might take. As was characteristic of him during the early New Deal, Roosevelt reserved his administration's ballyhoo and fanfare for administration programs that were going concerns, not those still on the drawing board. Where young people were concerned, he promised from the start that existing institutions, spurred by federal action to take a cooperative approach, would faithfully follow traditional approaches to the problems of youth.[2]

Behind the scenes, however, New Deal youth planners rejected so self-denying a position. The federal relief administrator, Harry L. Hopkins, had tapped architects of the New Deal youth programs from the fields of social work, American education, and industrial management who shared his own disrespect for the restraining methodologies of the same professions (respectively, "case work," inflexible local control, and engineering for profit and efficiency). Working with each other, such men as Hopkins, Aubrey Williams, Clarence M. Bookman, and Jacob Baker cobbled together the latest generation's ideas about "the youth problem" along with their own disrespect for precise models and established norms of procedure. The result was a program that functioned according to a set of recent and new ideas. Silently in 1933 and 1934, and publicly thereafter, the New Dealers hoped to realize the old objectives of these three powerful professions by shaking them free of their failed methodologies.[3]

Even Franklin Roosevelt's public promise to conserve youth cooperatively was not easily accepted by an America that liked to think of its past in individualistic terms. If Americans had known the full range of hopes that New Deal youth planners had invested in their work, conservatives would have had even more reason for alarm. To an unprecedented degree, the national youth agency they were planning would address itself to the needs of the historically undereducated and seek to supply those needs by permanently reforming the existing institutions of American education. The rhetoric of the first New Deal prepared America for a "junior" Works Progress Administration, not an unprecedented effort to train youth in democratic values and to spur education reform. Spokesmen for the relief and recovery programs of the administration stressed recovery by solidifying and working through the powerful organizations of the past: business trade associations, organizations of large farmers, and state bureaucracies and their social service constituencies. For a nation whose economy was on the brink of collapse, the first New Deal waged war on the depression with surprisingly familiar and modest weapons. The titles of New Deal legislation bore such words as "emergency," "relief," and "conservation," suggesting fondness for the economic structures that had failed the nation in the 1920s.[4]

The Roosevelt administration, dependent at first on a fractious coalition of competing interests, was reluctant to stir controversy by singling out youth from adults for special comment. Early in the New Deal, few Roosevelt advisers spoke publicly of their desire to superintend young people's education, even if for traditional goals. In fact, however, anyone who looked over the New Deal's emerging blueprints for the young observed an ambitious design. The architects of the New Deal for youth were drawing on memories and experiences older than the emergency of 1933, older even than the experience of World War I. These memories were inspiring them not to conserve but to dramatically reorder the politically delicate relationship between Uncle Sam, the schools, and the young. The hope that the Roosevelt administration invested in the NYA was as simple as it was unprecedented. The mere fact of federal training on an emergency basis, they hoped, would force educators to offer the same program on a more permanent basis within the schools. While working itself out of an educational function, the NYA would initiate the realization of Horace Mann's dream of equal educational opportunity for the poor and the rich and allow educators to garner the credit. But realization of this dream required that federal officials in 1933 and 1934 keep educators guessing about their intentions. The more educational problems assumed priority within the agenda of New Deal relief, the less was said publicly about these same plans. Accordingly, only a knowledge of the inheritance of the progressive reformers, the experience of Herbert Hoover, and the lessons learned by Franklin Roosevelt in the formative 1920s can account for a planning process so conservative in look yet reformist in promise.

HERBERT HOOVER and Franklin Roosevelt, while differing markedly in temperament, thoroughly agreed with progressivism's conviction that young people were Uncle Sam's special charges. Presidents from Theodore

Roosevelt to Hoover had honored the notion that young people occupied a special class. Exalting in speeches the idealism of youth, they had commissioned studies and conferences to explore the needs of the young. By supporting research alone and providing no direct line of aid to youth, the federal government paid homage to both the tradition of local control of education and the nascent national appreciation for youth as a group.[5]

Far from a spontaneous concept of the Great Depression, the New Dealers' assumption that the young were different from adults in more than size and skill was a product of late nineteenth-century urbanization and industrial growth. Americans of that age shared the Jeffersonian belief in the healthful effects of nature on human character (that nature *was* nurture). They retained an emotional distance from the city even as they moved there in increasing numbers. City life first brought masses of youth together in the schools, marking them off for special attention. The city, meanwhile, focused popular attention on the troubling lures popularly perceived to be lurking downtown. According to John and Virginia Demos, "the city loomed as the prime source of corrupting influences for the young." Moreover, not only did Americans believe that the city created special problems for young people, but the very fact that more Americans were residing in cities helped give rise to the *idea* of adolescence itself. The old pattern of life on the farm, where children and adults had shared similar tasks, militated against a conception of youth as a distinct group. But there was to be no returning to this pattern. Rural America was swept by an economic crisis of its own between 1890 and 1910, whose symptoms were increasing farm tenancy and out-migration. These problems and others spawned writings (such as those of Hamlin Garland and Harold Frederic) that identified rural America not as a romantic haven to which urban dwellers should return, but as an afflicted member of the body national. If the city offered the young only opportunities for corruption (as in Theodore Dreiser's *Sister Carrie*), the country offered no compensating refuge, no safety valve. In the city, moreover, young people had fewer economic functions and greater contact with their peers, a condition necessary for the development of a "youth culture." The chief (but by no means only) example of this urban phenomenon was the high school, where young people spent much of every day, rigidly segregated from their own youthful peers according to age. The Demoses traced the origin of this culture to the late nineteenth century.[6]

Meanwhile, the ideas of psychologist G. Stanley Hall and his followers gave immense scientific support to the concept of adolescence. Hall suggested that youth was a time of profound "storm and stress," in which the individual, through his emotions, "recapitulated" the most recent stage in the evolution of human development. Inspired in part by Darwinian principles, Hall theorized that nature forced on the adolescent a succession of conflicting psychological experiences through which each individual had to pass in order to gain the characteristics of a strong adult. In this volatile life stage, a youth was hyperactive one moment, apathetic the next; sociable in the morning, sullen and withdrawn by noon. Hall believed that for adults to avert this process of development, by requiring youths to concern themselves with the problems of adulthood, would be to deny the young people the emotional resources they would need in order to cope as adults. Given the nature of the city—which forced on too many youths a life of early industrial employment inconsistent with healthy play and emotional expression—adults did have a positive role to play in Hall's scheme. Through adult-sponsored youth organizations, young people would be shielded from the adult world. The recapitulation theory, which suggested that young people acted out the behavior of early man in the age of migration (with its patterns of superstition, myth making, and sagas), lent adults a model of action. They must send youths to the country, there to learn the ways of the wild and participate in communal games and storytelling.[7]

Groups such as the Boy Scouts (created in England in 1908 and extended to the United States in 1909), boys' workers of the early twentieth century, and leaders of Protestant youth-serving organizations (also known as "muscular Christians") eagerly seized on Hall's notions to justify their activities. They believed that young men required physical conditioning because their home lives were soft and their bodies flabby. The designation "young men" is appropriate because, almost universally, these organizations were aimed at boys, not girls. A Young Men's Christian Association (YMCA) publicist described psychology as "boyology." Lending support for Hall's ideas was the movement to encourage playgrounds for urban schoolchildren. The originator of the playground movement was Joseph Lee, an upper-class Bostonian who believed with Hall that youth's primitive instincts and potential lay in imaginative exploration of the environment through physical activity, and that the work world deprived them of it. The influence of machine work also drew Jane Addams's fire, and for the same reason. In *The Spirit of Youth and the City Streets* (1909), Addams expressed outrage at "the lack of public recreation" and "the connection between the monotony and dullness of factory work and the petty immoralities which are often the youth's protest against them."[8]

With a growing awareness of the special problems of children, reformers of the progressive era (1900–1920) waged a battle for the creation of juvenile courts, reform schools, and child labor legislation. By World War I the battle was far from won, but progressive efforts to aid children had achieved broad national support. Looking back on the successful struggle to achieve the Children's Bureau between 1903 and 1912, Lillian Wald characterized the era as a time when "intelligent interest in the welfare of children was becoming universal." It is quite clear, however, that progressives made a distinction between children and youth. The dividing line was well understood. As Representative M. Clyde Kelly of Pennsylvania put it in 1914, "The most priceless asset of this Nation . . . is the army of children, 30,000,000 strong, *under the age of fifteen years*, who live in this land of ours."[9]

The establishment of the Children's Bureau in 1912 indicated that progressives intended to attack specific institutions and problems that, for the sake of the children, needed to be reformed. The bureau was charged with investigating "the questions of infant mortality, the birth rate, orphanage[s], juvenile courts, desertion, dangerous occupations, accidents and diseases of children, employment, [and] legislation affecting children." But in the next seventeen years, and even into the depression, the movement to address the specific problems of children began to lose followers. Clarke A. Chambers has shown that steady gains were made in the 1920s in the mothers' pension movement, in the establishment (through the Federal Maternity and Infancy Act of 1921) of public health centers and prenatal clinics, and in the drive for mandatory school attendance laws. While such efforts improved children's position in American society, they did so indirectly, primarily through the agencies of the family, the school, and the clinic. The child-centered approach of the progressive education movement, led and publicized by John Dewey, itself exemplified the proliferation of attempts to model the child more effectively outside the family as a seemingly necessary supplement to the work within the home.[10]

World War I further encouraged a concern with children's well-being. Woodrow Wilson sponsored the second White House conference on children in 1919, setting a decennial precedent for such conferences that has continued down to the present day. The conference was spurred on by the world conflict, which reinforced the prewar trend toward greater federal analysis and treatment of children's problems. As Julia Lathrop described it, the war represented an embarrassment to leaders of child welfare in America because it focused attention on Europe, where reform measures were more advanced. Even more discomfiting was the fact that Europe had forged ahead with child welfare reform during, and in spite of, the war. "It was seen that, under circumstances of such difficulty that we happily cannot conceive, the civilized populations of Europe were achieving new laws for the protection of childhood," Lathrop wrote. "It was felt that the second year of the war in the United States ought to show a popular sense of responsibility for child welfare in some degree commensurate with our opportunities."[11]

In reporting on the conference for the Children's Bureau, William L. Chenery wrote that society, "in order to assure its own sound future, if for no more lofty motive, must rear all its children with a wisdom and a justice which hitherto have nowhere been attained. . . . The memory of the dread season through which the world has struggled is a potent inspiration to all to create a happier future." Chenery spoke of the many international participants in the conference, whose advice had been assiduously cultivated. "This was done because it was known that despite the stress of war, a splendid advance in the nurture of children had been made in Europe during the years immediately past." Although the war did not initiate federal interest in sponsoring programs to reform conditions for children directly (that interest had been growing since at least the administration of Theodore Roosevelt), the war did accelerate a trend already very much under way. In addition to transforming the United States into the world's leading economic power, the war awakened the nation's social service community to an awareness of international developments in the profession.[12]

AS A RESULT of the severe recession of 1921–23, a lesson learned in World War I was reinforced: the concept that the best government was the least government had no place where the needs of children and youth were concerned. In 1923 the Children's Bureau had suggested that "unemployment, because it means lowered family standards, had a direct and disastrous effect upon the welfare of children." Grace Abbott, the bureau's chief, reiterated throughout the 1920s the theme that youth was a social and possibly governmental responsibility. That notion later played a large role in shaping the conclusions of President Hoover's White House Conference on Child Health and Protection (1930).[13]

Even as reformers grew doubtful that the welfare of the child could be improved before that of society itself, the problems of an older group of young Americans increasingly seized their attention. Young people in their teens and early twenties were noticed in the 1920s to a greater degree than they had been earlier. If the conclusion was widespread that society held the key to children's salvation, it seemed equally true that Americans on the cusp of adulthood held the key to society's disruption. A growing cry was raised in the 1920s that teenagers and young adults were guilty of a trio of elementary sins: disregard for authority, rebellion against tradition, and allegedly unprecedented forms of sexual behavior. Society searched for evidence that it held the key to unlocking youth's problems as well. There seemed to be easy answers to the problems of children, but was this true of youth?

Youths (that is, people aged eighteen through twenty-five) seemed to threaten society in a different way. As much as children they required a form of adult supervision, but one whose components still had to be improvised and worked out. Hall's psychological theories were still exerting influence on American social thought in the 1920s, still convincing Americans that the problem of childhood was that children required society's helping hand—through adult-supervised group work—to become mature adults themselves. The optimism of the New Era supplied a reassuring corollary to that conviction: if children's problems required a social response, society possessed both the answer (exposure to nature under adult guidance) and the experts (family, school, and church) required to supply that response. But the dissent of youth raised a more forbidding specter to Americans of that optimistic generation. While not children, neither were youths adults. By threatening society's traditions, they, no less than children, seemed to require adult supervision. As with children, the necessity of self-preservation compelled society to address youth's challenges.[14]

The foreboding reality was that no easy answer comparable to that suggested for children presented itself in the case of "the youth problem." Adult guidance was necessary, yes, but what kind of guidance? The strictures and scientific theories of Hall, so attractive to a "machine age" generation in search of mechanistic and complete formulas for treating social problems, were empty of ideas for guiding the youth population of the 1920s because that population's demographic characteristics were radically different from those of the youth group Hall had known. Americans, dimly aware that youth posed a problem with no apparent solution, were unable even to suggest an intelligible, integrated formula before the depression. They therefore employed alarmist rhetoric about youth, as in the popular journals of the decade, or renewed the quest for programs to treat the easier problems of the child, as with Hoover's 1930 Conference on Child Health and Protection. Even at this conference, however, Hoover hinted of an awareness that youth's problems were primarily attitudinal rather than physical, largely governmental rather than private. Bereft of solutions, Hoover and other Americans at least spoke, if haltingly, of a problem of which the demographics of the decade had made them more than dimly aware.

Even if the labels of Hall and his contemporaries had been appropriate tools for social organization in the early twentieth century (1900–1920), they offered no solution for the problems of postwar America. In the 1920s, women in ever greater numbers were graduating from college. At the beginning of the decade, in 1920, 16,642 women received baccalaureate or professional degrees. They constituted about one-third of the total number of recipients of such degrees that year (48,622). By 1930, 48,869 of the graduates of baccalaureate and professional degree programs were female, or about 39 percent of the total number of graduates in these programs (122,484). Meanwhile, the proportion of Americans employed in "nonfarm" jobs rose from 63 percent to 73 percent during the 1920s. Young people were represented in the urban work force. The twin facts of a greater number of women in higher education and the rising importance of nonfarm employment in an urban nation discredited many of the inferences that Hall and others had drawn from *Adolescence*. Outmoded was the sexual bias implicit in such "causes" as "boyology" and "muscular Christianity," as well as the idea that the path to maturity lay in physical toughening. It became harder to believe that by placing young people in a setting of nature the instinctual seeds of adulthood planted in each youth's character would germinate as a matter of course.[15]

After 1920, moreover, the youth problem seemed to be less one of adults abdicating their responsibility to organize young people into groups than one of young people repudiating their superiors and initiating rebellion on their own. The titles of articles in middle-class periodicals of the decade betray a belief that young people, completely on their own, were flouting social mores and upsetting tradition ("Is Modern Youth Going to the

Devil?"; "This Wicked Young Generation"; "They are Hell Bent"; "Youth's Pagan Religion"; and "Motors and Morality"). Adults of the 1920s, certain that Stanley Hall had correctly perceived the need for adult supervision of youth, were now alarmed because youthful behavior seemed impossible to supervise through the older methods of Boy Scout camps and military drills. An approach to youthful *minds* now seemed necessary. Even before the Great Depression, when youth's economic problems would assume precedence over all other youth problems, concern about morale was beginning to grip a national conscience that once worried only about youth's morals. After the Crash, there was less talk about hip flasks and houses of prostitution on wheels, and much more on the prospects of a generation experiencing psychic disintegration with undesirable long-term social implications.[16]

It was the combination of youth's changing demographic profile with their peculiar behavior in the 1920s that increasingly convinced adults that teenagers and young adults represented a separate social species. More than ever before, young people were living and working like their parents and behaving in leisure time like aliens. As Robert and Helen Lynd noted in *Middletown*, the overly scandalous behavior of young people concealed a fundamental, middle-class conservatism. Girls who in dress and leisure time mimicked the flapper behaved with the utmost propriety at home and at church. This kind of artificial behavior was engaged in because young people, like their parents, accepted the Hallian notion that they constituted a separate, age-based culture, even as the external reality of the situation in education and employment increasingly mocked such a view.

In the 1920s, when more youths were involved either in the industrial marketplace or were receiving more advanced forms of education than their parents had received, young people were becoming the intellectual equals of adults at an early age. At the same time, they were segregated from adult society for a longer time. The result was the creation of an artificial youth culture, which young people accepted and embellished with inconsequential, if "shocking," behavior in their off-hours. Because it offered them the trappings of youth culture, such behavior enabled young people, like adults, to continue to believe in the appropriateness of the "group" conception of adolescence and young adulthood. Because it was artificial, their actual beliefs and important life decisions continued to be based on a value system differing little from that of adults.[17]

Yet, ironically, the more objective reality revealed the adultlike character of youth activities, the more young people appeared to "matter" to the rest of society as a separate age-defined class. The objective reality that young people were working, learning, and thinking like adults could just as easily have convinced observers that youth as a life stage had disappeared altogether. Instead, observers responded by drawing the conclusion that youth's adultlike behavior, in the context of their never-questioned "special needs," required even more adult supervision. The continued appeal of Hall's ideals in part accounted for this reaction.

But an enduring respect for Hall's ideas was not the only reason why the demand for adult supervision of youth became more audible in the 1920s. The notion accorded well with what many leaders of adult-directed institutions wanted to believe. The ethic of the Progressive movement, which Arthur S. Link has shown was very much alive in the 1920s,[18] identified reform as the replacement of the unfettered individual with a national community of cooperating organizations and groups. A more specific example is "social education," a reform pushed by a group of imaginative educators roughly between the years 1910 and 1925. Educators grew convinced that their schools must become socializing institutions, for such an undertaking seemed a viable response given the ever-larger proportion of American youths forced into the schools by compulsory attendance and child labor laws. Social educators hoped to transform the school into a regulator of youthful behavior. They also hoped to condition young people for life membership in a series of socioeconomic groups. One analyst of social education wrote in 1929: "The modern community is not real enough, not sufficiently organized to provide the old-time social integration as a matter of course."[19]

In the 1930s, leaders in government would find it but a small step to enlist the socialization techniques in the service of the state as well as the society. If the 1920s generation seemed to ignore this possibility, it was only because American society, not American government, seemed to require assistance. The depression put strains on both and gave social work administrators the idea of organizing young people into groups in order to provide instruction in the nature and value of their government.

IN THE YEARS before and after World War I there had been a heightened awareness of the problems of children and youth in America. By the end of the 1920s, however, an ironic situation had developed. While social workers and government leaders continued to write, study, and seek solutions for these problems, they now concluded that children would benefit far more from programs designed to assist the family (and ultimately society) than from direct efforts to reach children. The result was that Americans lost interest in sponsoring government efforts to assist children directly, even as they expended time and money to examine the plight of the youngest Americans. Meanwhile, the plight of youth increasingly drew the attention of American political leaders but not the resources they controlled. The nature of the 1930 White House conference and the view on children and youth of the president who sponsored it provide one illustration of these paradoxes.

When Herbert Hoover noted, in his news conference of 2 July 1929, that he would convene the nation's third White House conference for the study of child-related problems, his listeners must have been surprised less by the idea than by the scope of the endeavor. The president announced that the conference would study "problems of dependent children, of regular medical examinations, of school or public clinics for children, hospitalization, . . . maternity instruction and nurses . . . , facilities for playgrounds and recreation, voluntary organization of children, child labor," and "scores" of other subjects. He added, however, that whatever recommendations were made would have to be implemented by private citizens, not the federal government. Indeed, the conferees themselves were "representatives of the great voluntary associations." The Hoover conference was funded by $500,000 collected from "purely private sources," and its purpose was to develop measures "for more effective and voluntary action and coordination" in an effort to protect and care for children.[20]

Although Hoover's public comments sometimes suggested otherwise, a generation of thinking about young people was subverting his own attachment to voluntarism in this one area of American life. Hoover preferred that the conference do nothing more than assist the real experts in child socialization (the family, school, and community) in their self-directed roles. The conference would only "advance those activities in care and protection of children which are beyond the control of the individual parent," he promised. The responsibilities of parents would not be "invaded," for the government did not know as well as they what was best for children. The society could do no more (but should do no less) than give "its mite of help to strengthen mother's hand [so] that her boy and girl may have a fair chance."

At the same time, however, Hoover believed that federal assistance to the family was an obligation the nation owed itself. Aid to the family was something akin to an act of national self-preservation. More than the interests of the child were at stake when the government assisted the family. For, as Hoover declared, "anything that strengthens the family and gives a deeper significance to family life is salutary, not only for the family, but for the nation. . . . The problems of the child are not always the problems of the child alone. In the vision of the whole of our social fabric, we have loosened new ambitions, new energies. We have produced a complexity of life for which there is no precedent."[21]

Hoover shared with leading sociologists of his day the idea that America's generational, racial, and ethnic groups were so many potentially warring elements in society, made dangerous to the whole by "cultural lag." The definition of the "problem" of "cultural lag," as coined by William F. Ogburn in the 1920s, lent an added sense of urgency to its solution. The theory held that modernization in technology had always advanced at a pace that exceeded the ability of people to adjust their ideals, values, and beliefs to those same changes. The dizzying technological advances of the consumer age of the 1920s widened the gulf even further. The implication of cultural lag theory was that social integration required some sort of federal ordering of the discordant elements of society until culture could catch up with technology. The alternative to such mastery was a national drift leading to disorder and all manner of social problems. Some kind of federal assistance was needed to assist, not coerce, social groups to keep pace with rapidly changing technologies. At issue was the social peace of the whole society. Accordingly, even as Hoover's native opposition to direct federal intervention in individual affairs appeared in his speeches, he committed the federal government to examine needs of the child formerly ignored by Washington. In other ways the Hoover conference was placing the presidential imprimatur on a concept gaining intellectual currency: the idea that federal involvement in the socialization of youth was as vital for the harmony of the society as for the individual youths themselves.[22]

Hoover found it impossible to keep the youth problem off the agenda of a conference on children. The rhetoric he employed suggested that he regarded young people, even more than children, as security risks to the nation. He further suggested that youth required supervision of their attitudes as much as their physiques, and not only for the sake of each youth's individual future but for the sake of American democracy.

When children became "youths," Hoover argued, their primitive nature rendered them potential threats to political stability and an appropriate concern for government. Efforts to restore young Americans to physical health would not by themselves guarantee their mental and physical well-being. Hoover employed the imagery of nature to characterize young people, casting them in elemental, romantic terms. "Each of our boys," he said in 1930, is "a growing animal of superlative promise, to be fed and watered and kept warm." Unlike children (who could not immediately retaliate for improper care), the youth group might either be "a joy forever" or "the incarnation of destruction." Young people were at once "the problem of our time and . . . the hope of our nation." They therefore required a more extensive contact with nature than currently was their lot in a predominantly urban nation.[23]

Hoover did not believe that youth would seek consciously to undermine democracy, but that young people would be unable to uphold its fragile structure without the proper kind of education. The time before adulthood, he wrote, "is the plastic period when indelible impressions must be made if we are to continue a successful democracy." He hoped that along with the "three R's," educators would add one other, "responsibility—responsibility to the community—if we are not to have illiteracy in government." In 1930 the president praised both the Boy Scouts and America's teachers for "guiding our children in the first steps of democracy." The common task of all Americans, he added, "is to give every child the opportunity to grow up with a healthy body, a trained mind, a disciplined character, a cheerful faith in himself, and a devotion to our form of government."[24]

Hoover's words implied that something would have to be done to salvage the physical and spiritual health of young people. If the city provided the young with "stunted" and "morbid" minds, an improper diet, and an unnatural play place, then surely action was needed either to transfer the youth to the country or to bring the valued features of the country to the youth. Far from merely implying this, Hoover explicitly demanded action. "Some of the natural advantages of the country child," he said, "must somehow be given back to the city child—more space in which to play, contact with nature and natural processes. Of these, the thoughtless city cheats its children."[25]

Of course, it was Franklin Roosevelt, not Herbert Hoover, who called for the creation of a Civilian Conservation Corps (CCC) to send the unemployed from the city to the forests, there to receive good food and renewed hope. Although the problems Hoover associated with youth (poor diet, a difficult home life, and inadequate contact with nature) were among the problems the CCC ultimately confronted, Hoover never countenanced federal action to deal with them. In his few veiled references to the New Deal youth agencies, he suggested that these programs, while advertised as job-training initiatives, were creating a class of Americans permanently dependent on welfare. Under the Works Progress Administration (WPA), he declared in Kansas City on 28 September 1938, "great numbers of self-reliant people are being inexorably moulded into the hopelessness of a permanent army of relief. . . . And American youth is being poured into this mould." Two years later, Hoover insisted that solutions for a national unemployment rate whose "hardest impact has been upon youth" would only come when "we . . . reverse our national drift toward State-ism [and] resolutely turn from government spending to national thrift."[26]

Yet Hoover's precise attitude toward the role of the federal government in education and recreation was not so clear as these pronouncements seem to suggest. When asked by a friend late in 1933 whether he would have signed most of the New Deal legislation of the "hundred days," Hoover thought a moment and replied, "I think I would." As Albert U. Romasco has demonstrated, it was Herbert Hoover who first denied what had always been an article of faith in national policy: that cyclical oscillations in the economy were either impervious to federal correction or constitutionally beyond the federal government's jurisdiction to control. Hoover intervened to reverse the economy's downward spiral. If the intervention was inadequate in scope, it nevertheless was an important symptom of a new attitude toward the federal role, one Franklin Roosevelt would elevate to a new plateau, but not create. As Hoover noted in November 1938, he, no less than FDR, wanted "increasing public health services, spread of medical attention, hospitalization and education. All these and many more resolute objectives of progressive men were going concerns before the New Deal was born. The New Deal deserves credit wherever it has in reality advanced them."[27]

Hoover steadfastly believed that local or private groups (teachers and Boy Scout leaders among them) could maintain, in all its fullness, young people's abundant faith in the democratic processes of American life. The implication, however, was that if the latter assumption proved incorrect, the federal government would have to assume the burden of "saving" youth, since the Constitution (as interpreted by presidents from Lincoln to Wilson) provided the national government the authority to ward off political threats to itself. Although Hoover never drew these conclusions from his ideas, the ideas themselves (reinforced by the weight of tradition) nevertheless indicated a new perspective on American youth. Later, those same ideas could be, and would be, used to support the creation of New Deal programs to aid the young. Herbert Hoover's conception of adolescence, then, far from indicating old ways of thinking, pointed the way toward the perspective of the New Deal on "the youth problem."

THE FORMATIVE ideological influences on New Deal youth planners were not simply ideological or institutional, to be found only in progressive ideas or the legacy of Herbert Hoover's "New Day." They were also to be found in the personal experiences of those living in the 1920s, experiences that were in some cases searing. Franklin Roosevelt's own intimate encounter with one of that time's most dreaded ordeals of youth, poliomyelitis, had implications that added to the significance of the 1920s as the seedtime decade for New Deal youth policy.

Roosevelt's direct personal involvement in New Deal youth planning dated from the spring of 1935, after the politics of two years of upheaval had rendered a "national youth administration" almost inevitable. Although the president's overt influence on administration policy toward young people came rather late, Roosevelt's indirect and long-standing role in the NYA's evolution may have been just as important. His idea of what American society and government owed its disadvantaged youth had been developing since the war. In 1922 Roosevelt headed the New York Boy Scout Foundation, then actively engaged in purchasing a mammoth summer camp in Sullivan County for New York City boys. That year about seven thousand boys from the five boroughs of New York City and surrounding counties had attended the foundation-owned Kanohwanke Camp in the Palisades Interstate Park. Only about twenty-five hundred boys could be accommodated at any one time, however. Dissatisfied with the scope of their effort, foundation officials in 1927 purchased eleven thousand acres along the Delaware River in Sullivan County. They planned to build a camp large enough to serve ten thousand boys simultaneously. While this goal was still a dream when Roosevelt became president of the United States, the camp was built and did assist thirty-five hundred boys each day. Purchased for $300,000, the campsite consisted of eleven thousand acres located about twenty miles from Monticello, New York. The tract encompassed three large estates, 104 buildings (including hotels and bungalows), and twelve lakes. The camp served as an example in microcosm of what an organized group might accomplish with finite resources. The foundation's success in acquiring such a large campsite no doubt fortified Roosevelt's faith that the federal government would not be overextending itself in launching the nationwide camp system that became the CCC.[28]

Roosevelt's interest in the Sullivan County camp and in scouting in general probably owed itself in part to the political advantage of being identified with an undertaking so obviously uncontroversial and beneficial to the community. But what may have originated as a politically useful diversion became something more in the years after he was stricken with polio in 1921. For several years after his illness, Roosevelt's opportunities for the kind of continued public exposure so critical to any politician were usually limited to the intrastate and philanthropic endeavors that the Boy Scout Foundation offered in abundance. Indeed, long after he had passed the critical stage of his illness and had recovered his mobility, Roosevelt worked to cultivate the image of a recuperating statesman. Such a stand spared him involvement in the internecine battles between rural and urban elements of the Democratic party. Given the political restrictions he chose to accept, one of the few activities that remained open to him was his work with the Boy Scouts. Moreover, his own ailment, because it was popularly regarded as a children's disease, no doubt generated within him a deeper appreciation of the problems of the very young. As for his interest in scouting, that too may have achieved a personal sort of poignancy after 1921. The final known photograph of Roosevelt walking unassisted was taken at a foundation meeting in the Palisades camp during July of that year.[29]

Roosevelt felt a special kinship with those who shared his affliction, most of them children. After establishing Warm Springs, Georgia, as a center for rehabilitation from the disease, Roosevelt made special efforts to accommodate the social as well as the physical needs of young adults. At the Warm Springs Foundation, all patients were encouraged to strive for self-reliance regardless of their age. According to Hugh Gallagher, "The youthful patient population at Warm Springs added to its vitality. Roosevelt is said to have felt strongly that these young people needed to be encouraged not only in their social life but in their sexuality." Boys and girls hired as wheelchair "push" persons took patients wherever they wished to go, encouraging a sense of independence and mobility. In terms of their rehabilitative needs and activities, the youth of Warm Springs were often as much an inspiration to FDR as he was to them. An empathy for the problems of youth could easily have emerged from this unusual relationship.[30]

Roosevelt's tenure as governor offered him the opportunity to translate these concerns into functioning examples of governmental oversight of youth. Some of the first relief ventures planned in Albany involved the employment of young men. When New York amended the state constitution in 1931 to provide $20 million for reforestation over twenty years, Commissioner of Agriculture Henry Morgenthau worked with FDR on a conservation program. They thought of such things as the conservation of human resources and the need to prevent social alienation among those more susceptible to it. They agreed that youth represented the charges of society whose conservation seemed most likely to benefit society for the longest period. John M. Blum believes that in two years the men experimented with programs that furnished the precedent for both the CCC and the NYA. Besides putting ten thousand men to work planting trees, Morgenthau pored over lists of idle youth provided by New York City social workers and sent these young men to the woods and back each day. Over the next four years, Morgenthau wrote, "We took the gas house gang, the bad boys who were loafing on the streets and getting into trouble, and we put them on the four a.m. train that ran up to the Bear Mountain area where they worked all day. Then, because there was no housing for them, we took them back at night." Meanwhile, on Morgenthau's suggestion, Roosevelt pushed for a state constitutional amendment calling for the expenditure of $20 million over the next twenty years for the reclamation of state lands outside the Adirondacks. These lands offered another potential setting for the employment of idle youth. The central place that young people occupied in Roosevelt's thinking about relief was demonstrated by the fact that the New Deal's first relief effort, the CCC, was largely an assault on youth unemployment.[31]

Ever sensitive to the approach of political dangers, FDR must have been keen to the fact that two utterly different ideas were on a collision course during 1933. On the one hand, the air was heavy with the conviction that a united nation ought to wage war on the depression with the resources of the existing industrial society. The National Recovery Administration empowered businessmen to lead the nation out of the economic collapse very much as the War Industries Board had marshaled industry for victory in World War I. As Thomas McCraw wrote, "the New Dealers talked incessantly of the 'public interest' even as their multitudinous agencies laid the institutional basis for its fragmentation among particular groups." In 1933 the New Deal may have brokered the demands of discordant groups by offering an alphabet agency to each. But Roosevelt's rhetoric revealed his understanding that the nation wanted to believe that the New Deal would forge a national consensus. Much of the nation desired a New Deal that would accomplish recovery not through discriminating favors dispensed to individual groups or the creation of a new America but through a unified national effort. Many wanted recovery to preserve, not recovery through change. That is one reason Roosevelt told the press in August 1933 that he was reluctant to set groups apart from the whole and provide special federal aid to teachers or students.[32]

Yet there was another climate of opinion with which Roosevelt had to reckon, one threatening a political storm over the New Deal if he did not approve federal aid to youth. This was the history of ideas stretching back to the nineteenth century that demanded a social ordering of youth's development. Psychologists such as Hall joined Progressives and presidents in urging private groups to take up their responsibility to shepherd young people to adulthood. The 1920s supplied the successive shocks of a thoughtful population of college-matriculating youth and a Great Depression against which traditional organizations like the Boy Scouts had neither answers nor resources. The newer sociological prescriptions offered for these problems—federal supervision of young people—dovetailed with the growing conviction that all individuals, old and young alike, could be rendered socially "safe" only through their treatment as members of discrete individual groups. As FDR declared in 1932, "Any neglected group . . . can infect our whole national life and produce widespread misery."[33]

Thus the New Deal could not deny or evade the influence of a long, formative heritage of ideas on the youth problem. Because they shared the conviction that unsupervised youth threatened the whole society, the

Roosevelt planners never doubted that an effort at federal supervision of youth was a New Deal right and responsibility. The peculiar political dynamics of 1933, however, simply rendered it impolitic for Roosevelt to discuss his plan for a parochial assault on the youth problem. Even so, the president's correspondents were writing him that the crisis of democracy made ideological maintenance an urgent national imperative. At the same time, relief planners were maintaining that a gap between graduation and employment was yawning ever wider as educators ignored their job-training responsibilities. Any New Deal announcement of a plan for ideological maintenance and direct federal job training would collide with the popular desire in 1933 for sacrifice, unity, and the employment of existing institutions, inviting the disaster of political misrepresentation and public misunderstanding. To do nothing, however, might invite the greater disaster of the loss of American youth to anomie and totalitarianism.

Roosevelt's answer was to permit the priorities of his relief administrators and the pressures of the public to set his youth agenda through 1933 and much of 1934. He decided to support publicly only a modest program for youth that already enjoyed a powerful and vocal constituency: college student aid. But as his advisers continued to bring to his attention the connection between young people and democratic dangers, Roosevelt came to conclude that a bolder approach to the youth problem might well be in order, provided it could be packaged in familiar wrapping. He then drew once again from the well of past ideas and permitted his relief advisers to plan a silent reconstruction of the nation's posture toward youth and education.

CHAPTER TWO

Schooling for Democracy,

1933–1934

As president, Roosevelt had a constitutional obligation to preserve the commitment of all Americans to democratic values and political procedures. As a humanitarian and a reformer, he had an additional deep desire to push the promise of equal educational opportunity closer to reality. During the first hundred days of the Roosevelt administration, however, New Dealers gave higher priority to recovery than to reform. Supremely confidant in the patriotism of American youth, Roosevelt had to be tutored in the connection between ideologies of despair and the idleness of depression youth. The president proved to be a quick learner, partly because it was so clear that educators were failing to meet even their traditional responsibilities in 1933. In 1934 the New Deal began to occupy the educational void and move against the interdependent problems of anomie and idleness.[1]

In 1933 and 1934, several of the president's correspondents and relief planners concluded independently that their deepest concerns might best be alleviated through a federal undertaking of certain historically local educational activities. Each of the two groups emphasized a different aspect of the youth problem. Nevertheless, both lobbied for different reasons for a federal training program for high school and college students. The first faction, a trio of unofficial Roosevelt advisers, presented FDR with a warning articulated best by one of the economic advisers in Roosevelt's

31

brain trust, Charles W. Taussig. Tyrants abroad, they agreed, were turning European youth against democracy, exploiting the idealism native to
all youth, and demonstrating how easily America's young might suffer a
similar experience. Taussig urged the president to make the New Deal
the political and ideological schoolmaster of those young people anxious
to graduate from high school or enter college but financially unable to do
so. These seemed to be potential converts to the class of the American
disgruntled, the young people most likely to voice doubt about American
institutions and democracy itself.[2]

Throughout 1933 Taussig and two other Roosevelt correspondents high
in business and academia and prone to theory were driven by completely
unrelated experiences half a world apart to warn Roosevelt of youth's sus-
ceptibility to demagogic appeals. Marching Hitler Youth in Germany and
quarreling Socialists and Communists in America were on the three different minds, but however different their recommendations for action,
all three advised that the dictators be defeated with their own weapon:
training in ideological values.

Roosevelt accepted the premise of these social critics that American
youth required ideological maintenance for democracy's sake. He rejected, however, their conclusion that the maintenance should take place
through the raw methods of classes in political theory or the mindless
regimentation of youth through their inclusion in NRA parades and New
Deal ballyhoo. Unknown to these correspondents and critics, a second
faction, the relief planners, were supplying FDR with a method for ideological maintenance honoring the American tradition by supplying youth
not a ready-made future but merely an opportunity to shape a future in its
own image. Relief officials favored a solution to the problem of democratic
values that mirrored the American past, not the European present. They
hoped to preserve the real meaning that the phrase "Go West, young
man" had held to generations of youth by offering youth the materials out
of which to carve a life according to their own design.[3]

Relief planners within the Federal Emergency Relief Administration
(FERA) were bringing to Roosevelt's attention a crisis in American education that at once threatened to compound the crisis of ideology and furnish
a solution to it. In 1933 and 1934, tens of thousands of youths, despair-
ing that the schools would ever offer them the job training demanded by
a depressed economy, were abandoning the schools. Leading educators,
obsessed by a crisis that existed largely in their own imaginations—the

myth of an imminent radical takeover of their profession—were largely ignoring the real crisis of angry but reluctant dropouts. The (unrealistic) ideological concerns of educators were threatening to create real battalions of disaffected youth. Indirectly a product of misdirected worries about the future of local control of American education, these numerous un-noticed young people might pose a real threat to democracy. The answer seemed clear: not ideological training but simply the provision by Uncle Sam of the kinds of skills both the young people and the existing econ-omy demanded. The result would be not only a thoroughly conservative and American re-creation of Horace Greeley's West of opportunity but an antidote to youth's radical tendencies that gave young people what they themselves wanted. The hope, at least in the White House, was that this effort would last only as long as the educators' shortsightedness in neglect-ing their own responsibilities. The New Deal would shield democracy and spur education reform, but only for the duration of the emergency within American education. The New Deal would merely pave a saving road between democracy and education, starting with aid to college students.

ALTHOUGH THE WHITE HOUSE came to share in the growing con-cern for youth's democratic loyalties, Franklin Roosevelt was resistant to such concerns from the start. The new president shared much the same cast of mind as the old toward the youth problem. Just as he retained a few of Hoover's Treasury officials to draft emergency banking legislation, Roosevelt drew on ideas as old as William James's concept of national service as "a moral equivalent of war" to create the CCC. Physical con-ditioning and the conservation of morals, not morale, were on his mind. Fresh air, hard work, three square meals a day—these would rescue young people, Roosevelt believed. Although, to Hoover, the CCC obliterated the necessary middleman between federal aid and assisted youth, the CCC was still the realization of Hoover's desire for a national program to keep the youth "fed and watered and warm."[4]

Nevertheless, the transition from an "interregnum of despair" to the action of the New Deal signaled a renewal of hope and intellectual fer-ment. At precisely the moment when the intellectual order was splintering into shards dangerous to America, the nation received a badly needed stimulus to its confidence in government's capacity to achieve a domestic order. No one could at first foresee the degree to which dictators abroad would mobilize young people behind their ideas, but the spectacle of the regimentation of the young fascinated Americans at the New Deal's outset. Roosevelt's foreign and domestic correspondents alike drafted letters and plans, instructing him that an American youth movement, under federal auspices, was both possible and desirable. Such a movement, they counseled, might be essential to keep youth aligned behind democracy. They were not the only sources of advice on the youth question, however. And Roosevelt's own hierarchy of objectives for the nation was crucial in determining the degree of credence and support he provided the different proposals for youth that others were bringing to his attention.

The old method of physical exercise and conditioning by which society looked after young people seemed singularly ill-designed to meet the threat of a Hitlerian world. No matter how elastic Theodore Roosevelt regarded the Constitution to be, he seems never to have considered stretching it to cover manipulation of young people's political thoughts. A rational, Victorian faith in the innocence of the young persuaded TR that youth's ignorance of political ideologies was neither a threat nor a concern for the nation. In the wake of World War I, however, pessimism about political stability and despair for the future became a theme unifying the writings of such otherwise dissimilar critics as Oswald Spengler, Albert Einstein, and F. Scott Fitzgerald. The indolent Harding and Coolidge administrations did not notice that young people, matriculating from college in growing numbers, might participate in the intellectual trend of devaluing individual autonomy in favor of the needs of the masses. Largely a phenomenon of the Great Depression, the radicalization of European youth escaped even Hoover's attention, harassed as he was by crashing banks and marching veterans.[5]

After 1929 there were mounting incentives for an ideological approach to what was increasingly labeled "the youth problem." How, after all, could training in square knots by the Boy Scouts or swimming lessons at home successfully compete with the popularity of demagogues shouting at youth to sacrifice, not play, and become the saviors of their nation rather than its burdensome children. By the mid-1930s, Germany, Italy, and the Soviet Union, as well as such Western democracies as Great Britain, France, Czechoslovakia, Belgium, and Switzerland, had established work camps for unemployed youth. Italian boys joined the Young Fascist organization on their eighteenth birthday, thus embarking on a regimen of political and military indoctrination. The Soviet Union provided "allowances" to assist university students to complete their educations. Through the Communist Union of Youth, Soviets trained the young to fill positions available in industry and agriculture and taught them military skills. Henceforth, the operative assumption in each nation was that the powerful hold of political ideas on young minds could no longer be doubted or ignored but must be considered in the design of each country's national security policy. The military aspects of most European youth programs would figure prominently in the minds of Americans pondering the fate of their own jobless youth.[6]

Such a concern for youth could scarcely have been more alien to most Americans, who identified youth (past and present) as the conquerers of the frontier and the creators of American democracy. Youth were to be loosed on the landscape, not reined in; prized, not feared. It was precisely this conviction that increased the shock of thinking Americans witnessing the popularity of antidemocratic ideas with German youth. Membership in the Hitler Youth soared between 1933 and 1939. A state-run organization that purported to provide young people a means of gaining fitness and a recognition of their importance in a supposedly "classless" nation, the Hitler Youth in fact attempted to regiment youth into an unthinking loyalty to the fascist regime. Not until March 1939 was membership compulsory, yet enrollment climbed from 55,000 in January 1933 to 3,577,565 by the end of 1934, and to 5,437,601 two years later. While the Hitler Youth conferred special favors on the enlistees and their parents, no one doubted the enthusiasm with which many took to Nazi ideas in an organization that by 1936 had become, according to Peter D. Stachura, "probably the largest youth organization in the world."[7]

The humane liberal democrats who advised the president did not quite know what to make of the Hitler Youth and its equivalents. That such programs warranted condemnation was never in doubt. The question was whether the New Deal ought to establish a democratic alternative to the Hitler Youth. In other words, an important thrust of the early New Deal was to hold adults to their patriotic loyalties by demonstrating that a democracy was just as capable as a dictatorship of fulfilling the health and employment needs of its people. Should not the New Deal establish a program to impart this lesson to the young? A significant faction in the New Deal thought the answer to this question was yes. While only a minority emphasized the problem of political radicalism as the decisive factor justifying action (most worried more about morale, unemployment, and the potential for anomie), they comprised a minority close to the president's ear and high in his respect.

What made this minority especially insistent that FDR act was the stark and frightening contrast between American youth's apparent disdain for the democratic reforms the administration had already advanced and the facility with which completely contrary ideas were holding European youth spellbound. William E. Dodd, Roosevelt's ambassador to Germany; Edward A. Filene, Boston department store executive and head of the Massachusetts NRA; and brain truster Taussig all subscribed to the "progressive" school of American history, the interpretation that America past and present was shaped by the slow if inevitable triumph of the democratic working-class interests over the conservative higher classes. Viewing conflict as inevitable and desirable, Dodd, Filene, and Taussig felt certain that they were on the side of an afflicted minority soon to triumph.

Dodd, an optimist, initially believed, in the words of Neville Henderson, that the "good" side of Nazi Germany would triumph as conservative leaders restrained Hitler, "the monstrous specimen of a debased humanity." "It is impossible to say whether the new regime is going to take a more liberal or more ruthless direction," he cabled in July 1933. All revolutionary movements, he wrote, tend to "swing a little bit to the right as soon as they are firmly fixed." Roosevelt, however, evaluated the regime with less hesitation. "I sometimes feel that world problems are getting worse instead of better," he wrote Dodd in November. Alluding to Walter Lippmann's theory, he suggested that "about 8 per cent of the population of the entire world, i.e., Germany and Japan, is able, because of imperialistic attitude to prevent [peace] on the part of the other 92 per cent of the world." Within a year, Dodd had lost some of his optimism and was nearing agreement. "The Hitler regime is composed of three rather inexperienced and very dogmatic persons," he cabled the White House, "all of whom have been more or less connected with murderous undertakings in the last eight or ten years." Not since ancient Rome, he said, had the world witnessed such a triumvirate, "and you probably recall what happened [then]."[8]

If, as Robert Dallek noted, Dodd eventually realized that "he was up against ruthless, unreasonable men" who would not be moderated by the course of history, his faith in that very course helps explain the longevity of his optimism. What did not fit in Dodd's schema of a struggling humanity against Hitler was the support given the latter by one of humanity's innocent (not debased) segments: youth. Thus Dodd sometimes seemed more alarmed and fearful of what the Hitler Youth implied than what the generality of Nazis might bring, and he told Roosevelt so.

By the end of 1933 Dodd had taken notice of the activities of the Hitler Youth and included some personal observations in his cables to Washington. What he saw so alarmed him that he felt obligated to report his observations to the State Department. In a letter that reached the president, Dodd described his travels to Nuremburg, Bayreuth, Berlin, and other German cities. In nearly every city or town he had observed the marching boys of the Hitler Youth. "In Bayreuth," their "marching and singing kept me awake nearly all the night." While he ate lunch in Hechingen, "at least 2000 Hitler *Jugend* marched past the hotel door."[9]

Just as Dodd was alarmed at the support given ultra-right-wing conservatives by a presumed liberal ally, youth, so Filene on a European trip was conditioned by his own NRA experience to grow similarly anxious. By late 1933, Filene, like his NRA chief, Hugh Johnson, had grown accustomed to enjoying grass-roots pressure enlisted *against*, not in support of, the extreme right-wing opponents of the administration. When Henry Ford, for example, refused to sign the NRA auto code, letters poured into the White House denouncing Ford's want of patriotism, urging FDR to "Turn the Hose on Henry," and promising to display Blue Eagle stickers proclaiming, "My Last Ford Supports NRA." Now, however, in Germany, youth were supporting a right-wing politician who made even the anti-Semitic Ford appear, by contrast, somewhat liberal. Danger appeared to be looming in these trends. Accordingly, Filene, Dodd, and Taussig rushed proposals to the White House sketching the contours of the action needed to neutralize these dangers.[10]

A few months before the end of 1933, Filene warned the president that the treatment of German youth had important implications for American domestic policy. On 7 September he wrote FDR of his trip to Germany that summer, where he had witnessed a march of "tens of thousands of boys and girls from eight years to maturity, organized in military fashion." Filene enclosed a snapshot of these youths, just to show how young some of them were.[11]

Alive to the impressionability of young people, Filene had returned home and attempted to organize Massachusetts youth into a movement to support the NRA. The young people he enlisted in his organization were pledged to "spend their pennies in stores flying the Blue Eagle," and thereby "directly influence their families to do likewise." As he explained, his trip to Germany had convinced him that children were a real force not only in shaping events but also in "influencing their parents and other adults." Young people thus posed a dual danger. Not only were they easy targets for the persuasive efforts of malevolent personalities, but, once misdirected, they possessed persuasive powers of their own in influencing adults.[12]

Filene hoped that Roosevelt would follow his lead and organize youth on a national basis. If youth's energies were directed into positive and constructive channels, he suggested, it would be impossible for some individual to organize them for destructive purposes. "Should we fail to do this," he warned, "it is conceivable that this great potential power may be diverted to dangerous selfish or partisan interests." He explained his ideas further:

Russia and Germany and the other countries show clearly how the youth movement can be diverted to partisan political ends. We learn from this enough to enable us to apply this force along constructive lines by first establishing a proper objective—the support of the NRA movement, and then building on this other objectives which are unselfish and non-partisan. By organizing the youth movement on this basis, we guard against its diversion to selfish purposes.[13]

Filene envisioned this youth movement as an organization formed to support the NRA and including in its ranks "religious groups, boy scouts, campfire girls and service clubs." Replying to Filene through his press secretary, Stephen Early, Roosevelt wrote that "it may be profitable to discuss this matter at length at a later date."[14]

Apparently no such discussion took place. It is unlikely, however, that Roosevelt's interest in Filene's remarks was feigned. Probably he was more interested in Filene's description of how German youth had been organized militarily than he was in the New Englander's advice on the best method of organizing youth at home. Filene had written of a problem and a danger the president could not ignore. Roosevelt was sympathetic to the idea of helping American youth find jobs so as to neutralize the attractiveness of un-American creeds. To be sure, Filene's proposal, while promising support for the NRA, left other important needs unmet: the need to relieve the overcrowded job market, for example, and the necessity of shielding the New Deal from charges of regimentation. Nevertheless, the separate conclusions of Dodd and Filene together helped crystallize concern about American youth's fidelity to democratic values. Dodd's report that American youth was a "marching nation" became salient to New Deal youth policy when the White House began receiving Filene's reports that young people were leading the Nazi procession.[15]

One man more than any other within the administration endorsed the idea of teaching young people the workings of the American democratic process. Charles William Taussig was one of that circle of university and college professors who advised Roosevelt on social and economic policy in the early New Deal. Although not himself an academic, Taussig, the thirty-six-year-old chairman of the board of the American Molasses Company, was familiar with the problems of adjusting production and consumption for the economic betterment of the nation. At the beginning of the New Deal, Taussig wished primarily to ensure the continuation of "liberalism," a term roughly equivalent to the New Deal's conviction that social welfare was an individual right sometimes attainable only through federal regulation of private activities. Taussig was convinced that liberalism could not survive unless the federal government helped persuade young people to participate in politics and educated them to the advantages of the positive state.[16]

In December 1933, Taussig, then a technical adviser to FDR on international political and economic affairs, composed a memorandum on youth problems for circulation within the administration. The context of his concern was the gathering in Washington that month of student organizations representing the entire ideological spectrum of politicized American youth. Even before the young Communists and Socialists gathered together that month with youths of more moderate opinions, there were unmistakable signs of a collaboration inimical to the interests of the New Deal and dangerous to democracy. By December the socialist Student League for Industrial Democracy (SLID) and the Communist-dominated National Student League (NSL) had broken from their habit of attacking each other and were speaking of forming a united front against war, fascism, and unemployment. While the SLID continued to spurn communist appeals for complete confederation, the organization's mouthpiece, *Student Outlook*, spoke favorably of "the vision of one, powerful revolutionary student movement."

Taussig was no doubt alarmed when the two groups did edge closer by joining the National Conference on Students and Politics (NCSP) in 1933.

The new organization's purpose was to concentrate the energies of its many supporting groups behind the goals common to all: peace and federal aid to education. Its educational board included national figures fully capable of gaining White House attention, if not access, including John Dewey, Reinhold Niebuhr, and Senator Robert Wagner (D., New York) among others. Such a focusing of radical energies was worrisome itself to the New Dealers. But by being welcomed into a predominantly mainstream organization such as the NCSP, the young Socialists and Communists might gain influence over the conservative youth organizations affiliated with the new political group, including such innocuous groups as the YMCA and YWCA. The young radicals did not remove all the barriers to their joint affiliation until December 1935, but even before the Popular Front accelerated the Communists' search for conservative allies against fascism, the trend toward common cause was visible enough. As one historian wrote, "If there was a date when the student movement became official, it would probably be December 1933." Taussig's memo was to be the New Deal's initial salvo in its defense against this disturbing development.[17]

In Taussig's view, young people had to be taught the basic rationale for democracy, for in this way the New Deal would at once neutralize the radical appeal to youth and render democracy secure. In his memorandum he proposed a program to interest university students in the politics and social problems of the nation. Each participating college or university within the program (the number he envisioned was fifty to one hundred) would send a different student to Washington every two weeks, there to take a "two-weeks course in the objectives and the economics of the New Deal." The students' travel expenses would be privately funded, but the federal government would pay for the classes in political education. As part of their coursework, students might attend NRA code hearings. At the end of the brief course, the Taussig plan would enable each student to attend a presidential press conference. They would even be permitted to ask questions "in the same manner as the press do." Classes would be taught by professors and economists currently employed in government service.[18]

At first glance the plan's purpose appeared blatantly political: to preserve the Roosevelt administration's political existence beyond 1936. Taussig had written that "with a nucleus of say three to four thousand men and women who would participate in the Washington classes the first year, it should be possible to create an intelligent group scattered throughout the country of from fifty to one hundred thousand, most of whom would undoubtedly be aggressively sympathetic with the purposes of the government."[19]

While Taussig hoped that young people would support the Roosevelt administration, the goal of political education, he believed, was to develop support for a principle (that of the positive federal state), and not a party. To be sure, his curriculum could not justly be described as nonpartisan. Unlike some advocates of civic education, Taussig did not see political activity among young people as a worthy end in itself. Instruction was valuable only if the political activity it encouraged promoted an active national government. In general, of course, the New Deal promoted this goal, and so Taussig tended to support it wholeheartedly. But he was no blind supporter of the administration, especially when it seemed to violate his own principles. At such times he could be quite critical. In a 1933 passage worth quoting in detail, Taussig wrote:

> The major weakness in the recovery program is not the minor miscalculation of some detail in this or that economic measure, but rather the failure to prepare the country to assimilate new and revolutionary economic and social concepts. We have no youth movement, no group to whom we can look to carry the banner of intellectual liberalism. Having failed to educate the people to accept, we try to sloganize them to comply. "We Do Our Part" is a splendid sentiment; it would have been more splendid if the nation knew precisely what it meant. . . .
>
> The lack of active interest in politics and social problems on the part of university men is peculiar to this country. In a crisis such as we are now passing through, it is essential to arouse this interest, unless we are to return once more to our attitude of "*Laissez-Faire*."[20]

Nor did Taussig care whether the professors appointed to teach the classes in political education were Republicans or Democrats. The task was to turn apathetic young people into citizens aware of the changes taking place in their government and anxious to participate in these changes. Even in 1933, then, while he proposed a youth program designed in part to preserve the Roosevelt administration against the onslaught of laissez-faire, Taussig was equally concerned with the future of a broader and more important ideology—democracy itself. He explained in December 1933 that "it should not be essential that all those who go to Washington be sympathetic with the ideas and ideals of the present administration. It is quite probable that some of the community forums that develop may not prove sympathetic, but if the work is properly conducted, at least their opposition will be intelligent. . . . [The students would return home] with a feeling of being a definite part of the government."[21]

No one in the administration seems to have encouraged Taussig to pursue his plan. In the first six months of 1934, however, he revised it. Taussig no longer spoke of the plan as one designed to turn apathetic young people into Americans "aggressively sympathetic with the purposes of government." Instead he transformed it into a program more nearly designed to involve youth in the general workings of the democratic process. Now convinced that American democracy, and not merely the New Deal, was threatened by youth unemployment, Taussig had come to believe that youth must be taught to understand and influence current American political trends.

Taussig had probably been concerned about the future of representative government earlier than others within the administration, and for good reason. He had had greater contact than most of his colleagues with the grievances of student groups and their leaders. A second-echelon figure within the Roosevelt brain trust, and regarded as such by some members of that body, it was natural that Taussig would seek support for his ideas from those more interested in youth problems. Thus he was especially interested in sounding out Eleanor Roosevelt's views on the subject. Beginning in 1934, the two held long discussions about youth's condition. At the same time, he met with youth leaders and joined a Christian pacifist youth group, the Intercollegiate Disarmament Council (IDC).[22]

Membership on the council, which focused almost exclusively on efforts to prevent war, doubtless left Taussig unprepared for what he encountered when he met with leaders of a newer youth organization, the American Youth Congress (AYC). The AYC was an organization of college students formed in 1934, ostensibly to champion antiwar efforts and pressure the administration to drastically expand the scope of federal student aid. Nevertheless, many of its members were more interested in debating, if not trumpeting, the idea of replacing American capitalism with some novel alternative. After meeting with AYC leaders Taussig grew more concerned about the changing political complexion of the nation's young people. According to George Rawick, he was not yet aware that Communists dominated the leadership of the congress, but he could see all too clearly that the AYC had a radical orientation and that its members seemed more interested in debating the future of capitalism than the agenda of the New Deal.[23]

The change Taussig thought he observed in American youth convinced him that his own youth plan required modification. Since young people were now questioning the very fundamentals of the American economy—particularly its capitalistic basis—the only program of education likely to interest youth would be one that dealt with these basic foundations of society. Thus, although the program had obvious value as one that could educate young people into the advantages of the New Deal, Taussig believed it was at least as valuable as a means of teaching young people about the merits of democracy. As he told members of the Baltimore Rotary Club, a federal youth program was necessary to ensure that young people did not embrace communism.[24]

In the spring of 1934 Taussig proposed that the IDC organize discussion sessions on the campuses of the nation's colleges and universities. Students would debate "all questions involved in the administration of our federal, state, and local governments." In the words of one of Taussig's friends, the New Yorker's purpose was to help students "learn to distinguish facts from propaganda so that . . . they may decide intelligently the issues on which, as voters, they must be informed." Taussig believed that similar discussion groups might be organized at meetings of alumni and in connection with classes in adult education.[25]

One of Taussig's objectives was to organize independent voters into a nonpartisan group that would act as a "whip" to force the major parties to heed their wishes. It was possible that the New Deal would not benefit from such organization; independent voters might support whatever policy they wished. Democracy would surely benefit, however. For one thing, independent voters, as they gained power, would grow more confident of the efficacy of democracy. Furthermore, the plan would heighten political action, not only among the normally somnambulent independents but also among those whose commitment to democracy was most fragile—the young.[26]

Taussig, Filene, and Dodd were not the only Roosevelt advisers to conclude that the New Deal youth problem was a malady of the mind. Recognition was emerging of a national problem of youth unmeasurable by crime statistics and exhibiting no visible symptoms. The attitudes of young people shut off from opportunity and schooling were also drawing the attention of relief planners within the FERA. Whereas Taussig and other advisers feared for the democratic future, Aubrey Williams, Harry Hopkins, and other architects of relief policy were intent on bringing to present realization the old American objective of equal educational opportunity. That both goals might be achieved through the same program lent the concept of a national youth program virtually a momentum all its own.

ROOSEVELT NEVER APPROVED of Taussig's proposal for ideological training of American youth. Although he believed that something had to be done to both support and justify youth's faith in a democratic society, Taussig's method seemed certain to stir up a hornet's nest of conservative and anti–New Deal sentiment. Moreover, it placed excessive faith in the ability of a few bright youths (those attending Taussig's classes) to transmit their renewed faith in America to the thousands of idle young people who wanted only a skill and a job. The dynamics of Taussig's argument suggested to other New Dealers that young people had to be reached not ideologically but vocationally, through job training. These conclusions did not come immediately in 1933, but only after eighteen months of debate by relief officials planning a New Deal for education from within the FERA.

More important, the conservation of democratic values through education reform may have received Roosevelt's support more because he understood its political value than for any shared faith in its possibilities for success. The FERA argument was that educators could be cajoled to assume the job of morale building through job training; a federal job-training program of sufficient duration would be all that was necessary to generate an educational reform movement that would then be self-perpetuating. Whether it succeeded or not, it could be attempted at little political risk. Faced with a need to choose between education programs with visible public support and those more likely to target values for maintenance, Roosevelt generally tended to cripple the ideological cause by supporting the former. Indeed, Roosevelt's distaste for educational controversy was exhibited by his decision to initiate educational reform through a college aid program that bypassed the group of greatest concern to those worried about ideology: high school dropouts. College student aid possessed more grass-roots support than any other federal training concept, but it lacked the attributes the FERA planners considered indispensable to broader educational reform.[27]

The New Deal often had less to do with ideas than with indignation, for it frequently mirrored the personalities of those who plotted its assaults on depression distress. Harry L. Hopkins, Jacob Baker, Aubrey Williams, Hilda Smith, and their cohorts were iconoclasts of social work who sought to do much more than minister to the poor. Most had had unusually broad life experiences, exposing them to ambitions that led them to define their FERA duties as broadly as possible (among many other unusual ventures, Baker had founded a publishing house, Williams had joined the French Foreign Legion, and Smith was a poet). Ultimately, it was the personalities and experiences of these New Dealers that determined their approach to education.[28] Like the president they were sympathetic to reform but cautious about unnecessarily disturbing conservative sensibilities. They realized that silence was the best policy while they planned how to reform education through relief. So explosive was the issue of local control of education that Roosevelt usually insisted on his loyalty to the principle even as he worked to convince educators to reorder their priorities to the FERA's liking.

BY DEED AND WORD, Roosevelt left a record during the early New Deal suggesting that he shared the idea that the secondary schools were too elitist in their emphasis on college preparation at the expense of vocational training. Almost to a man and woman, the personalities Roosevelt placed in charge of education planning regarded dropping out as the rational act of a student wise to the fact that school curricula were of little relevance to his or her needs. Even Roosevelt himself, in his infrequent comments on education, let this attitude slip out to the press, though it was anathema to many professional educators.

The New Deal's impulse toward educational reform arose in part from the hostility to stultifying conventions that was native to the Roosevelt relief planners. Hopkins, the federal relief administrator himself, personified that pragmatic style. Son of an irreverent, sharp-tongued father and a mother of strong missionary fervor, Hopkins borrowed without discrimination the dominant traits of both parents. His mannerisms were so obvious as to enter the realm of cliché by 1934. The newspapers pegged him accurately as a man for whom bureaucracy, rank, and the hours on the clock were obstacles almost as intolerable as the human suffering he felt driven to relieve.[29]

Hopkins "enjoyed nothing more than cutting through red tape," wrote

Irving Bernstein. Though "not anti-intellectual, he put people into two categories, the 'talkers' and the 'doers,' and he proudly claimed himself among the latter." Perhaps the most celebrated descriptions of him (as ulcerated, sarcastic, and direct) often obscure more than they reveal. Until failing health and presidential ambitions commanded his attention in the later 1930s, nothing so concerned him as the American without a chance, from the slum dwellers he faced working out of New York City's Christadora settlement house in 1912 to the four million federal workers he enrolled in 1934. Hopkins saw no reason why poverty and people had to coexist in America. For that reason he rejected theory, spent no more time than necessary on administration, and participated actively in every phase of FERA planning, including early discussions about education.[30]

Hopkins expected his aides to spend only as much time on relief as he himself was willing to devote. In 1933 and 1934, that meant that lights in FERA headquarters, the old Walker-Johnson Building, often burned long into the early morning hours. FERA administrators either left early or signed on for the duration, adoring Hopkins and working as hard as he. By and large, Hopkins, for all his dynamism, did not earn this loyalty; it came naturally from men and women who rivaled him in energy and compassion. Along with Lewis R. Alderman and Cyril F. Klinefelter, the leading planners in education included Jacob Baker, head of the Works Division, John H. Millar, a specialist in vocational education, and two young graduate students on leave from law school, Elizabeth Wickenden and her husband, Arthur ("Tex") Goldschmidt. In 1934 they were joined by a University of Michigan professor, William Haber, an unemployment statistician and expert on the marshaling of private funds for its alleviation. Throughout the next year and a half they devoted their time partly to drafting a battery of plans for youth, and partly to combating plans supported by local educators and originating from within the U.S. Office of Education (USOE). Above all, they were led by Aubrey Willis Williams, the Alabamian who, since August 1933, had been Hopkins's chief deputy within the FERA. This cohesive crew developed the remaining New Deal programs on behalf of unschooled or untrained youth. Under Williams's lead, they constituted a wing of the New Deal that possessed an ever-expanding, indeed a seemingly inexhaustible, agenda of reform for the nation's youth.[31]

Williams was one of a rare and remarkable group of Americans: a southerner who preferred to be ostracized within his region rather than accommodate to its racial conventions and practices. Born in 1890 in Springville, Alabama, he observed the contours of racism and poverty from the Birmingham blacksmith shop of his father. Acutely sensitive to the ways in which racism warped the lives of white and black southerners alike, Williams saw the ministry as a source of change. Not until age twenty-one (when he completed his first formal year of education) did he see an avenue for escape. A divinity school in Tennessee, Maryville College, offered an accelerated high school program and college education, and Williams served there as a student pastor from 1911 through 1916. World War I convinced him that a more secular form of service suited him better. A stint overseas with the YMCA, the French Foreign Legion, and the U.S. Army turned him toward a career in social work. After taking a degree in social service from the University of Cincinnati in 1921, he spent the decade of "normalcy" as executive secretary of the Wisconsin Conference of Social Work, helping to liberalize Wisconsin's state aid program for dependent children. After 1931 Williams worked for the American Public Welfare Association (and later the Reconstruction Finance Corporation), making relief loans to the states of Mississippi and Texas. In one of his first actions as federal relief administrator, Harry Hopkins appointed Williams to the post of FERA regional representative for seven southern states. In August 1933 he was appointed deputy director of the entire agency.

If possible, Williams was even more committed than Hopkins had been to the principle that the impoverished deserved immediate aid regardless of the political costs. By the late 1930s Hopkins had developed political ambitions and had begun to enjoy the circle of some of the president's wealthier friends, a circle in which they accorded him a place of honor. If such a change was a mistake, it was an error Williams never committed. Perhaps poverty and racism were too personal for him ever to forget them, the New Deal too remarkable (and improbable) an opportunity for service for him to dare to slow his reform efforts or to believe that it might long continue. Ten months after joining the New Deal, he explained to a southerner why he couldn't leave the federal service: "I think that this man Roosevelt is something unusual." Williams was right. The New Deal coincided with the only twelve years of his life when his opinions did not isolate and ostracize him from powerful means of social reform. Before the New Deal slowed to a halt in 1938, he helped ensure that his relief agencies were the most racially enlightened (in terms of policy and personnel) of all the alphabet agencies. Williams went so far as to force the NYA state director of Alabama to integrate social gatherings of the agency. In addition, he tactlessly urged WPA workers to "vote to keep your friends in power," a remark that barred him from the leadership of that agency in the late 1930s.

By the time Williams moved on, in 1943, nearly five million of the nation's unschooled youth had filled some of the New Deal jobs he had helped create. Without question he was the leader of the group of New Dealers who discovered almost immediately that training for youth could be secured only at the cost of alienating one of the most vocal factions within American education.[32]

ORGANIZED EDUCATORS and New Dealers under Williams's lead possessed mutually exclusive conceptions of the uses of education as an antidepression panacea. To the NEA, "depression" meant unemployment for teachers and closed schools for young people.[33] To Williams and Hopkins, it meant joblessness for adults and young people, problems young people were making worse by taking the jobs of older employables. The educational deficiencies of young people were chalked up to the failures of educators. For the New Dealers, no educational cure for the depression was worthy of the name if it failed to remove young people from the labor market and provide education under the supervision of employers, not the teachers who had failed at the job.

The year 1933 gave little hint that the remainder of the decade would witness conflicts between Uncle Sam and the schools. Although the educational scene, with schools closing and teachers unpaid, was anything but placid, at least the federal government seemed to respect the authority of professionals in matters educational. Had not Roosevelt selected as commissioner of education forty-eight-year-old George F. Zook, head of the USOE's Division of Higher Education in the 1920s and a staunch foe of a Department of Education? C. R. Mann, director of the American Council on Education since 1922, would soon lecture his school colleagues for "failing to achieve as satisfactory results as [had the] political and economic experiments under the New Deal." Eunice Fuller Barnard wrote in the *New York Times* of the likelihood that New Dealers and educators would march together with joined hands toward a reconstructed America. "Never," she wrote, "has the outlook been brighter for the dignifying, the clarifying and the extending of the work of the Office of Education in the nation. . . . All agree that we seem to be on the verge of acquiring a consistent national policy toward education."[34]

Events of the next two years mocked Barnard's hopes for a single mind in education planning. Convinced that the United States could tolerate experimentation with many different plans for economic reconstruction, Roosevelt supported both conservative thinkers and proponents of national planning. Planners from Lewis Douglas, on the right, to Jerome Frank and Rexford Tugwell, on the left, received presidential support. The same willingness to experiment evidenced itself in the New Deal's approach to education. When Zook resigned on 18 May 1934, Roosevelt appointed John W. Studebaker to succeed him. Studebaker had served as assistant director of the Junior Red Cross during World War II, and then reorganized Iowa's school system as superintendant of schools from 1920 to 1934. More important, his pet idea was the creation of guidance and adjustment centers, federally funded but locally controlled, where private educators could dispense all manner of educational services, from adult education to training of jobless youth. Even though Studebaker opposed federal training from the start, Roosevelt retained him as commissioner through the remaining eleven years of his administration.

On the other hand, FDR seldom followed Studebaker's advice and cut USOE appropriations in most years of the 1930s, actions at variance with his rhetorical support for traditional forms of educational control. Relief agencies for youth such as those offered by the CCC and FERA continuously met with the president's avid interest. From the CCC (which FDR saw as his pet project) to the FERA (which evolved a surprisingly diverse array of educational services for youth and others), the New Deal role in education seemed heavily weighted toward relief and federal administration.[35]

Nevertheless, there was a consistency about Roosevelt's approach to education, and, whether critical or supportive of the New Deal, most educators agreed on what it was. Roosevelt, through the CCC and FERA, had started down the road toward transforming the federal government from a mere financier of the schools to a schoolhouse in and of itself. What was unique about the New Deal was that, from the start, the CCC and FERA provided training (not just relief) under federal auspices. The CCC paid teachers to hold classes after work hours, with attendance voluntary. FERA officials directed supervisors of New Deal–supported students and out-of-school youths to provide the kinds of jobs and guidance that would help youth develop skills demanded in the marketplace. Nor was it possible for educators to reassure each other that job training under the New Deal had "just happened" beginning in 1934, and was not the product of a plan. To be sure, Roosevelt's speeches on education were confined to clichés extolling the glories of local control of education. But by 1935 FERA planners were going public with their conviction that Washington must help a group ignored by the schools: youth of low-income families.[36]

Until the New Deal launched its first series of attacks on illiteracy and student distress, most American educators regarded the Great Depression, not the federal government, as the greatest problem of their time. The Great Depression overturned, at least briefly, traditional attitudes that school leaders had had about the federal government. Specifically, it raised the possibility that Washington might be a source of rescue for the educators rather than a source of trouble.

By creating an image of the businessman as a charlatan and by posing problems for which economic orthodoxy had no answers, the depression encouraged educators to repudiate their business allies and fall back on political reform as a panacea. Politics, after all, had enabled education to become professionalized in the first place, through the reforms of Horace Mann and other antebellum New England reformers. Looking back to politics for an answer, educators broke from the 1920s mold. They could do so without acute reservations. They still considered themselves conservatives "reminiscent of the nineteenth century educational crusaders, who also had hoped to use the schools to remake the world . . . according to values in which they had transcendent confidence."[37]

In February 1932, George S. Counts, a professor at Columbia University's Teacher's College, asked a question his peers regarded as one of the most crucial of their era: "Dare the schools build a new social order?" Counts advised teachers that they must choose between socialism and capitalism. As he explained it, the present economic system had led directly to the present disarray in education, simplifying the decision facing the teachers. Counts's injunction struck educators as a burning question. They heeded his demand for an answer with alacrity, though not with the results he wished. They did choose sides, but as the attacks on capitalism intensified, most educators only grew more confirmed in their allegiance to the tenets of the free enterprise system. Such traditions as local control of education and federal aid without strings assumed, for many educators, the image of barricades protecting the entire structure of American education. Paradoxically, then, most educators were of two minds toward the federal government during the depression. They found themselves pleading for federal aid while denouncing federal control; they were among the staunchest defenders of capitalism but the most vitriolic critics of the capitalists.[38]

In 1933 and 1934, even conservatives who would become some of the New Deal's fiercest educational opponents venomously attacked business practices of the day. Although in no way aligned with those who supported Counts (the "reconstructionists"), these educational conservatives nevertheless wrote in a style reminiscent of populist tracts. Joy Elmer Morgan, editor of the *NEA Journal* and an educational moderate, denounced agents of "'the Wall Street power trust' oligarchy" for denying the schools badly needed tax revenues in order to salvage their own reputations. Writing of the same group in a contribution to the NEA's annual proceedings, Willard E. Givens, president of the California Teachers Association (and a future foe of the New Deal) said of the businessmen: "Money has become their God. . . . We have built great temples of marble and granite in which to worship these man-made gods. We have called some of these temples stock-exchanges." Having fought for generations with businessmen against the growth of federal power, many educators were stung by what they perceived as businessmen's attempts to transfer the onus of responsibility for the depression onto educators.[39]

As might be expected, the reconstructionists were no less fulsome in their criticisms of business practices. S. A. Courtis, a professor of education at the University of Michigan, praised Mussolini and Stalin for partially "remedying the very evils that plague our people." Questioning whether freedom and individualism were "as desirable as they seemed," Courtis called for "a new definition of liberty," one that emphasized the individual's obligation to submit to national planning for the good of the whole. Education is a "socialistic enterprise," he added. "The school must train future citizens in social methods of adjusting opportunity to capacity and of preventing the misuse of opportunity for purposes of personal exploitation of others."[40]

Within and without the educational profession, the year 1933 witnessed a conservative counterattack against the reconstructionist point of view. Right-wing critics of alleged school radicalism included publisher William Randolph Hearst, union organizer Matthew Woll, and the Daughters of the American Revolution. Prominent educational reconstructionists and critics of capitalism such as the historian Charles A. Beard were especially targeted for conservative attacks.[41]

In the depths of the depression, the central issue for many educators was the need to commit the government to vastly increased education funding without precipitating the slightest encroachment on the principle of local educational control. Educators combed vainly through Roosevelt's speeches in search of incontrovertible evidence as to FDR's position regarding this philosophy. But Roosevelt was uncomfortable with aligning himself behind creeds in general, especially because doing so cost votes; on this particular issue the president preferred to straddle the fence. Roosevelt's real interest in education was often overlooked because it was not part of the contemporary debate among educators. He wished to earmark resources toward the education of a larger proportion of the nation's youth than had previously been reached by the schools. The plight and ignorance of the young, not the fiscal problems of educational administrators, was the problem he hoped to alleviate.

Sometimes Roosevelt seemed to be a conservative on the subject of federal support for education. His early speeches revealed only that his ideas were not frozen in time, but underwent change under the pressure of events. On 2 March 1930, for example, Governor Roosevelt had declared:

> Wisely or unwisely, people know that under the Eighteenth Amendment, Congress has been given the right to legislate on this particular subject [prohibition], but this is not the case in the matter of a great many other vital problems of government, such as the conduct of public utilities, of banks, of insurance, of business, of agriculture, of education, and of social welfare and of a dozen other important features. In these Washington must not be encouraged to interfere.
>
> The preservation of this "Home Rule" by the States is not the cry of jealous Commonwealths seeking their own aggrandizement at the expense of the States. It is a fundamental necessity if we are to remain a truly united country.[42]

Such words soothed educators long after they were uttered, which was one reason subsequent presidential pronouncements often voiced the same theme. Yet, had Roosevelt really felt he was bound to this creed, he would have vetoed most of the "hundred days" legislation or never sent it to Congress. Roosevelt's words were designed to build an ever-growing constituency while leaving him free to forge a new federal style in education.

Often, as president, Roosevelt called for more dollars to support local schools, locally controlled. On receiving an honorary degree from Washington College, Maryland, on 21 October 1933, Roosevelt declared "that we are seeking, in time of depression, to prevent further attacks on our educational system." FDR's listeners were left to decide for themselves whether he regarded the "attackers" to be the federal government or economy-minded businessmen. The following March, writing to George F. Arps, organizer of an Ohio State University conference on educational problems, Roosevelt attributed school closings and the elimination of "highly essential services" to a decline in funds. In November 1934 Roosevelt implied again that it was his administration's policy to increase funding of education and "to improve the standard of living in this country as a whole. . . . Better education is very, very important."[43]

Through rhetorical gymnastics and adroit public presentation, Roosevelt succeeded in convincing educators of his conservatism even as he supported assaults on their most sacrosanct shibboleths. He did so by declaring that reform would take place within the context of a federal commitment to exercise fiscal restraint and maintain local control. To Arps, FDR expressed confidence that "after careful deliberation you will be able to formulate a plan of action." Perhaps because he ultimately decided that the need for federal training of youth would exist only for a brief time, Roosevelt felt it unnecessary to explain that there would have to be exceptions to the rule of laissez-faire in the arena of education. To be sure, there were moments of frankness. He once spoke of federal efforts to "stretch" the law in helping those in school and employing the federal government as an "entering wedge" in the field of education, words educators regarded with the deepest suspicion. More often FDR spoke in a kind of code that permitted federal training as a national imperative without announcing that as the procedure he favored. In 1933 he mused that "if we could provide in the Nation for an adequate education for everybody, the spirit of the country would be vastly safeguarded." Given the millions of youth who, by the president's own estimate, were beyond the schools' reach, this goal was unattainable without federal training and aid.

Later, Roosevelt explained why he was both a reformer and a conservative. All "appropriations which have been made had one single objective— relief. . . . We are trying to keep the relief part of the budget as low as we possibly can." But, he added, "in these entering wedges, we have started a general education program."[44] More than any previous president, Roosevelt wanted to be an innovator in education. It was a fact he never denied but often left unstated. The many educators who chose selectively from his addresses the phrases they wished to hear would be ill-prepared for the New Deal's decisions of 1934 and 1935.

CHAPTER THREE

The Entering Wedge
of College Student Aid

T he New Deal's 1933 approach to the fiscal plight of schools and their students betrayed a reluctance to group all youths together for unified and common treatment. Nearly every conceivable New Deal agency offered something to those involved in the system of American public education. Yet there was no central body within the New Deal charged with coordinating these efforts; no central "plan" imposed rationality and a common purpose on the administration's disparate educational programs. The NRA banned child labor, creating a new constituency for the schools. The Agricultural Adjustment Administration (AAA) created vocational education programs to instruct farmers in the technicalities of production control. And the CCC hired fifteen hundred education advisers to provide basic education for 300,000 young men. Community center schools were built through a $25 million appropriation to the Federal Subsistence Homestead Corporation. The CWA building program resulted in the construction of schools and playgrounds.[1]

By early 1934, planners within the FERA and the USOE regarded this ad hoc approach to American education as a source of educational difficulties in America rather than a salve. Before 1933 was over, Harry Hopkins voiced concern that the NRA, by working to expand employment opportunities for adults, had created a population of formerly employed children now uninterested in attending school. Many of these children turned to the FERA for help, revealing that one New Deal agency might create problems for another and give rise to job difficulties for youth at the very moment it was expanding job opportunities for adults. In addition to Hopkins, Lewis R. Alderman, the director of emergency education in the FERA, and John H. Millar, the director of vocational education within the Office of Education, within a matter of months recommended to their respective agencies that an identical approach be adopted to solving the youth problem. Concluding that New Deal agencies had in many cases exacerbated the problem, they urged that all of the agencies send representatives to confer on a coordinated response to the ills that had originated from policies of the federal government. Thereafter it would be possible for the New Deal to evolve a purposeful, coordinated plan to deal with the youth problems arising from local conditions and the American economy.[2]

Such a conception indicated that there was little disagreement within the New Deal over the nature of the youth problem. Nevertheless, whatever agreement there was concerning the definition of the problem, the necessary solution remained a bone of contention between officials in the FERA and those in the Office of Education. Coordination was possible only if all agencies involved agreed on the course all would have to follow as part of the joint response. And the USOE emphatically disagreed with the FERA on the key question regarding which agency (USOE or FERA) should administer federal funds, or whether there should be any federal administration at all. Unity within the New Deal would exist only as long as the Roosevelt administration persisted in defining the dimensions of the problem. By the spring of 1934, the administration was poised to develop a solution. The president would then have to oversee a sharp debate within his own administration, one that would reflect the debate between educators in higher education and those within secondary and elementary education. From that moment on, the New Deal style in education would be a deeply divided one. Ominously, the New Deal would have to choose between an approach favoring educators at the district level and one involving federal direction and administration. With that choice the administration would alienate profoundly one or the other faction within American education.

All of this was in the future in August 1933, when the FERA unveiled its initial education program. A concern with youth as a distinct group did not characterize early New Deal planning, partly because officials recognized that 1933 was the worst year of the depression so far. Consequently, adults in dozens of professions seemed as worthy of federal attention as young people (even hungry children, since parents and children were starving together). In 1933 the FERA had a full plate ministering to the transient unemployed, illiterate adults, Americans working in cooperatives or participating in a barter economy, farmers, and women. Before reaching out to young people, the New Dealers lent a helping hand to each of these groups through, successively, the transient relief program (begun in 1933), the Emergency Education Program (initiated in August 1933), and the self-help and barter program (introduced in January 1934). Finally rural rehabilitation, resident schools and camps for jobless women, and FERA sewing rooms were introduced by the late spring of 1934.[3]

The program offering the greatest range of services was the FERA's Emergency Education Program (EEP). Unveiled on 19 August 1933 by Harry Hopkins, the EEP originally proposed to hire forty thousand teachers on relief and give them the task of teaching rural schoolchildren (in communities of fewer than twenty-five hundred persons) and conducting literacy classes for jobless adults. In the following six months, Hopkins expanded the program with three separate directives. On 26 September 1933 he authorized use of FERA funds to hire teachers to provide vocational training for Americans over twenty-one years of age and rehabilitation training for the handicapped. As a result of an FERA directive of 23 October, preschool children of jobless Americans on relief began receiving instruction in their own homes, at FERA expense. Four months later, on 2 February 1934, Hopkins announced the final expansion in the program, permitting the distribution of FERA funds to non-profit-making colleges and universities for the purpose of providing part-time jobs to seventy-five thousand students (up to 10 percent of their full-time enrollment) who would otherwise be unable to continue their education. This was an extension of an experimental program conducted by the FERA at the University of Minnesota in December 1933. The same press release disclosed that teachers would be hired under the EEP to instruct students of rural secondary as well as elementary schools in communities of fewer than five thousand persons.[4]

In its totality, the New Deal response to the nation's education crisis was impressive indeed. Yet, somehow, the dominant constituency in America's educational system—adolescents and young adults as well as children—seemed neglected in the EEP program, for they were denied priority treatment over other groups in the scheme. In fact, the program seemed to deny that young people formed a social group requiring special treatment. The EEP treated youths as nothing more than members of the educational community, along with adult illiterates and jobless teachers. In other words, they were treated like the unemployed generally. As the director of the EEP, Lewis R. Alderman, noted, "to these hundreds of free classes come persons of all ages—so long as they are unemployed they can have teaching and training to fit themselves to be better producers and wage earners when jobs open up."[5]

THE EDUCATORS most likely to applaud these initial ventures into federal aid were those in administration who were struggling to balance increased expenditures and shrinking budgets. Yet the seemingly planless nature of the New Deal's educational approach, especially its unspoken assumption that the government need go no further than providing young people the opportunity to attend school, disturbed many commentators, particularly students and administrators in the field of higher education. Just as relief officials saw the specter of poverty behind every educational problem, educational administrators were equally inclined to escalate the importance of their own profession (education), identifying its future with the fate of democracy itself. Their concern with ideology would soon be shared by New Dealers, if only because an uneasy fear for the future of representative government was widespread in 1933 and 1934.

In June 1933 the secretary for student employment at Harvard University, Russell T. Sharpe, penned a biting satire on the folly of government inaction in the face of rising student withdrawals. Sharpe concluded that in the absence of government aid, only one method remained to reduce "the volume of need" on campus: limit "the number of needy men admitted to college." With tongue in cheek, he argued that this solution would effectively silence those who continually prattled on about the importance to democracy of equal access to education. "Only a confirmed and sentimental believer in the popular notion of democracy would take issue on this point. . . . As long as nature is capricious enough to endow one child with uncommon ability while denying the gift to the next, there can be no unrestricted democracy in education." Sharpe added, however, that government would do well to recognize what it had so far ignored:

that a "selective policy . . . may well be prophetic of the course which American democracy itself is to follow in the years to come."

By the end of 1933, officials of the nation's colleges and universities had become convinced that a "new deal" for higher education was required. The entire financial structure of collegiate education had reached a crisis stage. In this crisis, college presidents sympathized with the plight of their students. During the 1920s the economic condition of college students had become an important consideration of administrators as a greater cross-section of the American people began extending their education beyond high school. Enrollment in baccalaureate or professional programs had risen from 582,000 in 1920 to 1,054,000 a decade later, invalidating to some extent the stereotype of the college student as a child of the rich. It seemed that a larger percentage of students were vulnerable to the effects of economic depression in 1929 than had been the case in 1923, the previous period of "hard times."[6]

A 1928 survey of fifty-five colleges revealed that only 5 percent of the male students (and 4 percent of the women) who had dropped out of school left because of financial problems. Seven years later, however, a majority of the dropouts in ten of twenty-five surveyed colleges had been forced to leave school as a result of financial difficulties. The change was occasioned in part by the depression itself, and in part by the democratization in college attendance that had occurred in the 1920s. The latter development brought more and more students with precarious finances to the colleges and universities. Thus, if university officials expected their institutions to remain economically viable in the depression, they could no longer expect students to pay their full tuition unassisted. This lesson was reinforced by the 10 percent decline in college enrollments that occurred between 1932 and 1934.[7]

Thus, during the "hundred days" when the Roosevelt administration was sending legislation to Congress to assist labor, business, and agriculture, one voice was raised in behalf of the politically weak student group: that of college officials. They increasingly called for federal action because the states were proving obdurate in the matter of funding. In fact, the states were largely responsible for the low budgets of public universities. In 1932, for example, the Ohio legislature slashed its appropriation to Ohio State University from $9,879,206 to $7,938,926. Although university president George W. Rightmire predicted a crisis on campus unless funding was increased to $10 million, the state cut the university's appropriation still further the following year, to $6 million.[8]

Ohio State's case was not an unusual one, and many college presidents, including Rightmire, sent requests to Hopkins for a federal program to assist their needy students. As Aubrey Williams recalled many years later, "mostly it was the college presidents who brought the pressure on Congress and the President, to do something for 'unemployed youth.'"[9]

The U.S. commissioner of education, George F. Zook, sympathized with the plight of college administrators and was determined to respond favorably to their demands. For nearly ten years, since 1922, he had directed the USOE's Division of Higher Education, and he counted many college presidents as his friends. Unlike his successor, John Ward Studebaker, Zook's attitude toward education meshed perfectly not with educators in the local school districts, who viewed the federal government as a threat, but with college administrators, who saw Washington as a source of rescue. Desperate for student aid funds and accustomed to receiving public revenues at the state level, college heads knew what they wanted from the New Deal: financial aid to entice students back into the schools. Zook was prepared to support them in their demands.

During the summer of 1933 Zook invited some of America's most "prominent educational leaders" to attend a USOE-sponsored conference he had scheduled for 8 August to consider what to do for the hundreds of thousands of high school graduates facing the depression. Twenty responded favorably and attended the conference, including Robert M. Hutchins, the thirty-two-year-old president of the University of Chicago; Mordecai W. Johnson, president of Howard University and later a member of the NYA's National Advisory Council; Harlan Updegraf, the former president of Cornell; and Charles R. Mann, president of the American Council on Education.[10]

After one day of deliberations, Zook announced that the conferees and the USOE had agreed that the FERA should "set aside funds for a Nationwide program of educational work relief." Zook described as "a matter of national concern" the "deplorable" condition of the nation's high school graduates. "Many of them with excellent preparation and native capacity are unable to continue their education." The commissioner estimated that about a million of these youths were insufficiently trained to acquire jobs. He called for the allocation of $30 million to provide a dollar a day for each of 100,000 youths, from families on relief, willing to return to the schools.

Each student could continue to receive funds for ten months. This was a considerably more generous student aid program than the one the FERA ultimately provided. Yet Zook believed that many more youths than the 100,000 were in need of schooling. Therefore he suggested that the FERA spend an additional $12.5 million to hire jobless teachers to train 400,000 youths deficient in education but ineligible for student aid (that is, not from families on relief).[11]

Officials in the relief wing of the New Deal had their own reasons that month for supporting the principle of federal student aid. Although some of these reasons differed considerably from the considerations advanced by the USOE, they too pointed to support for the idea. The Roosevelt administration's major concern in 1933 and 1934 remained the problem of relieving unemployment and speeding economic recovery. The consensus was that reform would have to await the emplacement of the economic recovery program. In planning for a revised youth program, then, FERA officials sought solutions that would not only assist youth but would simultaneously stimulate employment and recovery for the rest of society. A youth program was particularly attractive because it offered the possibility of relieving the crowded job market of the workers least likely to secure employment (the unskilled young), thus easing the job competition for the remaining adults. The goal of decongesting the labor market was one of the two most important objectives of the FERA youth programs.[12]

The administration's inclination to take groups out of the labor market grew stronger when it became apparent that an old American evil—child labor—might be wiped out in the process. One of the age-old causes of unemployment among adults was the employment of children under sixteen at substandard wages. By prohibiting the hiring of the young, the New Deal would release these jobs to adults. Federal regulations would ensure that adult workers received a living wage. Meanwhile, the newly unemployed youths, instead of burdening the federal treasury by moving to relief jobs, presumably would return to school and gain the skills with which they could later compete more successfully for employment.

It was thus envisioned that a youth policy designed to promote recovery and reduce unemployment might have the added advantage of inaugurating child labor reform. Furthermore, this could be accomplished without contradicting the administration's oft-expressed desire to achieve a balanced budget. The machinery necessary to attain this goal already existed in the form of the NRA. Accordingly, NRA regulations were adopted prohibiting all parties to the code agreements from employing children under sixteen years of age. The New Dealers were determined that such a reform would do more than abolish child labor. In September 1933 Harry Hopkins noted that "one of the main purposes of the NRA . . . is to spread employment among adults and release children to continue their education."[13]

Unfortunately for the New Deal design, many of the "children" proved uncooperative. With many school districts operating on shortened terms, and others closed entirely, even those who were willing to return to the classroom found it impossible to do so. Since countless schools were operating on reduced budgets, vocational course offerings suffered. Young people expecting education to render them jobworthy were likely to find such schools unattractive. Families with a father or mother out of work often could not afford to allow a child the luxury of an education, regardless of what the NRA decreed. The predictable result was that children remained in the job lines and businessmen began applying for exemptions from the minimum age provisions of the codes. The Roosevelt administration steadfastly refused to grant these requests.[14]

By August 1933 the administration had been largely unsuccessful in its effort to use the NRA to ease the pressure on the job market. The New Dealers' hope that students would return voluntarily to the schools had proven groundless.

Meanwhile, by 8 August, with the USOE proposal for a student aid program already in hand, the FERA was presented with the means not only to accomplish what the NRA had failed to do (draw young Americans out of the labor market) but also to meet the demands student leaders and university presidents were pressing on the administration.

Those demands became even more vocal and concentrated in August. On 15 August Robert Hutchins was scheduled to return to Washington as chairman of the advisory council of the Congress-related Federal Employment Service. In addition, Hutchins was representing the college presidents, for he carried with him a draft of a student aid plan. As it happened, Roosevelt was scheduled to meet with Hopkins and NRA chief Hugh Johnson that same day in a session called to more effectively coordinate relief and recovery activities. Whether Roosevelt, seeking perhaps to preempt Hutchins's demands, directed Hopkins to prepare a recommendation on student aid for use at this meeting, or whether Hopkins independently prepared a memorandum in light of Hutchins's imminent visit (and the growing pressure of the college presidents) is not clear. But on 14 August Hopkins prepared such a recommendation for the president. And on the following day Roosevelt met with Hutchins to discuss the propriety of using federal funds for such a purpose. Since the president also placed the proposal before the National Recovery Council the following day, it is clear that Roosevelt was not as late in supporting the idea of a federal student aid program as many historians have charged.[15]

The Hopkins memorandum that the president took with him to his meeting with Hutchins, Johnson, and the FERA chief is worthy of extended analysis. As an expression of opinion within the relief wing of the New Deal, it affords an opportunity to compare and contrast the thinking of FERA personnel and USOE officials on the question of youth planning. The Hopkins plan was largely a duplication, with some expansion, of the Zook proposal advanced on 8 August. Hopkins advised Roosevelt that a program should be established to offer work relief to young people willing to enter, or remain in, school. He recommended that the program be made available to college students but not those in high school. It seemed wise to test the experiment of federal student aid at the colleges, since they were fewer in number and more readily observable than the high schools. Furthermore, college officials were exerting more political pressure than secondary school leaders.

Hopkins wrote the president that half of the 1 million new graduates of the nation's high schools were looking for work but willing to continue their education if assisted. The fact that these youths continued to occupy the nation's labor market was harmful for both themselves and the nation. These young people "would normally be under educational auspices," he explained, and they were "not adequately prepared for work in industry, commerce or the professions." By providing work relief to enable students to go to college, the New Deal would offer a real service to American youth. "At the same time," he added, such a program would help relieve the job market, since the 500,000 youths were "actively competing with heads of families for available jobs."[16]

Further agreeing with Zook, Hopkins recommended that the federal government employ forty thousand professionals and assign them to university extension departments, where they would teach 400,000 youths in a variety of "vocational and cultural subjects." These students would receive free instruction but no work and no income. Work relief would go to 100,000 college students. Hopkins hoped that student jobs would "remove these young people from industrial competition for a year and . . . give them the educational opportunities which under normal conditions they would receive." In addition to these components of the plan, Hopkins included within his recommendation two plans that had taken shape before the USOE conference and had received the prior support of the FERA. He urged the president to approve the use of FERA funds to hire teachers to conduct classes in rural elementary schools as well as to teach adults to read and write. Further, Hopkins suggested the placement of fifteen hundred to sixteen hundred jobless teachers in the CCC camps to alleviate the unexpectedly high rate of illiteracy that had been found to be characteristic of CCC youth.[17]

Perhaps it was not surprising that Roosevelt approved at once only those portions of the proposal that had originated prior to the USOE conference. At heart a fiscal conservative, and always anxious to move with extreme caution in acting boldly, Roosevelt was aware that the employment of forty thousand teachers would cost less than a work relief program for 100,000 students. Then, too, the teachers would provide vital instruction to young children at a critical stage in their development, whereas college student aid would go to only a fragment of America's student population (those in college), at a time when less than 8 percent of Americans aged eighteen to twenty-four attended institutions of higher learning. An administration concerned with assisting "the forgotten man" and the dispossessed of the nation moved slowly to assist what it, perhaps unfairly, regarded as a strata of the wealthier segments of the middle class.[18]

As Roosevelt mulled over Hopkins's plan, an additional consideration was his trust in Hopkins, with whom he had worked in New York State and whose judgment he respected. Aid to teachers was an idea FDR had had time to consider, and Hopkins recommended it as a relatively inexpensive way of lifting educational spirits and teaching "plastic" minds. The Zook plan, by contrast, was conceived largely by outsiders and dropped suddenly into the president's lap. Finally, the mere promise of college student aid in the future (which the president preferred) would please Hutchins and the college presidents for the time being. Hence, when FDR met with the press two days after receiving the Hopkins memo, he admitted that college student aid was under serious consideration but almost certainly likely to be rejected for the moment. The president was holding out hope to those in favor of the idea while simultaneously satisfying the conservative proponents of inaction. "Watchful waiting" offered a risk-free alternative to immediate action, one that would always furnish an opportunity to act if the emergency (and the pressure) continued, and to quietly table the idea if they did not.

From the moment Roosevelt approved of the concept of federal student aid to the period of final drafting of the plan, caution characterized the New Deal approach toward what would become the core program of the National Youth Administration. Some of the events that preceded the program's announcement suggest that it was in large part a political gesture designed to quiet the demands of adamant college presidents and their students. In August, September, and October, the pressure for action intensified rather than abated, forcing the administration to consider reluctantly an immediate revival of the concept. On 15 August, for example, the *New York Times* reported that Hutchins was to meet with the president to discuss student aid, an account that convinced college and student leaders that a favorable moment had arrived to press their case yet again on the administration. Robert L. Kelly, executive secretary of the Association of American Colleges, wrote Hopkins on 16 August that the FERA, as "a work of high statesmanship," should fund and support the Office of Education's plan to provide work relief for students. Richard S. Burington, an instructor at Case School of Applied Science, urged the president to put students to work on public works or on projects of the army and navy to help them "finance all or part of the expense incident to attendance in college." On 15 August the president of the National Student Federation, John H. Lang, wrote Hopkins endorsing his "plan to send college boys back to school through federal relief." [19]

Others lined up behind the program. Speaking of "perplexed and discouraged" high school graduates, Newton D. Baker, secretary of war in the Wilson administration, called for an end to budget cuts at the expense of students. "It is our duty to see that work for boys and girls throughout the country is unimpaired by the disaster in which we adults have been plunged, and for which we alone are responsible." Meanwhile, explaining that he had come "reluctantly to the conclusion that the Federal government must take an active part in public education," Hutchins himself that same month called for the creation of a cabinet-level Department of Education. "I have never," he added, "heard of any argument advanced condemning one child to illiteracy because he was born in one part of the country, whereas another born in another part may at public expense proceed from the nursery school to the highest scholarly degrees." [20]

Given the evident popularity of the idea of student aid, and the obvious hostility to federal administration of the program, Roosevelt characteristically was inclined to push for a program offering something for everyone. Decentralization, therefore, was as essential to the program's popularity as the program itself. To draft the evolving student aid plan, Hopkins selected EEP director Lewis R. Alderman and Cyril F. Klinefelter, Alderman's assistant. Together they worked out the full provisions of a program that would integrate youth's needs more centrally in an endeavor that had been launched as a means of aiding collegiate finances.[21]

THE DEBATE within the administration over the proper method to proceed with student aid concerned precisely this question: Should student aid be designed primarily to aid students (and hence serve as a "youth program"), or should it primarily help university finances? The New Deal's genuine humanitarianism focused on the former objective, while its equally real political concerns stressed the latter. Reflecting the president's own ambivalence on this issue, Hopkins vacillated over the question. In his 14 August memo he expressed hope that student aid would provide an "educational opportunity for those young people who have been denied this opportunity because of the economic depression." He was thus one of the first to suggest that New Deal youth policy be designed to eliminate obstacles to educational opportunity for low-income youth as well as to relieve the pressures on a crowded American job market. These would remain the guiding principles of the New Deal on the campus.[22]

Nevertheless, while Hopkins was genuinely concerned with the plight of low-income youth, his student aid proposal placed priority on removing pressure from the job lines of America. He advised FDR to present the plan to the public "first, as a means of taking one-half million young people now looking for jobs in competition with heads of families out of the industrial market," and only second as a proposal to help relieve youth's financial woes. Moreover, while it offered work relief to the 100,000, Hopkins's measure was presented in the guise of a scholarship program. Hopkins proposed having

the relief offices of the United States select 300,000 high school graduates who in their judgment would benefit by formal college or university training. These 300,000 children would be given a competitive examination, the highest 100,000 would be matriculated in the various schools of the United States and given work relief to the extent of about twenty hours per week so that they could earn approximately seven dollars a week.[23]

Roosevelt, however, eventually proved resistant to the idea of providing work relief to superior students. Characteristically, his motives were both reformist and political. To have required a certain degree of intellectual performance as a prerequisite for eligibility would have prevented the New Deal from achieving what a correspondent from DePauw University regarded as its objective: the neutralization of "an aristocratic educational system in the United States." From 1933 until the abolition of the CCC and NYA ten years later, Roosevelt spoke of how these agencies had helped democratize educational opportunity by extending it to those least likely to partake of education: the poor. Scholarships would have limited the opportunity to those of high intellectual ability.[24]

At the same time, the president was well aware that a requirement of superior scholarship would interfere with the New Deal recovery program. Such a rule would limit the number of young people taken from the job lines and increase the likelihood of squabbles with Congress. For example, when Hopkins proposed modifying CCC policy, Roosevelt countered: "You will realize that all three proposals will mean less people taken from the unemployment rolls." In December 1935, long after the idea of providing scholarships had been abandoned, Roosevelt explained why he had opposed such a scheme. "Much as I would like to, I cannot see my way clear to approve placing these boys and girls at work unless they come from needy families," he wrote Williams. "If I open the door here it will reopen the whole question in relation to CCC camps and a number of other government projects."[25]

Hopkins's proposal revealed that FERA officials had been careful to create a youth program that would operate on past precedents and offer benefits to groups other than the young. The possibility of offering loans and scholarships to students was considered briefly. Both of these forms of student aid had been provided by the colleges for many years and might have engendered less criticism than work relief, even if provided by the federal government. To be sure, Hopkins proposed that the 100,000 scholarship "winners" work for their relief stipends, but even the work relief aspect of the scheme was not as novel as it seemed. By August 1933 FERA officials had already expressed a preference that relief recipients work for their benefits. Thus, in a sense, extending such benefits to college students was following rather than establishing precedent.[26]

A policy of requiring students to work had the added advantage of serving the labor needs of college and university officials. According to NYA administrators, "college budgets did not have the funds to keep their physical equipment in the best possible shape [or] to hire the clerical, library, and laboratory assistants needed to serve an increased number of students." Federal work relief not only would help students continue their education; it would offer the financially embattled college presidents a labor force at no expense to themselves. This is not to say that federal relief officials viewed student aid primarily as a means of aiding educational institutions rather than students. In fact, they sincerely desired to extend educational opportunities for low-income youth. As Alderman later wrote to a Kansas newspaper reporter, "the idea of providing part-time employment for needy college students was not to aid institutions as such." The checks were sent directly to students, and only to those students who would otherwise "be obligated to quit and compete on the open labor market with unemployed adults." More succinctly, Alderman warned one college president anxious to pay existing college workers with FERA funds reserved for students that "this policy is primarily to afford work to needy students rather than directly to aid colleges themselves." Alderman and his associates in the EEP believed, however, that their goal of aiding low-income youth would be largely accomplished once the students were enabled to remain in school.[27]

Alderman and Klinefelter were not the only New Deal relief officials who possessed deep concern for the special problems of youth. Like others, however, they had to subordinate these concerns to the New Deal's commitment to help other social groups first. As administrators of the EEP, Alderman and Klinefelter hoped to refine the concept of college student aid into a program more beneficial for young people than for the institutions in which they worked. In part this change reflected their own preferences, for both men had had lifelong experience working with students and professional educators at the district level, rather than with university leaders. As a result, their own personal preferences lay with a program designed to help students, not college budgets. Alderman was sixty-one in 1933; he had been superintendent of schools in Portland, Oregon, and, since 1925, had served as chief of the service division and adult education in the USOE. Between 1933 and 1935 Klinefelter was also "on loan" from the Office of Education. Like Alderman, he possessed more than a decade of experience working directly on the problems of young people of secondary school age. From 1920 to 1933 he was a member of the staff of the Federal Board for Vocational Training, an agency independent of the USOE prior to 1933, working on the board's trade and industrial education service. At the time he was appointed to the FERA position he was serving as editor and educational consultant for the USOE's Division of Vocational Education.[28]

In spite of their professional education backgrounds, however, in late 1933 both men were serving within the FERA and were compelled to follow policy. As of 15 August that policy was to plan a college aid scheme but not to unveil such a program until absolutely necessary. "Necessity" was defined as collegiate pressure of an extent that could no longer be ignored. By definition, then, the task posed for Alderman and Klinefelter was one of assisting colleges to meet their needs through the employment of students (not a plan primarily designed to help youth), and only to help the colleges when it became obvious that college heads could not meet their own needs unassisted.

Several months passed before FERA officials decided that that time had come. Documenting the course of inaction is, by its very nature, nearly impossible. But the response of FERA leaders to continued pleas for action indicates how and at what pace the college aid scheme was drafted, and why the plan assumed the form it ultimately achieved. On 12 September an impatient John Lang wrote FERA's assistant director, C. M. Bookman, of his intention to visit Washington and "talk over the matter of the college relief plan" with him. Bookman's secretary replied that there had been no change in FERA policy since August, and hence there was no need for a visit. Nor did FERA thinking change in the following six weeks. One who hoped the FERA would move more rapidly to approve an aid program for students was Minnesota's governor, Floyd B. Olson, a member of the left-wing Farmer-Laborite party. As early as August, Olson had appointed a committee of thirty-one state leaders to propose ways of helping some of Minnesota's 250,000 jobless youths to occupy themselves in college. He had traveled to Washington that month to urge that federal monies be devoted to this purpose. The FERA turned a deaf ear to Olson's pleas, both in August and October, when he asked the FERA for $100,000 to pay the "sustenance" of a thousand college students. Alderman advised Bookman to draft a reply disillusioning Olson of any expectation of such aid. "This is not in accordance with our releases or our policies," Alderman explained, "and if granted will open the gates for a flood of requests and will bring to our doors a continuous fight between public and private schools."[29]

Continued pressure from university presidents helped convince the FERA that the time had come for action. So, too, did an awareness that aid to teachers, adults, the handicapped, and preschool children had all been introduced by October 1933. The danger of further inaction was that the public might question why nothing had been done for college-age students. With Hopkins's go-ahead and the assistance of the USOE, Alderman and Klinefelter began drafting a revised student aid program in November, one calculated to assist more needy youths than the Hopkins plan and to be even more decentralist in operation. The plan retained the provision that students must perform work supervised by college officials. Rejected were both the concept of loans and scholarships and the idea that either state or federal officials should select the students to be aided. Scholarships and loans were considered counterproductive in a scheme designed in part to equalize educational opportunities for rich and poor students alike. Historically, scholarships had been provided to students "of outstanding scholastic achievement," while the prerequisite for receiving a loan had often been resident status on the campus. In the pursuit of such awards, many needy students were likely to be at a serious disadvantage. Under the plan submitted by Alderman and Klinefelter, no student would be eligible for an FERA job unless his "financial status" was such as to "make impossible his attendance at college without this aid."[30]

In December 1933 the plan (perhaps because of Olson's persistent requests) was developed and tested at the University of Minnesota. There was little doubt, however, that federal aid would be extended to all "non-profit-making" colleges and universities in the nation. After only two months, Hopkins announced on 2 February 1934 that the FERA program would be made available to 100,000 college students nationwide. Between $5 and $7 million would be sent to the colleges for this purpose, far less than the $30 million suggested by the conferees of the USOE's August 1933 youth conference. Not only would college officials rather than state or federal administrators assign students to FERA jobs, but the colleges would create the jobs on which students would labor.[31]

Other provisions of the program were designed to ensure that as many needy youths as possible be removed from the labor market. Unless tuition was lowered, some students would require more than fifteen dollars each month to remain in school. Accordingly, the FERA initially required all participating institutions to "waive all fees for registration, tuition, laboratories, and other purposes for the student receiving federal assistance." When some colleges refused to participate under this requirement, it was replaced with a recommendation that colleges lower the tuition costs of FERA students. The FERA officials also attempted to guarantee that a minimum number of youths in the college aid program be students who hitherto had never experienced college life. Regulations stipulated that one of every four federally assisted youths be drawn from this group.[32]

As FERA officials interpreted their mandate, they were to help the widest possible array of Americans, old as well as young, with their "youth" program. Therefore, the planning program resulted in a succession of draft proposals, creating collectively one ongoing proposal with an accretionary body of beneficiary groups. This result clouded the question of FERA priorities. Were youth to be the primary or secondary beneficiaries of "college student aid"? The commitment to youth shared by the FERA leadership did not assert itself at this time, but not because the New Deal possessed a disregard for youth; it did not. Rather, the Roosevelt administration possessed a positive determination to confront the entire unemployment problem at once. This decision in turn left FERA personnel no choice but to draft an omnibus venture that hid their private preferences.

Thus a college student aid program that seemed to slight youth emerged from the pens of officials who, in their other writings, voiced persistent concern for the plight of the young. For example, by providing part-time jobs to students, Alderman and Klinefelter recognized that they were helping to stabilize enrollments in higher education and offering college officials a no-cost labor force for college improvements. So long as the workers hired were students, college officials could use them to maintain and improve university grounds and buildings, and otherwise to perform labor of value more to the institutions than to the students. The FERA enacted safeguards against this possibility, but the safeguards were initiated not by Alderman and Klinefelter (who were working to alleviate college conditions) but by the college officials themselves. In a passage that suggests just how instrumental the pressure of college presidents was to the creation of the student aid program, Alderman wrote some months later that "the various committees of college presidents which assisted materially in this office in drawing up the conditions of this February 2, 1934 FERA press release were agreed that such a condition was necessary.

They pointed out that unless such a condition were inserted, some institutions would merely transfer such students over to the Federal payroll, thus preventing other needy students who were equally in need and had not had opportunity previously to engage in work while attending college to receive such help."[33] Many college presidents exhibited an impressive willingness to place the goal of helping college students ahead of what appeared to be the New Deal's predominantly institutional concern with helping the colleges even at the expense of the young.

The New Dealers possessed considerable concern for the needs of youth as well. After all, Klinefelter and Alderman readily conceded the need for the stipulation suggested by the college presidents. It was the FERA, not the college heads, who had established the student aid program and provided it the funding with which to operate. But at this juncture FERA leaders were as anxious to help the colleges as the young, and wished to shore up the old foundations of American higher education as much as to build a new educational foundation for American democracy. In January 1935, when a correspondent wondered whether the student aid program would be continued the following autumn, Hopkins argued that America's future as a democracy would be ill-served by any other decision. As the federal relief administrator put it, aid to college students was "a tangible expression of the New Deal in permitting financially embarrassed young men and women to develop their talents and be in a position to exert a leadership for democracy that otherwise would have been impossible." And yet, to those who drafted the program, the initial justification for student aid involved its usefulness in promoting activities of importance to the colleges. Furthermore, by taking the young people out of the labor market, the measure helped adults find work more easily and thereby aided the New Deal's recovery program. Federal officials at first considered, then abandoned, the idea of offering scholarships. In each case, however, a consideration of what youth required was not the only factor. Scholarships were tempting because they were traditional, but work relief won out because it would take more youths out of the labor market.[34]

Once enough low-income students had been helped to pursue an education, FERA officials believed their work for the student group had been accomplished. Whether New Deal jobs matched students' interests and were vocationally useful, or whether they merely offered the universities a labor force for projects of interest only to colleges, did not alter the fact that the federal government's primary purpose was being fulfilled: student workers were in the colleges rather than on the streets. During the New Deal's first two years, federal planners made only one attempt to guarantee that student jobs had vocational value for young people. They stipulated that students be assigned to new projects, not those planned and funded in previous university budgets. Beyond this gesture FERA officials would not go. The FERA college student aid program thus offers further evidence that, from the beginning, the Roosevelt administration possessed vaunted ambitions for introducing federal initiatives on behalf of young people but retained its characteristic caution in translating those hopes into reality.

CHAPTER FOUR

The Inner War
over Youth Policy

The crux of the debate between conservative educators and New
Dealers lay in their definition of the capacity of the schools to meet
the needs of low-income youth. At the Chicago convention of the
NEA in 1933, NEA secretary J. W. Crabtree insisted that the financial
crisis was not too great for educators to continue to fulfill their responsibilities. Their work, he added, had an essentially conservative intent. In
facing "the blasts of the worst storm in the history of our nation," the profession had "succeeded in salvaging many of the essentials in our American
system of education which will serve as a basis for readjustments and re-
building to begin as soon as the dark clouds and the fury of the winds
have passed." He concluded that "the profession led by local, state, and
national associations is 'weathering the storm' in a remarkably effective
manner," and without federal assistance.

But educators did more than claim that they were competent to reach
out to low-income youth. They assailed the New Dealers for forgetting
their obligations to all other young people within the nation's economic
class structure. A variety of NEA officials accused the New Deal of "class
favoritism," arguing that the Roosevelt administration had rejected a general appropriation of federal aid to the states in favor of the creation of
relief agencies that would assist only the poor. The inference was that general aid (the so-called principle of money on the stump) would go equally

to all Americans, while the New Deal, through the CCC and FERA, was restricting the federal government to advancing only a segment of the population. Thus, in the eyes of the NEA, the New Deal was establishing not only a wasteful and parallel system of education (training youth who could be served by private educators) but also a "class-conscious," and therefore un-American, one.[1]

Hopkins and Williams developed a counterargument to this thesis: the professionals had had their opportunity to provide job training to low-income youth, had rejected it, and therefore had abandoned the working class, the poor, and the blacks to a form of education that failed to fit them for work in a depressed economy. Educators, they believed, were training the young in the wrong kinds of skills: white-collar education in a blue-collar work world. Even worse, their pleas for federal aid and their denunciation of federal control seemed wasteful of time—time that might have been better devoted to improving educational services. "The educators have a great lingo," Williams wrote early in 1934; "they talk glibly of [our] not supporting the one-room school. I suppose . . . it doesn't make any difference whether it is one room or a hundred rooms—it is what goes on in the rooms."[2]

According to a seminal study of public education in the depression, Hopkins and Williams believed that educators had written off the low-income group. This group comprised the very Americans for whom the New Deal relief officials had targeted their overall "social justice" objective of getting "help as quickly as possible to those who needed it." If private educators were already fitting middle-class youth to the white-collar jobs they expected, and if the New Deal was to help Americans do collectively what they could not do individually, it followed that the Roosevelt administration must address the needs of the ignored—the poor. By lifting the low-income youth to the status of his or her middle-class peer (the status of one given a job-oriented form of education), the New Dealers felt they were merely reforming education and rendering it "class-neutral." Far from being un-American, they regarded themselves as truer servants of the older traditions of American democracy than the educators who they believed had abdicated their responsibility to both American democracy and American youth.[3]

Whether the president of the United States would accede to the wishes of the FERA planners under Williams or gratify the hopes of the conservative educators depended on more than Roosevelt's personal inclinations.

Insofar as the latter was concerned, the president's appointments to the agency, in background and philosophy similar to Williams, signaled his approval of the Alabamian's views. But the political winds in America were changing that spring as well, buffeting the New Deal and the FERA in new directions. The new directions, like the new personnel of the agency, would point the New Deal away from conservative ventures and toward a National Youth Administration bearing the signature of Aubrey Williams's ideas.

IN ITS FIRST YEAR the New Deal seemed designed to assist the most vocal and politically potent constituents within the national community. American youth were aided in much the same way. The first "New Deal youths" were, of course, those in the CCC. The public perceived the young CCC enrollees less as youths than as idle men wandering the streets and threatening social stability. In 1934 the sociologist Thomas Minehan, in describing them as "boy and girl tramps," emphasized the social costs of their deterioration and despair, not their personal misfortune or their educational deficiencies as "youth." Further, the forty thousand teachers hired in September were voters, and no one doubted the political influence of those college presidents who increasingly demanded aid for college students. In aiding seventy-five thousand such students, Hopkins was meeting an important political need as well as ministering to a pressing human need. Both considerations, in fairly equal measure, guided the New Deal throughout 1933.

As a result, during its first year the Roosevelt administration sponsored no measure beyond the CCC (which employed only males, and no more than 250,000 of them in any one month) to address the problems of high school dropouts and out-of-school youths. Having already grown accustomed to the tales of idle youth and wandering men told in 1932 and 1933, most Americans seemed not to notice the estimated four million young people unoccupied in school or workplace. Thus the New Deal turned its attention first to more pressing problems and more vocal constituencies.[4]

After February 1934, the balance scales in the register of New Deal concerns began to tip toward a more serious effort to relieve the plight of America's politically voiceless youth. A number of factors weighed heavily in the balance on behalf of the out-of-school group. First, the disparity between the millions of idle youths in America and the less than one million aided by the New Deal in 1933 could not be unnoticed for long. Second, a period of new inspiration was developing within the FERA during the spring of 1934. On 31 March the Civil Works Administration (CWA) was phased out of operation and the quest for a successor began. For the immediate future, the old FERA practice of permitting the states to provide both jobs and direct relief was allowed to continue. But planning for some more permanent and ambitious work relief program, modeled after the CWA, was also initiated within the labyrinths of the FERA.

In addition, the FERA underwent a curious and little-noticed transition, in which the first-year administrators tended to be replaced by men and women of very different backgrounds and priorities. In 1933 the major policy decisions had been made by people who had spent most of their professional lives creating relief bureaucracies at the city, state, and national levels, working to raise the standards of social service work in the direction of "professionalism" and work relief. In addition to Hopkins, the architect and first chief of New York State's Temporary Emergency Relief Administration, the early leadership of the FERA included Frank Bane (onetime executive director of the American Public Welfare Association) and C. M. Bookman, who had for a generation served as executive director of the Community Chest of Cincinnati and Hamilton County. By 1934, however, Bane and Bookman had departed and Hopkins was spending more of his time testifying before congressional committees. In addition to seeking larger appropriations for relief, Hopkins spent much of 1934 tackling the political problem of state governments unwilling to supply their fair share of relief, and generally overworking himself. On the president's insistence, he reduced his workload in late spring and took a vacation to Europe that July. Never again did Hopkins, to the degree that he had in 1933, take charge of the FERA's day-to-day planning.[5]

Aubrey Williams took over in Hopkins's absence. Just as sensitive to the plight of needy people as Hopkins, he was more insistent that, regardless of the degree of political pressure, action for the out-of-school group ought no longer be delayed. Unlike Hopkins, Williams had once worked to alleviate the problems of young people; he wrote model child-labor legislation for the Wisconsin Conference of Social Work in the 1920s. Williams was assisted by men and women who possessed backgrounds not in relief philosophy (and in some cases, not in relief at all) but in fields that involved daily contact and concern with the problems of youth. The two USOE planners on loan to the FERA, Alderman and Klinefelter, were joined

by ex-publisher Jacob Baker and ex–graduate students Elizabeth Wickenden and Arthur Goldschmidt, two planners of FERA transient relief. In
addition, Williams received advice from Hilda Worthington Smith, the
FERA's specialist in workers' education. Smith, who directed the Summer School for Women Workers in Industry at Bryn Mawr in the 1920s,
received authorization from Hopkins in the spring of 1934 to establish
a program of educational schools and camps for jobless young women.[6]
Others advised Williams on planning throughout 1934. What most had in
common was firsthand, if not professional, contact with young people and
their problems.

As for Williams himself, he went to work with a will on the task of devising a new relief program for the FERA. By March, his typical workday
was running to eleven hours or more. Unlike Hopkins, he was not disposed
to conciliate the organized educators, within or without the FERA—men
and women he believed were knowingly or unknowingly denying to blue-
collar youth the industrial work skills they so desperately required from
the classroom. He suspected, however, that they sought federal aid less
to improve educational services than to strengthen themselves organiza-
tionally. On 13 March a friend, Professor Joseph K. Hart of Vanderbilt
University, wrote Williams of his suspicion that the public was about to
be "gouged" in the allocation of federal money for education. The wrong
would be committed, he predicted, "not by the men in Washington" but
by school officials making "persistent and specious pleas for the schools.
Here, in this state, the school officials are spending money like drunken
sailors, for the most ridiculous things." Hart sought reassurance that the
federal government was developing a plan to prevent fraudulent use of its
funds. "So far, I've seen absolutely no evidence that the public school man
[sic] have any other program than the perpetuation of the machine."[7]

Williams made no attempt to reassure his friend, for Hart's doubts approximated his own. As Williams told the professor, when he opened his
letter, "Klinefelter, who assists Alderman, happened to be in my office,
and I had just gotten through telling him that a lot of these places [sic] were
trying to take us for a ride." Williams added that he would do all he could
to make the schools pay more for their own support. Employing a word
that the president would use in assailing conservative educators (at a 1942
press conference), Williams concluded that the school men spoke "glibly"
when they talked of the glories of the independent one-room schoolhouse.
In 1937 and 1940 Williams assailed educators for lacking the "guts" to

teach the facts about maldistribution of wealth in America. He blamed them for developing "a hereditary caste system whereby only the children of the well-to-do might enter the professions and the children of the now less honored occupations should remain permanently bound to follow in their parents' footsteps." Without federal intervention, he added, millions would be denied free education; it was "another thing that we find ourselves romancing about." These bitter comments of the future were well in the process of formation in 1935, and they provide a hint of the deep animosity Williams felt toward those who stood in the way of federally supervised education for youth.

Williams's animosity toward American educators could only grow deeper in the months ahead. For the most part, his feelings were understandable, if not wholly justifiable. While the educators maintained their opposition to any work relief program for youth involving training, by March Williams had concluded that the entire structure of federal relief in America would collapse without an integrated plan of attack on unemployment in which a federal jobs program for youth was an absolutely indispensable component. Conflict with the educators was unavoidable. That meant conflict within his own agency, since several of its personnel were determined to champion the conservative educational philosophy.[8]

Williams was in a fighting mood. He was prepared to do battle with the conservative education philosophy, whether expressed by outside critics of the New Deal or reformers within his own relief administration. Some within the FERA worked openly that spring and summer to incorporate the educators' wishes into the evolving youth plans of the FERA. As he worked his eleven-hour days in March, Williams began drafting an article for the *New York Times* as a means of publicizing his plans for a new national program for relief. Teachers were "indispensable to the kind of recovery toward which we strive," he jotted down in the manuscript for his article as a gesture of conciliation. But the date of publication, the first of April, lent silent irony to Williams's ultimate determination that the teachers would do no more than assist a federal government striving and leading the way toward reform.[9]

When a principle seemed at issue, Williams went to work. Characteristically, he sought arguments and confederates. Neither was absent in the spring of 1934. For one thing, it was difficult to ignore the fact that New Deal "recovery" programs, such as the NRA, had retarded the reemployment of young people by discriminating against them in such areas as hiring practices and child labor proscriptions. AAA crop-reduction subsidies had reduced employment opportunities on the farm, and Public Works Administration (PWA) policies had banned youth from public works. These policies seemed to obligate the federal government to a campaign of redress. On 11 April 1934 Commissioner Zook announced that such difficulties had convinced him to call a "Conference on Youth Problems" to meet during the first two days of June and plan a coordinated response to the problem. "In the National recovery program," he explained, "the position of youth is particularly unfortunate. Even as employment increases, young people do not in general get jobs." "Federal responsibilities" seemed "peculiarly involved" in the problem.[10]

Zook's call and the conference itself created precedents that Williams could point to in support of his ideas. Zook invited people from more than a dozen government agencies to attend, or send representatives to, the conference. Invitations were sent to Harry Hopkins; Robert Fechner, director of the CCC; Milburn A. Wilson, director of the AAA's Subsistence Homestead program; Assistant Secretary of Labor Oscar L. Chapman; Grace Abbott, head of the Children's Bureau; and Frank Persons, the director of the U.S. Employment Service. A variety of representatives of the USOE were invited as well, including Assistant Commissioner Bess Goodykoontz, Fred W. Kelly (chief of the office's Division of Higher Education), and J. C. Wright, the adviser on vocational education. Far from being united behind Williams's proposition that the federal government must create new jobs programs for youth, most of those invited hoped to prod localities and communities to use more ingenuity in solving the youth problem themselves. All agreed, however, that the federal government must serve as a national spur to action. Zook's move aided Williams by serving notice that, until complete victory over youth unemployment was won, the burden of determining where the federal government must stop in achieving the goal lay with the opponents, not the supporters, of federal action.[11]

If issues and conferences proved useful to Williams in support of his brief, other FERA officials were indispensable to its chances for adoption. Among the most important was Hilda Worthington Smith, the FERA's specialist on workers' education. At Bryn Mawr Smith's Summer School for Women Workers in Industry had not been designed to institute "social control," as some historians have suggested; instead Smith had tried to break down one of the barriers between classes and obstacles to national progress: the ignorance of American economic conditions. The labor school had been designed to increase working women's activities as reformers and their intelligence as social critics. Women were trained in economics, the origin of labor problems, and social problems generally. School revenue declined sharply by 1933, however, prompting Smith to write C. M. Bookman, the FERA's deputy administrator, requesting federal aid.

Although the FERA provided no immediate funding for Bryn Mawr, FERA officials recognized that Smith might provide more help for the agency than vice versa. Smith was hired in September by the agency and directed immediately to plan a federal program to assist working women in some manner comparable to the procedure worked out for men under the CCC.[12]

Smith's draft proposal, completed later that same month, indicated that she, earlier than most agency officials, recognized that the federal government's responsibilities for exacerbating youth unemployment entailed a corresponding obligation to fund federal antidotes to the rising problem. The "NRA program will throw out of employment no less than 1,500,000 young workers," she wrote. "It is clearly a responsibility of the National Government to meet the needs of this group of workers affected by the National Industrial program."

Smith made it clear that the federal government must bypass the schools in a physical sense if it hoped to restore both educational standards and, more important, the morale of young people. As much as possible the FERA was to reemploy school personnel, for it could not do without their expertise and wide experience. As for the setting where the emerging education should take place, the FERA, she continued, should avoid existing schools at all costs simply because young people were apt to do so with equal determination. Smith was adamant on this point and emphasized repeatedly the problem of morale. Low morale, as she defined it, posed no immediate political dangers but promised to result in crime, alienation, and inadequate social integration, problems equally grave.

> Because of [youth's] lack of previous elementary education, these young workers cannot be easily adjusted in public school classes and will be behind their grades if they should return to school. Moreover, after years of practical working experience, they will be reluctant to return to classrooms, and

impatient of any attempt to restrict their freedoms. . . . They are pitifully unequipped through lack of education to meet the problems of modern life and play their part later as responsible citizens.

Without special provision for education, these young workers will be an easy prey for gangsters, for exploitation in street trades, a serious problem in their homes and to the police and social agencies in their communities.[13]

The chief opponent of Smith's plan and Williams's ideas was John H. Millar, the FERA's assistant on special projects. Millar and the FERA officials who shared his views on youth planning nearly all possessed backgrounds in bureaucratic administration, engineering, and other noneducational pursuits. Their perspective on federal policy toward youth nevertheless approximated the position of the conservative educators. Assisting Millar in drafting and selling his approach were Perry A. Fellows, an administrative assistant to Jacob Baker; the FERA's chief engineer, John Carmody; and regional engineers Willis Wissler and Colonel J. J. Phelan. Professional educators Alderman and Klinefelter found their ideas persuasive, but they were far less enthusiastic supporters of the group's approach than Millar himself, whose dynamism on behalf of an idea he believed in was one of the few traits he shared with Williams.[14]

Millar hoped that Washington could somehow fulfill its responsibility to increase youth employment while placing itself on record as abandoning the field to local and state educational professionals. By tapping the resources of existing federal, state, and local programs (such as the CCC and college cooperative education programs), the federal government might simultaneously draw young people off the labor market and provide training, and at the same time blue-pencil the federal government out of the business of education. As men who emphasized decentralization of administration as the highest priority for the agency, these conservative FERA officials saw their task as providing relief with one hand while preparing at the earliest possible moment to dismantle the agency with the other. Some of Millar's group conceded that American society required reform and regarded their New Deal tenures as extensions of their lifelong commitments to help establish such reform. Nevertheless, although reform must be encouraged by federal officials, it was to be carried out by private and state agencies.[15]

Between April and June 1934, Millar and Williams drafted separate proposals for new federal initiatives on behalf of youth. At the core of Millar's draft proposal was a plan to provide public service apprenticeships to high school graduates anxious for further education, and work relief in abandoned CCC camps for those not educationally inclined. Williams regarded these ideas as useful but too limited. Indeed, it was Williams himself who brought to Millar's attention the idea of using old CCC camps as a setting for youth work projects under the FERA.[16]

The two men worked harmoniously through the summer. When both plans were placed side by side for consideration in June 1934, an observer comparing the terms of the two might have concluded that the Alderman-Williams "suggestions" draft constituted little more than an expansion of the Millar plan. Both men regarded decentralization as a virtue. The "suggestions" went further than Millar's draft, urging the creation of vocational education classes for the one million out-of-school youths to be aided under his plan. In addition, Alderman and Williams urged an increase in the number of college students provided with FERA jobs (from 75,000 to 200,000) and the inauguration of a similar aid program for high school students. Although Williams did not realize it until later, these additions were unacceptable to Millar, whose intent was to assist in the removal of the federal government from the business of education, and ultimately from relief itself. Indeed, Millar regarded CCC camps and public service apprenticeships as alternatives to college student aid, useful primarily as means of prodding the federal government to reconsider, and possibly abandon, its commitment to the college student aid program itself. While Williams found Millar's proposed programs appealing, he did not believe they went far enough, and said so in June and July. The fact that both men sought decentralization further concealed from Williams their broad differences. What Williams sought, of course, was the subtraction of the youth group from the labor market, not the subtraction of the federal government from the resolution of the youth problem. Only in the autumn of 1934 would the dimensions of the dispute become clear, and then the FERA became the site of heated and bitter arguments.[17]

MILLAR'S DRAFT was inspired by the imagination and determination of local officials to provide their own programs for youth. On 12 April 1934, William Haber, then a member of the Michigan State Emergency Welfare Relief Commission, wrote Williams of a plan by three thousand jobless citizens of Michigan, aged eighteen to thirty, to solicit funds to educate themselves while producing goods and services in a camp setting. "The specific suggestion they have made is that we authorize the erection of three or four camps in the Upper Peninsula for single men." The men might learn vocational trades within the camps, produce items for use by Michigan families on relief, or engage in "stream improvement and work somewhat similar to the CCC camps we now have." Haber asked whether $150,000 of federal money could be invested in such a program. Williams gave the letter to Millar to draft a reply, and the latter wholeheartedly endorsed what became known as the "Michigan Plan." In his reply to Haber, Millar exulted, "Any contribution that you make in Michigan toward the solution of the problem of what to do with these three thousand young people, and how to do it, will have value to relief administrators in every state of the union."

On 19 and 20 April Millar discussed the implication of Haber's proposal with Fellows, Carmody, Wissler, Phelan, Alderman, and Klinefelter, and instructed Wissler to meet and consult with Haber in Michigan later that month. Millar had suggestions of his own for Haber to consider. Above all, he stressed the advisability of Michigan youth approaching existing agencies rather than seeking new federal programs. They might demand and receive federal aid, but the channel of federal relief should be through the schools and preexisting federal agencies. He suggested that "the University of Michigan, or Michigan State College, might make requests in the usual way for some sort of an extension program involving work, play and training for groups of young people in the state." At this point, Millar did not seek ways to dismantle previous federal youth agencies but rather to encourage their support as means of discouraging the creation of new federal programs.[18]

The Michigan Plan was structured to meet the needs and exploit the resources of a particular state. Developed by local officials, it could do no more than illustrate one local group's ability to reduce unemployment without federal involvement. Prompted by outside advice, Millar sought something more: a new federal youth program, applicable to the entire nation, which would be sufficiently comprehensive to supersede, and therefore replace, previous FERA youth initiatives. He hoped the plan might bear a New Deal acronym, for with sufficient drama of presentation its conservative intent would be at once concealed and accomplished. A plan that bore the symbols of federal intervention (boldness, a commitment to act, and a national scope) might win the approval of the FERA even as it reversed the trend of New Deal relief and placed the tasks of administration, funding, and control beyond the reach of federal officials. From April to June, Millar's plan became known within the FERA as the "apprenticeship" or "subsistence fellowship" program.[19]

Further inspiration for the apprenticeship idea came to Millar in an April letter from Columbia University professor Nels Anderson. Disillusioned by what he believed was the indifferent supervision offered to FERA students and the make-work character of their campus jobs, Anderson suggested that students be given work under the direction of those who supervised others for a living, not under college instructors on the campus. Anderson described FERA college aid as "poor relief and not too well administered. The students are put to various research jobs (so called) and I fear are being demoralized through left-handed indifferent guidance." Anderson called instead for the government "to take into its services for a few months each year a large number of young men and women as apprentices. Have them work on subsistence fellowships and work while they watch. Then let them be returned to the universities to study some more. After that let them be placed in some service or held in reserve. If they are not used, they will be none the poorer, nor will the country be poorer for the experiment."[20]

Millar was fascinated by Anderson's proposal. It met Williams's demand for a plan to subtract youth from the labor market while it undercut the Alabamian's conclusion that the federal government had to become, for youth as well as adults, the employer of last resort. Within the FERA, Anderson's plan bore the suggestive title "a nonemployment program for college graduates." Millar, however, wondered how anyone could object to any program that, "by projecting education a year or two further in many lines," took "many thousands of young people out of the ranks of the job-seekers and at the same time fit them for more active work." By 26 April 1934 Millar had reworked Anderson's brief suggestion into a more specific set of proposals and began airing them before prominent education and federal officials. Eventually, about 140 individuals received copies of Millar's "Confidential Inquiry." The problem, he wrote, was the existence of a population of high school graduates deficient in the skills sought by the employers within a society that wrongly assumed "that some businessmen or other employer will want to pay for the privilege of furnishing the rest" of their training. The solution seemed obvious. "Might there not be an in between, transition period of a year or two, during which the young person would work for subsistence, under supervision and guidance?" Millar suggested an "arrangement whereby young people now unemployed could be given some work on some sort of an apprenticeship or intern basis in certain public or semi-public lines, such as planning, research, recreation, public administration, etc."[21]

Reaction to Millar's inquiry was almost uniformly favorable. Recipients who represented opposite sides of the political spectrum returned equally favorable notices. At a time when students were receiving only one form of federal aid (and that a program of uncertain longevity), it was to be expected that professional educators, impatient student leaders, and government officials alike would endorse Millar's concept. His plan to apprentice the unemployed promised to rescue from the depression both students and nonstudents alike. Since Millar specified no limit to the number of youths eligible to be employed or the precise relationship between the federal government and the supervisors, his plan was sufficiently shadowy that recipients could read into the proposal the most important features of their own pet plans. Whatever those features might be, the feeling was nearly universal that the plight of youth required a response both bold and immediate. It was not whether the government should act dramatically but how the drama should be played out that was the controversy. Millar clearly encouraged his correspondents to believe that their expectations would find fulfillment in his apprenticeship plan.

The result was a steady stream of congratulatory letters from people with diametrically opposed conceptions of the proper relationship between the federal government and American youth. Those who believed that Washington must be the servant of the young, obligating itself to find every young person a job, were as gratified by Millar's ideas as those who believed (as William James suggested in 1910) that the young ought to enlist in a peacetime army, spending their early adult years in a sacrificial "moral equivalent of war." Viola Ilma, founder of the American Youth Congress (an organization insistent upon the right of every student to federal aid) praised Millar as an advanced New Dealer leading the American people forward. "I think you are going a long way," she wrote, "and it is rather fun to have the jump on 125 million people whose vision must be more on black and white." As early as 4 May, Millar reported that "favorable replies to our 'Confidential Inquiry' (several good ones every day)" were coming from such experts on the problem as Herman Schneider, the father of American cooperative education and University of Cincinnati dean of engineering, and Berea College president William J. Hutchins (the father of Robert Hutchins, president of the University of Chicago).[22]

If Ilma saw the Millar plan as an offering to the AYC, and Schneider regarded it as a cooperative plan extended to the public service, others believed that it harked back to older, more conservative schemes. On 28 May C. R. Mann, the director of the American Council on Education, praised the plan's "remarkable educational possibilities" and described it as "an expansion of the enterprise developed by the War Department after the war, of giving enlisted men in the Army training that would fit them for stable occupations in civilian life after leaving the army. Further, it might well be made a realization of William James' idea of a type of Civil Service that would serve as a moral equivalent of war."

In the days after he received Mann's letter, Millar was drawn irresistibly to the dramatic symbolism of James's idea. Here was a way to package the plan for public consumption as a bold step forward for the New Deal. By looking back to James's conception of service, the plan would blaze with patriotism and be seen as a combination civilian-military venture much like the popular CCC. Millar wrote that consideration ought to be given the James concept and even invented an acronym for the proposal, the "Civil Work Corps." Millar obviously hoped that the plan might win favor with the public as a kind of CCC for students, while in practice ingeniously reversing the trend toward federal intervention begun by the CCC. By living at home and performing community service, students could be paid far less than CCC enrollees ($5 per month rather than $25). Moreover, each would be paid "by the local unit of government for which he would be doing public work."[23]

As he filled in the details of his plan, Millar's intentions became clearer. Gradually, the objectives of Ilma and Mann (not to mention James) were rendered completely unobtainable as the emphasis shifted toward the goal that had been his primary objective all along: the elimination of all forms of direct federal assistance to youth. Before giving up on his plan, Millar seems to have changed the title twice, to a "Civil Scholarship" scheme and then to a "Civil Training Corps" (CTC). These two plans are unattributed in the papers of the FERA, but they are so remarkably similar to the Civil Work Corps scheme that they seem likely to have been the product of Millar's pen. Whatever the name, Millar's objective was to enable local and state officials to decongest the labor market unassisted, and, in so doing, indirectly to eliminate all justification for the college student aid program. "Civil Scholars" had to be of high school or college age and "anxious to continue their education either in the customary school systems or under the auspices of cooperating governmental agencies." The program would raid from the college aid programs those students who would rather serve in public agencies, and provide them a maximum weekly income of $2.50.[24]

ALTHOUGH HIS PLAN pointed in the direction of drastic decentralization, Millar continued to insist that his program was the most ambitious one yet offered for youth by the FERA. "We need a comprehensive plan of action, with none of that spirit of mollycoddly in it," he wrote to Secretary of Commerce Daniel Roper. "This is a case where a big program of activity will be easier to put over than a piecemeal one." But even as he was reworking James's idea, Millar emphasized that his "big program" would work only if the government henceforth spent significantly *less* money than before. He maintained that "the spirit in which this whole problem should be approached [is one] in which we use ingenuity first and money only where absolutely necessary and as a last resort."[25]

Despite Millar's energy, his plan had little chance for adoption. Above him in the FERA hierarchy were three men who regarded fiscal economy and decentralization as desirable and appropriate objectives in a long-term, rather than an immediate, sense. Harry Hopkins, Aubrey Williams, and Jacob Baker believed that the FERA's immediate responsibility was to reverse the drift toward increased distress in America. The way to reconcile their fondness for decentralization and economy with the importance of meeting present need, they believed, was to act on that need while quietly planning some distant, future program to accomplish their long-term objectives. Millar, on the other hand, would have given priority to a goal his superiors regarded as presently unattainable: immediate decentralization of the New Deal for youth. Moreover, as one who believed that the youth problem offered the wisest setting for the solution of the nation's entire unemployment problem, Williams was determined to broaden the FERA program, like an umbrella, to take under its provision young people never before reached by the federal government.

As for Baker, a key architect of the work relief program, he was unlikely to convert to the proposition that federal relief would eat away at the self-respect of the unemployed. Constant contact with suffering had inured him to that. In a comment that indicated both the fact of, and the reason for, Baker's displeasure with Millar's plan, Viola Ilma wrote the latter that she could not seem to get through to Baker: "I met Baker but he had his mind on the drought situation." In yet another suggestive (and prophetically accurate) comment, Baker explained in 1935 why he had no patience with those who maintained that federal work relief was a form of boondoggling of less value than local "community work." "I think it is about time that the press and the general public should begin to learn that we have raked leaves and boon-doggled to such good purpose that our work in cement and stone, in increased public health and educational facilities and resources will be remembered in pretty nearly every community in the country for many years to come."[26] These were the men who would pass judgment on Millar's scaled-down panacea for youth.

The resolutions passed at the USOE's June Conference on Youth Problems helped convince Hopkins that support was growing for the inauguration of federal aid programs for high school and out-of-school youths. In May, Zook had predicted that the conference would address only problems in the areas of employment, education, and leisure time. Its objectives would center on "helping youth to bridge the disillusioning gap between school and employment." Following the conference, however, Alderman noted that this conservative, old-line federal agency had suggested other, hitherto unexplored youth problems that the New Deal might legitimately address: problems of "health and food," young people's need for "a better understanding of the social and economic order under which they are living," and their hunger for ways of producing "desirable modifications of this present day society through various types of social action." The conferees agreed, however, that the program must be administered by local educators and community leaders. It was clear that an enlarged federal youth program would win major support in the nation provided that its administrative arrangements were more fully decentralized.[27]

By the time the Conference of Youth Problems adjourned, Alderman had completed his own draft of a model youth program, one calculated to combine Williams's hopes for an expanded superstructure of programs for youth (including, for the first time, aid to high school students and dropouts) with a diminished federal role in administration. On 7 June, two days before the plan was unveiled, Hopkins was presented with a reason to be even more disposed to expand federal college student aid rather than curtail it, as Millar hoped. Zook wrote him that all fifty-one colleges

and universities that had evaluated the FERA program on their campuses
had pronounced it a success. All "urged its continuance for another year."
Some of the presidents called it the "most profitable and beneficial of the
Federal government's relief measures." Hopkins favored the idea of an
expanded federal presence in the schools, provided that greater decentralization of administration followed. Williams's understanding of this desire
was complete, but gaining an understanding of the problem was the easier
part of the planning procedure. Negotiating the tightrope between these
two objectives was the most difficult part.[28]

After scanning Alderman's proposal, Hopkins, although impressed, was
convinced that his deputy had not quite negotiated the tightrope successfully. Still, he directed Williams to head the effort at revising the
scheme. Alderman first presented his plan on 9 June. The draft called
for the creation of three new federal youth programs for three different
youth "groups": the population of needy high school students, students of
college age and aptitude who preferred on-the-job experience in public
administration to higher education, and young people who had departed
the high schools with no further academic inclinations.

High school youth struck Alderman and Williams as the group in direst
need of rescue. "What is happening here," Alderman wrote, "is that large
numbers of boys and girls between fifteen and eighteen years of age are
going to high schools with the meagerest amounts of clothing, food and
money. . . . Large numbers of children in relief families are not going . . .
at all because of lack of finances." Alderman thought it ironic that this serious injustice could be prevented by appropriating only $5 per month for
each needy high school student in the program. "For me," he concluded,
"it is more important that these students should be aided than almost any
other group." Alderman quickly added, however, that the existing aid program for college students deserved to be expanded, not contracted. In the
previous six months, the FERA had pledged to employ 100,000 students
but reached only 75,000. Alderman urged the FERA to provide college
aid to 200,000 students in the 1934–35 academic year and to accomplish
this goal by increasing the colleges' annual appropriations from $800,000
to $1.2 million.[29]

Having rebuffed Millar's proposal to dismantle college aid, Alderman
and Williams attempted to steal his thunder by adding the apprenticeship
scheme to the 9 June plan. Alderman recommended that the FERA offer
"activities of an educational character" to a million out-of-school youth be-

tween sixteen and twenty-five years of age. The offices of county surveyors, county clerks, and city engineers were to be provided federal funds to hire and supervise young people. In these and other city and state departments, young people would serve as apprentices and gain firsthand exposure to the workings of democracy and the operations of local government. The program would have the added value of providing the kind of decentralization so many Americans were expecting from the Roosevelt administration's next relief program.

Alderman exhausted his store of fresh ideas on the problems of America's student population. When it came to aiding nonacademic youth, the jobless young people out of school by choice, the EEP director proposed nothing more imaginative than the creation of more CCC-type jobs. Although he wrote that "work should be given a very large place" in the FERA program, he offered no new ideas on the kind of work projects appropriate for young people. For example, Alderman recommended that youth construct "cabins and camps in connection with recreation" in woodland regions. Nationwide, he predicted, young people could build "ten to fifteen thousand of these camps . . . adjacent to a lake site." For seven to eight months each year, the FERA could engage in "the construction of fire ranges and the elimination of brush and dead trees." While Haber's plan was receiving praise precisely for the stimulation it provided to local initiatives and the economy it promised to achieve by working through existing CCC camps, Alderman inexplicably proposed to eliminate the economical and decentralist features that were its chief advantages. Alderman's plan for out-of-school youth was afflicted by problems that did not characterize the remainder of his plan. In the process of raising the price tag for out-of-school youth, Alderman was proposing to retain the less-than-vocational, CCC-style woodland work which formed the least desirable feature of Haber's plan. Even worse, this feature of the plan would be federally administered, not, at this time, a selling point for Hopkins.[30]

Alderman's associates at the conference, including Hopkins, were displeased with the ambiguous, expensive, and overly federalized nature of the out-of-school component of the plan. Robert T. Lansdale hastily assembled an alternative and presented it to Williams in June. Lansdale pointed out that all the FERA officials wanted to maintain high standards by keeping the program under the control of professionals, as opposed to conservative local groups and educators hostile to the FERA. Educators were to be prevented from supervising out-of-school youth. The danger was that they would seek to lead youth where they did not want to go: back to school. At the same time, the FERA wished to save money, accomplish real decentralization, and safeguard youth's commitment to the democratic way of life. These were no easy tasks, but Lansdale thought they could be accomplished through a nationwide training plan to equip young people for "recreation leadership." First, the county relief commissioners would appoint young people to their advisory boards. Then, "as the young people develop in leadership," a recreation "program might be put entirely in their hands." By deciding themselves the forms of recreation in which young people would be engaged, enrollees would learn the ropes of democracy. By supervising other youths in games, the young people would themselves reduce the cost of the program. The program would be decentralized in the sense that counties would have control over its administration, but not so decentralist that schools would take over.[31]

Lansdale's suggestion was not approved. July passed with Millar and Williams each developing new strategies to meet Hopkins's objections without materially altering their respective plans. Millar suggested that the heads of eight federal agencies whose policies actually or potentially affected youth should meet and decide on a common youth program acceptable to all. Millar's idea seemed a concession. He appeared prepared to accept not only an alteration of his proposal but an alteration effected entirely by federal officials. "As I sense the trend of things inside the government," he wrote on 12 July, "the time is about ripe to get representatives of these eight agencies in a room together to consider how to coordinate activities" and plans. The identities of these eight agency heads are unclear, but most likely they were the principal invitees to the USOE's June conference on youth. These were Hopkins; Assistant Labor Secretary Chapman; Milburn A. Wilson; C. A. Warburton, the director of the AAA's Extension Division; Stuart A. Rice, the assistant director of the Bureau of the Census; and three officials involved in CCC planning: Fechner, Arno B. Cammerer (director of the National Park Service), and Fred Morrell, a public relations expert in the Forest Service. If so, Millar was conceding little. Most of these men agreed with the resolutions adopted at the USOE conference, which, like the Millar plan itself, asserted that local administration and control constituted the sine qua non of any ideal youth program.[32]

If Millar sought nothing more than to cloak his original plan in a guise designed to appeal politically to Hopkins, the same generalizations applied to the intent behind Aubrey Williams's maneuvers. On 10 July Williams informed Baker that he was sending him an assistant, Charles Kramer, to work on the final drafting of the apprenticeship plan. Williams asked Baker to appoint his own aide to assist Kramer in the drafting procedure. The designation of Kramer, who had helped Hilda Smith establish the federally administered women's camps and schools of the previous spring, hardly suggested that Williams was prepared to shrink the federal government's role in his own apprenticeship scheme. Nor did the man Baker chose to assist Kramer suggest that decentralization would be the denouement of FERA apprenticeship planning. That same day, when Baker contacted Arthur Goldschmidt—the latter an architect of the FERA's completely federalized transient camp program—Williams and Baker signaled their determination to maintain some significant degree of federal leverage over every aspect of the New Deal's next youth program.[33]

The result of Goldschmidt and Kramer's collaboration, a one-page proposal for "unemployed youth," was one of the more fascinating youth proposals ever to emerge from the FERA. Although this first draft seems clearly attributable to Goldschmidt, Kramer reworded many of the sentences to eliminate potentially controversial misunderstandings about the program; in addition, the latter deleted other phrases he considered impolitic. Kramer's objections may be interpreted as indications of the intentions of his chief, Williams. The first (Goldschmidt) draft disputed the notion that the need for college student aid might be reduced by the apprenticeship program. Since college student aid was "at best supplementary relief," Goldschmidt argued, "it can help only the student who already had his head and shoulders into the tent. An integral part of the youth program should be an attempt to provide college and secondary schooling to young people who can not [sic] afford to go to school otherwise."[34]

Having delivered a veiled rebuke of Millar's effort to scale down college student aid, Goldschmidt (and Kramer by assent) explained how prospective students and nonscholastic youth alike might be apprenticed in such a way as to enlarge, rather than retrench, the existing student aid program. Where young people lived in cities and at home, unnamed existing "facilities" would be competent to employ such youth and might properly be funded by the FERA. The "unattached" and "homeless . . . intrastate transients" required closer federal supervision, however. Because transients could be divided into two separate groups, they required two complementary systems of relief. In a passage Kramer rewrote (to tighten the grammar), Goldschmidt asserted that one group of transient youth could be trained by the colleges. "Selected students that [sic] could be integrated into campus life could be given congregate care on the campus of the cooperating institutions. This may mean bartering to get tuition and other fees waived for them."[35]

There was another group of transient youth, however, who were not academically inclined and would gain little through employment on college campuses. Goldschmidt proposed instead that such young people be sent to new federal camps established for that purpose and possessing the heightened federal control needed to ensure that they received the training they required. He added that this idea had come from his wife, Elizabeth ("Wicky") Wickenden, who was in charge of overall planning for transient relief. For these youth, Goldschmidt wrote,

> Special transient camps might be set up . . . to give modern vocational training in experimental lines. Young people might be transferred to these camps from existing camps and shelters. These camps would correspond to the *land schulheim* problem in Germany before the Nazis got in. The whole job would be considerably better than the CCC plan. Wicky, herself, suggested it and therefore you know that it is reasonable as a part of the present transient program.

The most important objective of the proposed draft, other than helping youth in distress, was to derail, before it went on track, Millar's proposal for complete decentralization. This was shown by the nature of Kramer's amendments, which were designed not only to refine the draft grammatically but also to polish it politically. His goal (and Williams's) was to sell the program to Hopkins as a politically safe alternative to the politically problematical "Confidential Inquiry." Whereas Goldschmidt suggested that the plan to send transients to college was sought as a "way of keeping them off the labor market," Kramer deleted this phrase, perhaps because it seemed exploitive of the young. For the same reason, Kramer found it expedient to refer to the *land schulheim* camps in Germany simply as an "arrangement," not as a "problem." In addition, Goldschmidt predicted that the extension of the college aid program would result from the plan to aid young people in their homes. Kramer modified the paragraph to suggest that all three programs—the program for young people at home as well as the "two arrangements for the unattached"—would "require extension of the junior college plan and . . . other activities on a large scale."[36]

Such expansive ideas amounted to a reworking of Williams's earlier idea in a way he hoped would secure Hopkins's imprimatur. Yet his basic objective of drawing hundreds of thousands of additional youth from the labor market under federal supervision remained intact. By appealing to Hopkins's interest in a plan that promised boldness without controversy, Williams hoped to secure in July what he had failed to achieve in June. Accordingly, the last sentence in the Goldschmidt-Kramer draft (over which both men agreed) zeroed in on the heart of the perceived political weakness of Millar's plan. "These activities," the two men concluded, "would be a lot better than this apprentice notion and would not get us into as much hot water."[37]

THEIR ENERGY and enthusiasm notwithstanding, Williams and his closest aides could not, by the power of their arguments alone, gain FERA approval for their unprecedented youth program. In arguing for an all-federal program to educate the out-of-school population, the Williams group proposed to fracture tradition in three places. Even though the exclusively federal CCC had previously employed men with no hope for rescue outside the camps, and offered incidental forms of training, never had a federal program existed that would have transformed Washington into schoolmaster, training men and women theoretically within reach of the schools. Education, the selection of the out-of-school group for rescue, and the federal nature of the proposed scheme were the core components of the Williams plan, which added up to a novel proposal indeed.

Arguments on paper, of course, would have failed to induce either Hopkins or the president to approve such a program had not young people's plight been sufficiently desperate to convince them of its urgency. From the universities and the social service agencies, worried analysts of American society began spreading the word that youth's situation demanded dramatic and quick action. Beyond the campuses, young people themselves seemed strangely silent, perhaps because their problems were too visible or painful either to allow for, or require, description. One college student lived in an "old Model T Ford sedan . . . fitted up as a house." Another borrowed thirty dollars from a bank to pay the twenty-two-dollar semester fee and live on the balance.[38] That the one had a car and the other a measure of credit, and both the means to enter college without government assistance, testified to the fact that they were among the luckiest of America's hard-pressed youth. In the process, however, they demon-strated the miserable state of the less fortunate. This fact, increasingly apparent, soon gave rise to grass-roots pressure on the Roosevelt admin-istration, enlisted behind the sort of idea the Williams group had already proposed.

CHAPTER FIVE

The Battle Won:
The NYA Takes Shape

M onths of planning during the summer and autumn of 1934 brought no resolution of the Roosevelt administration's youth dilemma. To guarantee young people's integration into the American society and economy, and to defuse the discontent bred by idleness, the government knew it must help young people bridge the gap between school and employment. But, paradoxically, this effort to preserve democracy might backfire if in its pursuit the New Deal channeled enormous sums of money into a new federal agency whose reaches extended to every town and community in the land. Such an agency might be branded the "Roosevelt Youth," an invidious image whose European counterpart was known to all. In order to shield the New Deal from such charges and to keep youth democratic, the New Deal required a democratically administered agency. Hence, decentralization had to be the hallmark of any new federal youth program. Furthermore, while its objectives were lofty, the New Dealers knew that the agency would have to be administered on a small budget, also to deflect criticism.

Between June and November 1934, Williams, Hopkins, and other FERA planners gradually became convinced that any new youth program should be designed to achieve three goals. Job training was a must, but so too were decentralization of administration and training in democratic values; that is, a program to help youth understand and appreciate the principles

of American democracy. Largely as a result of this public debate and discussion, it became FERA policy, beginning in November 1934, to give
local authorities a larger role in the administration of the evolving youth
programs. Community residents would hold membership in "local advisory committees," from which ideas for New Deal youth projects would
emerge. Such decentralization would counter charges of regimentation
and attract public support for the program.

By November, when Aubrey Williams unveiled the FERA's new youth
plan, it was evident that all these factors had been considered. Williams's
November draft proposed that youth be given something to do through
recreation, and that their employability and allegiance to democracy be
guaranteed through a program of education. All of these objectives were
to be achieved through a decentralized administrative framework. Significantly, however, the FERA hoped to avoid the expense and political risk
of a large-scale jobs program, especially with so many adults in need of
work. As late as November 1934, then, the FERA promised young people
education rather than work as a solution to their plight.[1]

IN THE MONTHS before October 1934, FERA planners had displayed
much imagination in their proposals to help the nation's jobless youth.
Williams, Hopkins, Lansdale, and others had conceived ideas for the extension of student aid to high school students, the absorption of the leisure
time of young people in general, and a new form of aid to college students
("civil scholarships"). Lansdale and John H. Millar had even proposed that
the federal government sponsor apprenticeships as a means of teaching
youth the workings of democracy. In suggesting that the FERA encourage
local governments to provide public service internships to jobless youth,
however, Williams was the first New Dealer to call for a program designed
solely to provide the out-of-school group with education rather than work
relief.[2]

And yet, in a more fundamental sense, little had changed since February
1934, when the FERA student aid program was launched on a nationwide scale. Aside from the Williams-Kramer-Goldschmidt draft (which
remained stalled), the FERA proposals that emerged between June and
October 1934 *proposed no new activities that the federal government
itself would have had to undertake*. In the student aid program, the New
Deal had simply channeled federal funds to institutions of higher learning,

while the colleges and universities alone had borne the burden of educating needy students. This pattern also characterized the youth proposals that emerged over the course of the following eight months. To be sure, in June Hopkins had considered the possibility that the federal government itself might administer high school student aid. Yet in spite of the fact that student aid in general was by then a working program (and hence not new), this suggestion was not adopted.[3]

Likewise, FERA officials were decidedly cool toward proposals that the federal government undertake job training and political education programs for youth. If the New Deal had to involve itself in such activities, Hopkins preferred that they take place, like the CCC, in woodland camps, out of sight of people in the young people's home communities. Moreover, Millar's internship proposal was received with little debate, discussion, or apparent interest.

By contrast, relief planners found much more appealing proposals either to extend programs already in operation or to create programs which, though novel, were designed to achieve old objectives. In June, for example, Williams's proposal for aid to high school students constituted little more than an extension of the college aid endeavor. The New Dealers devoted much attention to student aid, for it offered a way to aid young people without requiring the federal government to involve itself directly in their employment and training, as would occur with an out-of-school work program. Even Kramer and Goldschmidt, proponents of an enlarged federal role in youth planning, regarded work and training for out-of-school youth as "hot water" politically, especially in view of the nature of European youth programs. Thus, whenever FERA planners in these months proposed that the New Deal reach young people in a new and federally controlled manner, they made it clear that their purpose was entirely traditional: not to train youth for jobs or democracy but to remove them from the labor market. Equally characteristic was Lansdale's proposal to absorb youth's leisure time. No leisure time proposal had been advanced before, but, in approach and objective, the idea was hardly novel. Administered by the state relief administrations, it was to be designed primarily to decongest the labor market.[4]

Thus, beneath the feverish activity among the FERA youth planners in the summer and autumn of 1934 appeared evidence of a rigidity of thought and purpose. Although relief officials were *discussing* the need to decentralize the New Deal for youth and beginning to consider the need for job training and citizenship education, none of these proposals was adopted before October. Indeed, as late as October, Hopkins announced a plan that, while it offered education, decentralization, and an awareness of federal responsibility to keep youth democratic, was so inadequate as a solution to all these problems that even FERA officials found it unacceptable. It seemed immediately clear to relief officials that this preliminary draft for a comprehensive youth program was not comprehensive enough. It did not go far enough in the direction of job training, decentralization, or political education. They then began conferring on a revised program, ideally one without the need for the kind of direct federal control they consistently had been so loathe to provide.[5]

One of the reasons the need for such a revision seemed so clear to FERA officials was that leading educators, youth leaders, and social workers had during the preceding months called for greater federal coordination of youth-serving efforts. Between September and November 1934, meetings and forums for northeastern professionals in the fields of social service, education, and journalism were increasingly the setting for expressions of concern that the New Deal was not doing enough to work with state and local officials in guaranteeing youth's employability and allegiance to democracy. These individuals urged improvement in the techniques of organized adult guidance of youth (formerly undertaken solely in the home, the school, and by private organizations). They called on the federal government to provide more help along job-training lines, albeit within a framework of greater decentralization and community control. If the FERA endeavors seemed woefully inadequate to relief officials—who were aware of the spate of plans to aid youth between June and October—they seemed doubly so to many outside government. Interested commentators on the youth problem knew only too well that, whatever the situation on the FERA's drawing board, not a single high school youth was being aided, no young person's leisure time was being absorbed, and youth's faith in democracy remained unensured.[6]

The FERA planners recognized these demands and, in October and November 1934, worked to satisfy them. They badly misgauged public opinion in one sense, however. The public was becoming increasingly convinced that youth's many needs could only be met by a program to provide them work, not just relief or recreation. Such a program would require the kind of federally administered work relief program that the FERA had found objectionable earlier in the year. The FERA's revised

youth program introduced in November revealed that administration officials understood the public's demand for decentralization of New Deal
efforts to aid *students*. Unfortunately, the plan also bore witness to the
fact that the FERA continued to underestimate the demand for a federally
controlled work program for young people who were *out of school*.[7]

IN LATE 1934 and early 1935, that demand was coming alike from prominent eastern social service activists, journalists, and political leaders. Individual commentators on the youth problem had little power by themselves
to change government's and society's perspectives on jobless people. Yet
they were no less vocal for that fact. Their arguments, which grew more
frequent between September and November 1934, were characterized by
remarkable similarities.[8] In general, observers argued that changed economic conditions (often described as the disappearance of the frontier) required the federal government to put young people to work. They agreed
further that such a program was needed to preserve youth's spirit and
allegiance to freedom. On 16 September 1934 the "youth problem" was
discussed at the 1934 Sunday Forum over New York's WOR radio station.
Homer Burt, director of the Transient Division of the state's Temporary
Emergency Relief Administration, argued that young transients deserved
respect, not scorn. Like their fathers, they were struggling for success on
their own, but without the economic opportunity their fathers had known.
Rather than "hoboes" or "bums," they were "pioneers," Burt declared.
"They follow the original American formula for success, stated years after
it had been in action: 'Go West, young man.' . . . The only difficulty is that
the frontier has vanished."[9]

If youth could not achieve opportunity on their own, it followed that
the government had an obligation to assist them. The *New York Times*
suggested that the entire nation had reached this conclusion. The editors
traced the change to the closing of the frontier: "Forty years ago . . . there
was no such national or united concern. Whatever was done was local in
scope and neighborly in spirit. Now the whole nation is roused to a consciousness of a responsibility to the millions out of school and out of work
who are on the verge of manhood and womanhood but see no gainful job
immediately ahead."[10]

There was further agreement on the specific kind of assistance young
people required: work. In September, Lionel J. Simmonds, executive

director of the Hebrew Orphan Asylum, declared, "these youngsters do
not want home relief. They are tired of being dependent and eager to join
the ranks of labor." The same month, Benedict S. Alper and George E.
Lodgen, both of the Massachusetts Child Council, drew the same conclusion from a survey of 330 out-of-school, out-of-work Massachusetts boys
and girls, aged sixteen and seventeen.

> The first important thing here is that, above all, these young people want to
> work. The large numbers who have expressed dislike of school as a reason for
> leaving, the large fraction of high school graduates who feel they have gone
> far enough to entitle them to find work now. . . . All point away from a pro-
> gram purely educational in nature. This is not to say that an educational or
> recreational program could not depend from or hinge upon a work program.
> But work should be the core.[11]

Some agreed that the alternative to providing work would be a deterioration of youth's spirit. Home relief, Simmonds suggested, "takes from
them the vital spark of self-reliance so needed in these days." At the same
meeting, Robert P. Lane, executive director of the Welfare Council of
New York City, spoke of "a world in which values are shifting [and] cer-
tainty has become uncertainty. . . . [N]ot only those young people are
adrift who happen to be orphans. All youth are adrift today." Lane added,
"It is our significant duty to aid in developing a proper sense of values."
According to the New York Times, youth needed not food or shelter but
attention to the "needs of the mind and spirit." Their "character" had to
be preserved through work, not direct relief. Character was "something
more than meat or raiment [could] give."[12]

For these individual analysts, the seriousness of the youth problem required federal, state, and local authorities to offer a combined program of
work and training. Private youth-serving research and pressure organizations, primarily in the field of education, were rapidly arriving at the same
conclusion. The interest in such a program soon focused on John A. Lang's
proposed "Federal Youth Service." Although it would not be published
until October, the plan had been presented to the U.S. Office of Education the previous June, and was endorsed by many of its members. The
Lang plan in two respects presaged the proposal Williams would unveil in
November. Lang urged that "private organizations [be] asked to cooperate" with federal officials, and that "opportunities for apprenticing young
persons to public officials . . . be encouraged." Further, he proposed that

the New Deal establish "an advisory committee composed of representatives from all . . . groups interested in youth's problems" to direct the agency. Neither proposal would have seemed novel to FERA planners. They had already discussed the possibility of offering young people apprenticeships and had incorporated the advisory committee concept into their Civil Training Corps plan.[13]

Yet many educators were attracted to the Lang idea, while the FERA schemes received little publicity. In October, before the FERA plan was announced, Chancellor Harry Woodburn Chase of New York University wondered "why there should not be somewhere in the government an agency which is concerned with youth in this difficult time." Donald J. Cowling, president of Carleton College, pronounced the Lang scheme "a practical step of great promise," while Robert L. Kelly, secretary of the Association of American Colleges, considered it "a very thorough-going set-up" for the solution of youth's problems. University of North Carolina president Frank Graham pronounced it "sound in every respect." Other educators (including J. W. Crabtree of the National Education Association) praised the idea and even lobbied for it in Lang's behalf.[14]

It is easy to understand why educators would prefer the Lang proposal to any FERA scheme. The former contained several provisions that leaders of education very much desired but were unacceptable to FERA planners. Although it promised a federal solution to youth's problems, the Lang scheme lacked specificity and placed nearly all responsibility for its success in the hands of educators and local officials. His Federal Youth Service would coordinate rather than administer, and supply more information than funds. "Extensive studies, dissemination of information, coordination of scattered efforts and experimentation" would be conducted, Lang promised. Furthermore, the agency's "staff of experts and field representatives would be small and the expense involved negligible."

For those educators who looked to Washington for financial assistance—but feared federal control of education—such vagueness was more a virtue than a vice. The FERA planned to exert greater federal control to guarantee that funds were well spent. In addition, the FERA plans were in their final stages. Like all specific proposals, they could not avoid criticism from some quarters.

Although it was not announced until November, Williams's draft was too close to completion in October to take into account fully the rising sentiment on behalf of a work program to preserve democracy. But Lang's plan gave one more indication that this sentiment could not be ignored. The plan contained three features that had been demanded by Burt, Simmonds, the editors of the *New York Times*, and others in September and October: the promise of a comprehensive rather than an ad hoc solution to youth unemployment, a recognition that youth required work as much as education, and an emphasis on the importance of federal efforts to ensure youth's allegiance to democracy. Lang had despaired that national planning was offered to farmers and businessmen but not American youth. The FERA programs, he said, were "scattered and largely palliative. There is no well organized or coordinated program at present to help the young person find his place in the changing social condition." His programs would offer youth training facilities and a fair share of work, all designed to provide employment, education, and vocational guidance.

Finally, Lang issued a warning that would, in the months to follow, be echoed by federal officials concerned with the problems of youth. "To continue refusing an adequate response to the problems of the young has obvious dangers," he wrote. "There is power enough in this group for a revolution or for deterioration to the point where America will suffer from dry-rot for at least another generation."[15] A program that coordinated federal youth-serving efforts while providing employment and support for democracy could not fail to be popular in 1934 and 1935. The work of FERA youth planners in October and November indicated that they believed a program of education—for work and citizenship—was all that youth required, and that immediate employment was unnecessary. But the thrust of congressional and public opinion in the following months would lead them to change their minds. Only then did they adopt work, along with education for democracy, as integral features of the revised New Deal for youth.

IN OCTOBER 1934 the FERA came forward with a plan likely to provide the kind of education and citizenship training demanded by eastern educators and social welfare administrators. The contrast between this proposal and those of the previous summer (which stressed removal of youths from the job market) was great. Hopkins characterized it as a "comprehensive program to occupy the leisure time of young people sixteen to twenty-five years of age." To ensure decentralized administration, Hopkins directed the state relief administrators to develop a threefold program of work projects, recreational activities, and education. Washington's role would be confined to "establishing a special information service to make available to all states the experiences of those communities which are most success-ful in handling the problem of leisure time for young people." Hopkins also authorized each state relief administrator to appoint a director for the program as well as an official to administer the program in every city with more than twenty-five thousand people.[16]

In June Lansdale had spoken of the value of absorbing youth's leisure time as a means of decongesting the labor market. It was clear that the FERA's October proposal reflected different concerns. As Hopkins in-formed state relief administrators that month, "training and education shall be provided that will help youth to become and remain employable and to understand the problems of our rapidly changing social, economic, and political life." This program of vocational training and social and economic education could be offered to all young people because it did not involve the expense of work relief. Assignment to work projects would "be lim-ited to those who present a specific basis of need." By providing young people with something to do and learn rather than jobs, the New Deal would avoid antagonizing organized labor and other groups opposed to government competition with private industry. With little cost (political or financial) to the federal government, hundreds of thousands of youths could be confirmed in their democratic faith. For this purpose, Hopkins proposed that the FERA finance a recreation program of "sports, games, music, drama, reading, hobbies, and the like."[17]

Hopkins believed that his proposal met the requirement of training youth for work and democracy at minimal expense. He was unwilling to establish a separate fund for the undertaking, and instead directed the state relief officials to decide "the question of the amount of funds that should be put into this program." Yet the goal of decentralization, even in principle, was only half realized in the FERA's October proposal. Relief authorities at the state and local levels were granted authority over the program, but no control was given to public and private youth-serving organizations. Thus the idea of establishing these "Commonwealth Youth Clubs" (as Hopkins dubbed the state programs to be launched under the plan) proceeded only halfway down the road to decentralization. Local private organizations and community officials were given no voice in the program, an omission that was to trouble FERA officials in the weeks to come.[18]

Hopkins's directive of 3 October was not put into effect immediately. Its enactment was delayed as a result of continued dissatisfaction within the FERA regarding the outlines of the plan. Less than two weeks after Hopkins wrote the order, nine of the agency's leading planners held a meeting to discuss the future of the emerging plan.[19] These individuals included Jacob Baker (head of the FERA's work division) and William Haber. Joined by Alderman and Lansdale, the nine officials recommended that the work relief aspect of the October plan should be downplayed even further and that the educational aspect should assume greater importance. They agreed that a select number of youths should receive a cash allowance for their labors but that the program should be described as a measure to provide "vocational and educational adjustment to all unemployed persons under twenty-five years of age." Moreover, while the conferees recommended that state relief administrators direct the program, they urged that private groups, prominent local officials, and young people themselves be given roles in the formulation of policy. Specifically, they recommended that "cooperation with all existing public institutions, private and character-building agencies and educational institutions be urged and encouraged and the participation of young people and their organizations be invited."[20]

On 28 November 1934 Hopkins outlined a new set of directives on youth policy for the state relief administrators. In response to the caveats and questions raised at the October meeting of the nine FERA officials, Aubrey Williams had drawn up most of the guidelines the federal relief administrator announced at that time. In the following months this newest proposal came to be known as the "Williams plan." Williams proposed that, along with the democratic participation of young people and private agencies, the state relief administrators establish a small number of work projects for needy youths and classes in vocational education for the remainder. By offering recreation and education in social and economic subjects, young people would grow more appreciative of democracy. Meanwhile, the FERA would teach democracy by example—the example of a democratically administered program.[21]

Hopkins explained that in contrast to the Civil Training Corps proposal, the new scheme would offer vocational guidance "not by setting up new institutions, but by using existing facilities, e.g., high school facilities, and character building agencies." These would be donated by participating groups. Such a program would conform to the objectives of establishing a low-cost federal youth agency while furthering the goal of democratic participation and control. "The cost of administration should be very small," read the report attributed to Williams, "and local advisory committees should be organized . . . so that the resources of the community could be fully obtained and utilized for this undertaking." It seemed that both youth's educational needs and the nation's political security would be well served by the endeavor.[22]

That same month, Williams discussed his proposal with Fred J. Kelly, the chief of the Division of Higher Education within the USOE. Kelly immediately identified the program's central feature and, he believed, its central flaw: it offered training only, not jobs. Further, even the training was to be limited to those interested in continuing their education; the out-of-school group was not included. Williams had neatly summed up the program's objectives (to provide the young job skills and renewed faith in democracy) when he wrote: "It is a primary obligation of government that the skills and morale of these young people shall not be lost to the future." But only youth in school could benefit from his plan, since it was to be conducted in conjunction with high schools, vocational schools, and junior colleges. It would be impossible for out-of-school young people to take advantage of the work aspect of the plan, since work was to be integrated with classroom studies. The work, Williams wrote, "carries out the subject matter which they are being taught in schools. . . . [T]hat is, if they have been taught bookkeeping they will be given work as apprentices to bookkeepers; if they are being taught mechanical engineering, they will be apprenticed to construction crews."[23]

Kelly complimented Williams for some aspects of the new FERA plan. Two of its "very striking merits," he said, were its "combination of real work experience and education" and the fact that it would "require very much less money per student" than the present college student aid program. Further, more than the college aid program, the Williams plan promised jobs of greater educational significance to the students. Nevertheless, by involving only those young people "who care for an additional educational program," it limited its "application to a relatively small proportion of unemployed young people."[24]

Even more disturbing was the fact that the success or failure of the Williams plan hinged on the imagination and resources of the public schools. Even if the schools had the finances to administer an imaginative vocational program—which Kelly doubted—he believed they would be "none too quick to visualize the greatly enriched and varied program" required by "this great new army of young people." Kelly had broken with those of his associates within the USOE who favored the Lang plan and school control over a federal education program. Williams, Kelly wrote, was requiring the schools to "make the most heroic effort" to expand their youth services. Kelly simply did not believe that American public education was up to the task.

Nevertheless, Kelly fully agreed with Williams that the government should work to improve young people's morale and prevent their disaffection from others in society. Williams had once written that all that young people demanded of their elders was the opportunity to obtain a job, marry, and raise a family. By providing young people a small amount of spending money (five dollars a week) and a semblance of a job with educational value, the government could start them down the road to achieving these goals. Kelly believed it was "sound" to begin to meet youth's financial needs in this manner. He did not fault the fact that the program, as he believed, included "general cultural, artistic and civic courses, as well as vocational" ones. But it was precisely because he agreed with Williams that young people would grow disaffected without the opportunity to experience life's basic rites of passage that he found the program inadequate. In his view, a semblance of a job was not enough, especially when it was limited to students. Kelly believed more emphasis on the work aspect of the program was required: "When I think of the whole proposal, I am impressed with the fact that your fundamental contention is not well-served by it. You hold that jobs are the primary need of young people. With this I agree. Many of these young people are twenty to twenty-five years of age. A considerable fraction of them are married. Many others feel the natural impulse to marry and enter into their proper social life." Society's continued well-being depended on the provision of employment for the young. As he put it, "education, jobs for youth, and recreation are necessary concomitants of a program under which young people may develop in this day of complex social organization."[25]

By the end of the following month, Kelly's chief, USOE head John W. Studebaker, had carried these views to the president. Roosevelt remained noncommittal, but Kelly found room for optimism in the fact that the president's information sources, hitherto controlled by Hopkins and the FERA, were being vigorously supplemented by the ideas of his chief. "Glad you had the visit with the President," Kelly wrote Studebaker just after Christmas. "I have great confidence in the soundness of his reaction if he ever gets the youth problem adequately before him. I doubt if he has had it properly presented to date."[26]

Kelly had been correct in interpreting Williams's November proposal as primarily educational in scope; it did offer training more than work. In a sense, the overwhelming emphasis on education was puzzling to Kelly. He knew Williams believed that "jobs [were] the primary need of young people." If a new federal youth proposal, announced with fanfare and great expectations, merely prolonged the education of the young, it would fail to support youth's morale.[27]

Williams's thinking had not progressed to the point where he regarded work projects as a valuable means of solving the youth problem. Rather, he still saw such projects as something of a stumbling block to this objective. In common with his FERA associates, he was accustomed to viewing the youth problem as a problem of community and commitment to democracy. Work alone would do nothing in the long run to provide youth a social place, restore their faith in the future, or preserve morale. Kelly, however, like Hilda Smith, recognized that if work projects had an educational component, they would contribute to, rather than delay, the progress toward social integration initiated by the FERA education program. Williams would eventually fall into line behind this newer conception of the integrative potential of work projects for youth. In the meantime, Kelly could find no fault in Williams's concern with democracy and anomie. He merely emphasized that work rather than education should become a more fundamental aspect of the plan. The FERA had not had as much experience as other agencies in the matter of work relief, and therefore Kelly believed it "impossible for the FERA alone to develop a program adequate to meet the situation."[28]

Such an expression of concern was in essence recognition that young people required more in the depression than the mere promise of employability through job training. If the problem had simply been unemployment, federal assistance for vocational education—on a sufficient scale— would have been enough to alleviate it. Yet FERA officials had already moved beyond such a narrow conception of the problem when they proposed that a decentralized agency provide public service employment for youth. By teaching them the workings of democracy and showing how a democratically administered agency was up to the task of easing their plight, FERA officials were working to preserve youth's "spirit" and commitment to an ideology. Kelly was simply expressing his view that one of the FERA's own objectives, preventing social and political anomie, was ill-served so long as education received priority over employment. What young people required, he believed, was not the promise of a job but a job itself.[29]

BETWEEN JANUARY AND June 1935, planning for a revised New Deal on behalf of young people was aimed as never before toward training youth for work and democracy. In these six months, four influences helped give shape to the evolving agency. The draft proposals that culminated in the NYA revealed the influence of Congress, the Department of Labor, the USOE, and a group of unofficial advisers to the president knowledgeable about young people's relationship to the economy and to radical youth movements.

On 30 January 1935 Massachusetts Democrat David I. Walsh introduced a Senate resolution requesting the secretary of labor to estimate the extent of youth unemployment and outline the steps the Roosevelt administration proposed to take to ease the problem. Walsh decried the fact that millions of Americans aged eighteen through thirty were graduating from school into "a work-world where no opportunities have been open to them." He asked Secretary of Labor Frances Perkins to ascertain whether the Labor Department or the Public Works Administration could assist them through a special youth bureau. Walsh believed that such an office might serve as a clearinghouse for information regarding youth employment opportunities gathered from private employers, community groups, and public agencies. Through the collection and dissemination of this information, such a bureau might go far toward eliminating what Walsh called "this gravest of problems."[30]

While coordinating private efforts might help youth, Walsh believed that the federal government had a more important role to play than that. He called for a number of New Deal agencies to work together to provide the only remedy likely to end the problem: federally created jobs for youth. Not only could the PWA and the Department of Labor help, but the new agency to be created by "relief legislation now pending before Congress," the Works Progress Administration, might offer young people places on work projects. In Walsh's view, young people who had left school and been blocked from opportunities made up one of "the more serious aspects of the depression." This was particularly true of the highly trained and specialized college graduates. Like Lang, the senator warned that "this large group may become demoralized and disheartened, and thus constitute a dangerous addition to the discontented and radical-minded elements" in America. Youth offered a "challenge to the system," he concluded. For the sake of democracy and the future of youth, the federal government had a duty to expand opportunities for these people.[31]

In her report to Congress, transmitted on 30 March 1935, Perkins responded favorably to the Walsh resolution. Herself convinced that something further should be done for American youth, she was well aware of the youth plans prepared by the FERA. After acquiring a copy of Williams's November proposal for reference in preparing a reply to Walsh, she directed Children's Bureau chief Katherine Lenroot to expand on the Williams draft in order to more fully meet Walsh's demands. Lenroot's work resulted in a Department of Labor proposal that sought greater coordination of New Deal youth-serving efforts than FERA officials had anticipated. In addition, the Perkins proposal reflected a greater awareness that work relief and training for citizenship were as necessary for youth and the nation as a program of vocational education.[32]

In her reply Perkins disagreed with Walsh in only one important respect. She believed that the youth problem should encompass only those between the ages of 18 and 25, and not those as old as 30. Explaining the New Deal rationale for limiting federal assistance to persons between 18 and 25, she pointed out that the NRA codes and the depressed employment conditions had effectively raised the school leaving age to 18. Although it was true that many Americans under 18 had left school in search of work, these people required "a flexible and rich school program," not work relief. Meanwhile, young adults over 25 were "in the prime of earning life," and many had "family responsibilities." The median age at first marriage for males remained unchanged at 24.3 between 1930 and 1940 (the figure for women was just over 21 in both years). Thus it seemed wise to include Americans over 25 within the purview of New Deal relief programs aimed at adult breadwinners. By contrast, young people between 18 and 25 had exhausted their educational opportunities but lacked the family responsibilities necessary to qualify for adult work relief. With employment a cruel mirage for many of these youths, Perkins believed they were among the Americans most deserving of federal assistance.[33]

Perkins proposed that the New Deal spend $96 million to involve a variety of federal agencies in a coordinated effort to put young people to work. Recognizing that youth's spirit should be as vital a concern of government as the level of their skills, she spoke of young people's "susceptibility to demoralizing interests and experiences." In order to provide jobs, she proposed the establishment of "a combined junior work and educational program" attached to the WPA. Its purpose resembled that of Williams's November draft. Youth would be given opportunities for work, recreation, and education in their own communities. Yet, as an adjunct to the WPA, the major part of the program would be oriented to seeing to it that young people received jobs, not merely education. Student aid was provided for in a separate section of her report. Perkins estimated that it would cost $84,370,000 to provide work for 800,000 youths every six months; each young person would receive $15 per month. Since $72 million of this appropriation would go for wages alone, the training value of the program would be limited. Perkins's proposal expressed a philosophy not held by relief officials: work, in and of itself, would offer youth rich benefits.

In addition, Perkins proposed that the U.S. Employment Service be allocated $2.5 million for "the development of interviewing and referral services for young people in search of work." Meanwhile, the Perkins plan would provide the Federal Committee on Apprentice Training an additional $30,000 to facilitate its work in persuading employers to train unskilled youths for journeyman positions. Yet another proposal without parallel in the FERA scheme was Lenroot's idea of allocating $1 million to employ a thousand youths in one or two experimental camps. These camps would offer organized recreation, health care, and "a wider variety of work experience" than was provided or contemplated by the CCC. At the same time, the Department of Labor draft promised an expansion of the educational and guidance offerings of the CCC. Like the junior work and educational agency, all these proposals were new in the sense that they were designed, above all else, to ensure that more young people received jobs.

Finally, the Labor Department endorsed the FERA plans for expanded student aid and urged that all New Deal programs be integrated in a single, coordinated effort. Perkins would continue college student aid and adopt Williams's plan to provide part-time jobs (at $2 a week) to 100,000 high school students. In her view, the need for this assistance was unarguable. There were an estimated 860,000 youths aged sixteen and seventeen from families on relief. Many were not going to school, she wrote, only because they lacked "carfare, books, and necessary incidentals." By providing only $8.1 million for this purpose, the government could rectify this injustice.

Significantly, Perkins diverged from the Williams draft by recommending that the Office of Education be granted control over the administration of federal student aid. She did so for two reasons. Not only did she wish to broaden public support for the agency, but she hoped to include as many federal agencies as possible in a collaborative effort. Such a move would placate school officials who watched the developing plans for a national youth program with wary eyes, fearful of federal intrusion into local control of education.

Educators had praised the Lang plan primarily because its scope and accomplishments depended largely on the initiative of school officials themselves. It seemed good sense, therefore, to bring the Office of Education into partnership with the new relief agency expected to be ushered in by the Emergency Relief Appropriation Act of 1935 (the yet-to-be-announced WPA). Both agencies would be equal partners in the administration of the new youth agency. By doing this, Perkins believed, the New Deal would achieve what Walsh and Lang had demanded: a coordination of federal youth efforts for the purpose of providing youth not merely relief but education and jobs as well. Therefore Perkins proposed that her $96 million plan be administered through a national advisory council composed of representatives of all the federal bureaucracies involved in the program. The council would coordinate and centralize the administration of youth programs currently operated independently by a host of New Deal agencies.[34]

It apparently mattered little to Perkins, at the outset, which agency administered student aid. A consideration of public attitudes and the need to coordinate New Deal youth programs were enough to convince her that the USOE was a natural choice. But the officials of the new WPA and those of the USOE viewed the selection from a vastly different perspective. For them, it was a question not only of policy but of power relationships, of whether an agency exclusively beholden to the New Deal (the WPA) would administer the new program, or whether its direction would be determined by an agency long controlled by, and receptive to, the leaders of conservative education organizations (the USOE). To a degree, the question was one of politics mixed with pride. Certainly there was no more ambitious New Dealer than Harry Hopkins, head of the WPA.

And Commissioner of Education John Studebaker was equally prepared to fight to maintain his influence (however small) within the New Deal.

Roosevelt wished to avoid any decision on the youth program that would appear to lodge control in the hands of just one faction within the administration. Image was important. It was necessary to shield the New Deal from the appearance that relief officials alone were placing young people in government jobs. There was no chance that the president would permit an unconditional public victory for either Hopkins or Studebaker in their efforts to control the New Deal for youth. At the same time, however, Roosevelt quietly moved to block Studebaker's attempt to gain influence over the new youth agency. In addition, the president worked to ensure that the program would provide immediate relief, employment, and political education under the direction of Hopkins's staff. Thus, quite apart from appearance, Roosevelt exercised decisive influence in determining the real character and direction of the new program. Meanwhile, he continued cultivating the false, but politically advantageous, image that all executive agencies shared equally in youth program planning. Given the controversy surrounding any peacetime federal organization of the young, Roosevelt hoped to appear to be following tradition in his approval of the NYA. At the same time, he sought to meet young people's real needs, even if that meant breaking with tradition.[35]

In March the president appeared hopeful that all executive agencies would collaborate in the program. He directed Hopkins to "speak with Charlie Taussig and Dr. Studebaker about this problem of the graduates, school and college, of 1935." Meanwhile, he gave Taussig and Eleanor Roosevelt the task of chairing jointly an impressive but unofficial advisory committee of prominent businessmen for the purpose of providing industrial employment for young people, noncompetitive with private labor. In both cases he seemed slightly aloof toward the prospect of a new agency for young people and certainly above the battle breaking out between Hopkins and Studebaker. Historians (particularly biographers of the First Lady) have long regarded this as an accurate generalization of Roosevelt's role in the birth of the NYA, for it accords well with the larger-than-life tale that Eleanor Roosevelt personally inspired its creation. Yet, appearance is not the same as reality, as the events of the following two months revealed.[36]

On the surface, the breakdown in the movement toward a youth agency controlled jointly by several executive agencies seemed to be precipitated by Studebaker. At first Hopkins was willing to accept Perkins's advice that the New Deal provide apprenticeships and positions on work projects in addition to educational aid. On 11 April he promised FDR that the WPA would inaugurate a "special Junior Work Program to employ young persons between the ages of eighteen and twenty-five at one-fourth security payment in local projects selected especially for participation by young people." For the first time relief officials were willing to provide the young with jobs, not merely relief and education. The Walsh and Perkins initiatives had had a telling effect on Hopkins's thinking; in fact, he characterized his Junior Work Program as one designed to fulfill the functions and activities suggested in Perkins's memorandum. Hopkins made no mention of Perkins's suggestion that the USOE administer student aid under the plan. Undoubtedly he was hostile to the idea, and perhaps he preferred to let silence put it to rest. Nevertheless, at this time he made no overt move in the direction of conflict with Studebaker's office.[37]

The genteel maneuvering for control over the new youth agency came to an end a few days later when Studebaker announced the USOE's alternative to the Perkins plan. He recommended that the New Deal launch a "Community Youth Program" to provide vocational guidance and part-time work for 2 million youths, 1.1 million more than were to be assisted under the Department of Labor's plan. Studebaker hoped that the government would fund the creation of locally controlled "guidance and adjustment centers," where young people could go for job advice and recreation. In addition, young people might be assigned as assistants to public officials, teachers, social workers, "or to any public or quasi-public work." A community council, organized "at the invitation of public school officials," would channel federal funds to the character-building agencies and schools most in need of assistance. New Deal funds would not go directly to the young. Instead, both student aid and work projects would be administered wholly by educators, for the main purpose of expanding educational opportunities for the young people involved.[38]

For Hopkins and Williams, Studebaker's proposal created a new situation and changed the terms of the debate. The commissioner of education had appealed for public support on behalf of a one-sided proposal to lodge exclusive control over the New Deal for youth in the hands of private educators. In a radio address over NBC on 30 April 1935, Studebaker had even suggested that his plan more closely accorded with American tradition than the plans of the relief officials. "No American youth," he declared, "should be entirely disassociated from the educational system until he is properly placed in constructive activities." He promised that an educational program, by itself, would be sufficient to salvage the spirit of the young. It would serve, he claimed, as "an anti-crime movement, morale-booster, and youth conservation drive rolled into one."[39]

In the face of this blatant appeal for complete control over the youth program, New Deal relief officials saw the need for a more aggressive strategy to bring the president to their side. The polite entreaties with which Hopkins had sought FDR's support, suggesting some willingness to compromise with the USOE, no longer seemed adequate to the situation. From this point on, Hopkins and his assistant, Jacob Baker, criticized *any* USOE involvement in the program and pointed out every deficiency they could find in the Community Youth Program. More important, thrown on the defensive by Studebaker's move, they retreated to the position they had held in November. They no longer suggested that young people required jobs especially tailored to their needs. Rather, they defended Williams's November proposal and the idea of merely including young people with adults on WPA projects. Just as Studebaker had argued that education would meet all the needs of depression youth, the polarization of the debate led WPA officials to argue that young people required primarily existing forms of relief and education, not a novel brand of employment.[40]

Jacob Baker explained the revised position of the relief officials. On 29 April he wrote Hopkins: "Our program is set up to be closely joined with the work projects for adults, with the idea that groups of young people may be [included] in a good many projects that are operating for adults." He scoffed at the claim that the USOE plan could reach 2 million youths. In his view, no program could aid as many young people as one operated in connection with WPA adult projects. As Baker explained, "to attempt to have local Boards of Education set up projects for 2,000,000 youths in any reasonable length of time, particularly if they are set up apart from adult projects, is probably impossible, and I think it would be very difficult even to reach the 800,000 [*sic*] suggested by the Labor Department."[41]

Doubtless the president was disappointed by all of this shifting around of positions. At a time when demand was rising for a program to provide young people work, training, and political education, Studebaker's recommendation that education alone be provided was clearly inadequate. As Perkins advised Studebaker's superior, Harold Ickes, on 6 May, Studebaker was right that "the educational phases of the program should be under the direction of educational authorities," but he was wrong in assuming that "selection and referral of these young people . . . on work-relief projects" should also be under his control.[42]

The crux of the problem was that neither the WPA plan nor that of Studebaker could enable the New Deal to justify a federal program for the young. Roosevelt wanted a program that would achieve a novel objective (train youth for employment) in a novel way, but which could be billed as an emergency relief program for young people, thereby warding off attacks from educators.[43] While he was anxious to provide real jobs with vocational value, he was adamant that such jobs be noncompetitive with adult labor and provide a genuine return on the government's investment. Achieving such objectives was a tall order, requiring the new youth agency to steer a clear path, as it were, between Scylla and Charybdis. In fact, achieving them all was impossible. The attempt by NYA leaders to do so would severely limit the agency's effectiveness as a job-training and anti-depression measure. One thing was clear, however: neither Studebaker's nor Williams's plan resolved the problem the president had authorized Charles Taussig to investigate, providing jobs for 1935 graduates.

Perkins recommended that a committee be established to work out the differences between her program and those of Studebaker and Williams. She proposed that the committee be composed of Studebaker, Katherine Lenroot, "and someone to be designated by Mr. Hopkins."[44] Roosevelt did not approve this idea. As historians have noted, FDR seldom found Studebaker's ideas congenial. Studebaker's desire to establish a locally controlled agency that would work in the long run did not accord with Roosevelt's interest in creating a relief agency that would put money in young people's hands rapidly and achieve immediate results. Further, the Studebaker proposal was prohibitively expensive.

There was a more important reason why Roosevelt could not support a simple amalgamation of the Perkins, Studebaker, and Williams plans. None of these programs, in the president's view, could adequately fulfill the task of political education. Therefore Roosevelt intervened personally to provide this ingredient. As early as March he had directed Hopkins and Studebaker to discuss their ideas with the one figure within the administration who had been most deeply concerned with youth's ideological state, Charles W. Taussig. On 9 March Taussig had reported to FDR that he had "discussed with Dr. Studebaker the program for finding jobs for the graduates of 1935 (non-competing with labor)." The assignment was evidently not a new one for Taussig since he indicated that a finished proposal could be on the president's desk within two weeks. Thus, what eventually became the NYA's primary order of business—educating young people in the means to appreciate and defend democracy—originated from the personal intervention not of the First Lady but of the president of the United States.[45]

Even before Studebaker offered his program to locate full control over the youth program in the USOE, Roosevelt had taken steps to involve others in the drafting of the program. In March and April, with Roosevelt's authorization, Taussig discussed the youth program with Eleanor Roosevelt and leading political and business leaders whose advice Roosevelt respected, including James D. Mooney, chairman of the board of General Motors; Adolph Berle, coauthor of *The Modern Corporation and Private Property* and a Roosevelt "brain-truster"; David Sarnoff, president of RCA; and Owen D. Young, chairman of General Electric. At these meetings, attended at times by leaders of student groups, the conferees apparently came to the conclusion that young people required, in addition to noncompeting jobs in industry, student aid and apprenticeships of the sort Williams had recommended the previous November. Indeed, Taussig conferred with Williams at times in the drafting process. In mid-April, pleased with their work, Roosevelt instructed the Taussig group to continue with their deliberations. The relief group was merging its plans nicely with the plans of other people interested in young people's relationship to student aid, industrial employment, and democracy.[46]

By the end of April, Roosevelt could only have been steeled further in his determination to minimize Studebaker's role and invest control over the youth program in the hands of those concerned with youth's relief, job training, and ideological needs. While the president was working hard to meet a popular mood favoring a dramatic national effort to relieve youth unemployment and shield democracy, Studebaker was proposing an undramatic plan to meet only the needs of the young in academic education. Meanwhile, Hopkins had spoken approvingly of the idea of special jobs for young people. Roosevelt had little difficulty resolving the question of whom he would choose to control the new youth agency: Studebaker, a recent Roosevelt appointee, or Hopkins, who already was demonstrating the kind of rapport with FDR that would have such historic results during World War II. Roosevelt chose Hopkins.[47]

The president recognized that there was one further difficulty to be overcome. The program would provide some form of job training, though the president, anxious to get money into the hands of young people as quickly as possible, stressed the relief and decentralized aspects of the plan. The problem was that he might not gain recognition for the educational aspects of the program if the press emphasized Studebaker's utter defeat on the issue.[48] To try to gain the support of educators for the emerging NYA, Roosevelt hoped to provide the appearance of full administrative backing of the program. Thus he asked Hopkins to take all four proposals (those of Williams, Perkins, Studebaker, and the Taussig group) and combine the best features of each into one plan. Further, as with the CCC, Roosevelt approved the establishment of an executive committee to head the bureaucratic chart of the NYA. All executive agencies interested in NYA activities (including the USOE) were given equal positions on the committee.[49]

Significantly, the NYA Executive Committee, headed by Assistant Treasury Secretary Josephine Roche, possessed a purely symbolic role. Policymaking was reserved for the national staff in Washington and the agency's National Advisory Committee (NAC), a body composed of leaders of powerful interest groups in education, labor, and industry, and headed by Taussig. Characteristically, Roosevelt gave more to groups who could do him harm (labor and industry) than to the bodies he himself controlled (such as the USOE and other executive agencies). By placing the USOE in the NYA hierarchy but giving it little voice and less power, the administration hoped to have it both ways on the educational question; it hoped to minimize the influence of the USOE while retaining the goodwill of educators. Similarly, Hopkins's task of considering the Studebaker proposal was for public consumption only. Privately, Roosevelt told his alter ego that the Studebaker plan was too costly. As John Salmond observed, the very decision to give the task of amalgamation to Hopkins meant that the relief perspective in the program would win out. In addition, the decision indicated not only that Roosevelt knew in advance the direction New Deal policy would take, but that he himself had, by the spring of 1935, taken a firm hand on the rudder.[50]

The Taussig group completed its work by mid-May. Like Williams's plan of the previous November, their proposal recommended introducing student aid to 200,000 high school students, expanding the college aid program to 200,000 youths, and persuading industries and all levels of government to make apprenticeships available to the young. The number of young people to be aided under the job-training plan was 150,000. The group's contribution to the relief plan was a work project program, designed to reach 150,000 youths at fifteen dollars a month each, and a procedure (not just an objective) to achieve decentralization. Washington would appoint a state director and a state advisory committee (SAC) for each of the nation's territories and forty-eight commonwealths. Composed of the state's leading figures in higher education, labor, business, and municipal government, each SAC would collaborate with the state directors in determining policy—subject to national regulations. The state directors, in turn, would work broadly to develop work opportunities and job training for young people by securing the cooperation of "existing public and private agencies." In addition, they would appoint local advisory committees to perform the same task in individual towns and cities.[51]

These features were outlined to Aubrey Williams in a personal meeting with Eleanor Roosevelt and other Taussig committee members on 17 May. Nearly everyone expected that Williams would be appointed the agency's executive director. David Sarnoff informed him that the NAC's role would be to draw on the expertise of industrial leaders in devising ways of employing youths "aside from the way you have done." Eleanor Roosevelt added that the number of apprenticeships secured would depend on organized labor's attitude toward that aspect of the program. In the exhilaration of the moment, she seems to have suggested that some of the NYA projects might put young people to work building their own homes and constructing youth hostels and rural nursery schools. Williams must have come away from the meeting pleased after hearing the details of a plan so essentially his own.[52]

Franklin Roosevelt had a few more changes to make, however. In a memo dated 20 May (but sent to Hopkins a week later) the president turned down yet another proposal to provide "special arrangements" for "the substantial number of young men and women of inherent qualities of genius." Projects for adult workers under the WPA were acceptable, but white-collar endeavors for youths were too politically risky to countenance. Roosevelt preferred to support projects that emphasized the physical development of young people. In addition, he was receptive to the argument that the grass-roots institutions of a romanticized, small-town America (a place that existed more in the twentieth-century imagination than in nineteenth-century history) should be replicated under the NYA in order to maximize youth-to-youth interaction. He particularly admired a Taussig proposal to have young people build recreational and community shelters. These were to be "anything from an old-fashioned 'swimming-hole' to a complete center." In his own hand, FDR added "baseball diamonds" and "gridirons" to the activities of the community centers. Although the political power of groups demanding some program to reach young people's minds had helped persuade the president to create the NYA, he was more sympathetic to proposals to strengthen their bodies and souls.[53]

In general, the president was pleased with the plan. Work projects were to be limited exclusively to young people from families on relief, thus adding to the plan's image as an emergency measure immune from normal political opposition. Yet, by claiming to reach 700,000 American youths, provisions of the overall program threatened to neutralize this politically safe image. The administration was worried about the public's response to so ambitious a national organization for young people. Stephen Early warned that care was necessary in announcing the NYA's creation, lest it be denounced as a form of regimentation. For these reasons Roosevelt scaled down the numbers to be aided on the student aid venture. High school aid was limited to 100,000 students and college aid was pared to 120,000 youths. The president left untouched one novel feature in the Taussig draft: a proposal to provide work for 30,000 graduate students at a monthly income of thirty dollars each.[54]

On 26 June 1935 FDR unveiled the NYA to the nation. The NYA was called into existence by executive order (number 7086), not legislative action. Roosevelt hoped to conserve his political capital with Congress by making requests of that body only when specific action of the sort he desired could not be taken through executive channels. The Emergency Relief Appropriation Act of 1935 had allocated nearly $5 billion for relief. It was a simple matter to slice $50 million from the pie and locate the NYA under the WPA's nominal jurisdiction, from which position the new youth agency could legally spend the money. In measured phrases Roosevelt emphasized the program's decentralized character and limited, emergency nature. "This undertaking will need the vigorous cooperation of the citizens of the several states," he said. "[T]o ensure that they shall have an important part in this work, a representative [group of citizens shall be appointed to] a national advisory board with similar boards of citizens in the states and municipalities throughout the country." Only a "resumption of normal business activities and opportunities for private employment on a wide scale" would solve the youth problem, he warned. The NYA would minister to "the most pressing and immediate needs" of the nation's "most seriously affected" youths; it could do no more. The program was really one to aid America as much as her young. It was necessary because the nation could "ill afford to lose the skill and energy of these young men and women."[55]

Roosevelt's effort to maintain expectations at a reasonable level and defuse opposition had little dampening effect on Aubrey Williams, who had seen his proposal at last become reality. The president had promised to create a program that would serve "a great national need. . . . The yield on this investment," he added, "should be high." The president was ambiguous about whether the program would be a short-term relief effort or a great national campaign to reemploy young people and preserve their commitment to democracy. Williams's experience as the NYA's new director would supply the answer. Williams himself was buoyed by the news. "It is certain," he announced, "that we will be well underway in ten days, and I hope, in full swing by mid-July."[56]

But it was not to be so easy.

CHAPTER SIX

Facing Failure and Fascism

T he NYA's employment of young people on work projects and school campuses relieved much of the political pressure that had given rise to the agency. There were some rumblings of discontent in the first fiscal year (June 1935–June 1936), when the slow organization of the agency delayed the start-up of the out-of-school program.[1] In January 1936, however, the first out-of-school youths received NYA jobs. A president who conceived of the youth problem primarily in terms of health and morale, not education, and who looked to the NYA to provide baseball diamonds and gridirons, responded by turning his attention elsewhere. The NYA would go forward with little White House interference.

Like the president, the NYA officials in the Washington office viewed the NYA as a relief venture. Executive Director Aubrey Williams despaired because the NYA lacked the funds to undertake useful job-training and education programs, but he immediately set about the task of dispensing relief, and relief alone, to the out-of-school youths under his care. (The old FERA student aid program was continued as before, largely under the direction of high school and college administrators.) The NYA's first full-time deputy director, Richard R. Brown, a public school teacher who had become a sociology professor at the University of Denver, followed his chief's lead and administered the NYA as a relief program. Brown argued against the idealists tied to the agency—Charles Taussig and various state directors and members of the National Advisory Committee—who believed that the NYA could undertake sophisticated education programs.

The NYA idealists saw their agency as a watershed program in the history of American public education.[2]

By the end of the first fiscal year, nearly all NYA officials realized that there was one area in which the mere employment of young people would not suffice to realize the ideal of integration into the normal patterns of American life. This was the need for some form of training to counter the danger of fascism. Even when the hands of young people were idle, their minds were active. Fascism and democracy were not on the minds of most jobless youth, but fascism and young people were on the minds of NYA leaders. When the NYA produced its own house history nine years later, its founders recalled their conviction that youthful discontent was nationwide in 1935, and only required consolidation by some would-be Pied Piper to produce "undesirable changes in the American way of life."[3]

In order to keep youth democratic, the New Deal had to reach the minds of the young. Neither the physical labor offered by the out-of-school projects nor the academic instruction received from the best student aid jobs was enough for this purpose. Taussig had recognized the need for political education in his memo to Roosevelt in December 1933. Aubrey Williams had done likewise in his persistent push for an education curriculum tied to public service employment, under FERA auspices (a persistence that had puzzled Fred J. Kelly of the USOE). If the overwhelming dimensions of the unemployment problem had made relief seem more critical in 1935, and had thus stymied action on the education front, the situation had changed dramatically by June 1936. By then, a move was under way to make education for citizenship and democracy an agency priority.[4]

If every young person had the potential for political disaffection, it followed that all NYA programs needed to have a civic training purpose. Yet, although the existing student aid and work project programs were enough for middle-class youths who lived in the nation's more prosperous small towns and cities, they were not sufficient for the "backwater" rural youths who all too often remained beyond the reach of opportunities for institutionalized education. Middle-class youths had only recently left the schools; hence they were well educated in the tenets of American democracy. Many rural youths had never gone to school. Only through education could the NYA provide rural youths what the nation and its young urban citizens were receiving from NYA employment: integration into a more or less traditionally structured democratic society, sorely pressed for internal unity at a time of depression and dictatorship.

THE DIFFERENCES in philosophy between the reform-minded Taussig group and the relief officials in the Washington office were starkly evident at the NAC's first meeting, which convened 15 August 1935. Taussig portrayed the NYA's work as part of a virtual crusade to preserve democracy in America. Its primary task was not to dispense relief but to equalize educational opportunities for youths unable or unwilling to attend the schools. Since these youths were unreached by public education, Taussig did not expect educators to view the NYA as a competitor. In fact, he hoped to enlist their aid in an effort designed as much to strengthen the nation's internal security as to benefit the young. Five of his fellow advisory committee members were educators (three of them college presidents), a fact that made this expectation of support seem realistic. "Much of our work lies in the field of education," Taussig explained, "and it is to the educators of the country and existing educational agencies we must look to help solve these problems."[5]

Taussig doubted that American democracy would be well served by a program that reached youths' bodies, through work relief, rather than their minds, through education. "Unless we can educate the youth of today to function intelligently in a modern democracy," he said flatly, "a democratic form of government is doomed." While the older generation remembered clearly a time of international stability, the young had no such reference point. Older Americans could see Hitlerism for what it was, but the young people—watching "age-old governments crack up to be replaced by various types of dictatorships"—could not. "Our youth of today never knew the norms by which we judge the passing show," Taussig explained. If young people were apathetic, the nation could perhaps afford to ignore their plight. But it was precisely because the young were gripped by a new social consciousness, precisely because they were subjecting democracy to a "cruel analysis," that NYA officials would be ill-advised to ignore the importance of civic education. The problem of "restless and explosive" youth, he concluded, was reducible to the fact that "vendors of gilded substitutes [for democracy] are finding willing converts to political and social creeds that are destructive to all that this nation stands for."[6]

The members of the advisory committee were sharply divided in their reactions to Taussig's remarks. Some, such as athlete Glenn Cunningham, aviator Amelia Earhart, labor leader Sidney Hillman, and publisher Bernarr Macfadden, were appointed for political or public relations reasons and said little.[7] Those without experience in relief work, especially those who represented one or more broad fields (such as education or recreation) rather than a single interest group, endorsed Taussig's position that youth must be integrated into the social fabric through education rather than work relief. The chancellor of the University of Kansas, E. H. Lindley, pointed out that NYA student work on campus had value not only as a means of helping young people earn tuition funds but as an educational force in its own right. "We who are interested in formal education realize that there are many things which educate youth besides what happens in the college and community," he explained, citing as examples the influence of peers and press: "School mates and the radio and bulletin boards and the press, etc., are educating them constantly; and we realize . . . that many boys and girls interested in school want a job to get the maximum educational experience out of a job. . . . I have a good deal of interest in what we recognize . . . as a supplement to anything the colleges attempt to do."[8] Through the NYA, the nation would compete with students' peers in their education. Even outside the schools, then, the nation would be guaranteed a voice in the education of the youth group.

Other committee members—in business, education, and the field of recreation—agreed that the NYA must work to integrate youth in society through an approach to their minds; that is, through education. Work relief alone would not produce the kind of psychological uplift, personal growth, and leadership qualities spawned by education. Work relief jobs were acceptable provided they offered abundant opportunities for instruction and pointed the way to a rational use of leisure time. Committee member Howard Braucher, editor of *Recreation*, admitted that "we can't dodge that fact that youth want to work and anything else does seem a pretty sorry substitute."

Braucher recommended a particular kind of work for NYA youths, however: the construction of swimming pools, athletic fields, and tennis courts. Through such work, young people "appreciated the value of those things and get satisfaction in making things for their own group." He produced a letter from a Cleveland girl who wrote about her thrill in organizing a recreation project.[9]

Two other NAC members, Mary McLeod Bethune and Owen D. Young, agreed that through education the NYA could maintain morale and achieve social integration. They were not speaking of racial integration but of integrating an entire generation into American life. Bethune, the president of Bethune-Cookman College in Florida and a pioneer in work-study education for impoverished youths, pointed out that perhaps 85 percent of southern youngsters were dispersed from each other in rural areas. "Now we can't get these NYA projects scattered all over the rural districts," she complained to the committee members. In her remarks she anticipated the resident center program of 1938, which would provide a central urban location to which rural youths could come and learn the skills of an urban-industrial economy. Bethune wondered if "we may not put up huge, strong, outstanding training centers." The "graduates" could return to their rural neighborhoods and bring "awakening" and "stimulation to the thousands . . . who are famishing, awaiting [sic] for a little encouragement and a little hope." "You ought to work hard upon your Recreational centers," she concluded, "so that Negroes might be taught how to swim and to go out and teach others."[10]

According to Owen D. Young, lawyer, industrialist, and chairman of the board of General Electric, "the easiest but the most fruitful" way the NYA could help the young was through education. After all, he reasoned, "the next best thing to having . . . a job is the feeling that you are being educated for a job." Like Taussig, he believed that recreation was not an end in itself. Young feared that the NYA would diversify into too many areas and believed that through education "we can do most with the least overhead." Thus convinced that educational projects offered a highly effective and affordable solution to the youth problem, Young reflected the optimism of most in the Taussig group. "There's almost no field you can't reach," he glowed, "whether you are talking about forums, swimming pools, tennis courts or vocations; there is no place you cannot reach from the educational anchorage."[11]

By contrast, Aubrey Williams, the man who would determine the nature of NYA work projects, reacted gloomily to the contrast between the agency's mandate and its meager appropriation. The NYA was expected to aid a substantial portion of the millions of jobless youths with only $50 million. Earlier, Williams had proposed public service apprenticeships to educate young people in the workings of government. Now, however, with the NYA raising expectations that could not be filled,[12] with applications for work cascading into NYA headquarters, and with White House pressure building on Williams to launch the work program, his support for a risky and experimental educational program was weakening. The most vocal champions of the agency, including Eleanor Roosevelt, were emphasizing the number of young people in need of attention and were not breaking down the problem in terms of specific needs.[13] As the official most responsible for the NYA's fate, Williams felt compelled to fall back on the position that the agency could offer only work relief, helping as many youths as possible without regard for the kind of training they received.

Harried by the difficulty of launching a vast program from the ground up, Williams for the moment abandoned his reformist aspirations and insisted that the agency was nothing more than a temporary relief agency. To be sure, he often spoke of the need to integrate the young into the social fabric. Americans had to realize, he said, that young people "want to be part of the going arrangement." Yet, he added, "We won't be able to do much along that line." "We have no answers," he told the NAC members. "I don't know that there are any answers. This whole thing may be beyond any group of people, no matter how sincere and how earnest they are really to do very much about the situation."[14] The recreation proposals particularly nettled Williams. Ideally, they were fine, but in a real world where everywhere could be heard the call for jobs, jobs, and more jobs, he felt that leisure time and educational projects had to await the performance of the simple function of providing employment. "These young people want jobs, just like you and I want jobs," he said impatiently. "Now that is a big order." The people who wanted experimental recreational projects excited his deepest desire for social reform, and "we are arranging a group to get their ideas and help." But, he continued, "I don't know—I fooled around with recreation for a number of years, and I confess I get a feeling of being up against a blank stone wall when you think of what you can actually do. You always get back to the answer that what they want are jobs and money; . . . and it keeps staggering you."[15]

Williams implied that it was wrong for the committee to recommend ideally perfect programs when he had to make decisions based on limited funds and then answer for the result. "We have $50,000,000 and a year's life," he explained. "What happens then is not any of my business. It may be some of yours, if you want to make it. But I am thinking of what I am charged with doing today." Taussig was thinking more about what the NYA might accomplish for the nation by the end of its work than what might be done for young people immediately. Williams felt compelled to remind him, and those who shared his views, of the almost equally sobering conditions of depression America in 1935.[16]

Nevertheless, Williams always recognized the need for equal educational opportunities for all young people in the land. No less than the NAC members, he hoped that the NYA would integrate young people into the democratic way of life. Five days after the NAC meeting, NYA state directors gathered in Washington to listen to what the *New York Times* described as "pep talks" from the president and the First Lady. Williams got caught up in the mood of the moment and proclaimed that the time had come to start something significant for the young. Several weeks later, he telephoned Braucher and endorsed his recreational leadership scheme. Braucher explained that the program would place "80,000 of . . . those who have capacity for recreation leadership" in positions where they could train other youths, not on the NYA payroll, in "happy human activity." The real goal was integration. As Braucher explained, "they who have been given opportunity to know how abundant life can be . . . want, really want, others to live as they live themselves." Williams responded: "It is the president's purpose and my purpose to back the kind of work you people have been standing for through the years."[17]

Many of the state directors, unused to working in government, were euphoric at the possibility of charting a new course in the nation's youth-serving efforts. Williams, however, was an old hand at working within the limits of a relief budget, and he had grown accustomed to seeing lofty objectives founder on the shores of inadequate funding. As a result of these contrasting backgrounds, Roosevelt's remarks in the following weeks raised the hopes of NAC members and state directors while leaving Williams gloomier than ever. While others focused on FDR's hopeful remarks, Williams searched for the rhetorical equivalent of the fine print. It was not difficult to find.

Roosevelt told the state directors he expected "action" from them. Previous White House–sponsored meetings on education and child welfare "had very interesting discussions and . . . passed very nice resolutions." Afterward, "everybody went home and little, if anything, resulted from their efforts." Roosevelt recognized that the NYA was an experiment, but he promised that "we are going to get something more than mere resolutions out of it." Seeking to keep expectations at a reasonable level, he went on to say that the NYA could help only the 2.9 million youths from families on relief. The NYA's work would remain unfinished until it enabled them "to share equally with their fellows the normal blessings of our traditional American life." Roosevelt hesitated to predict the future, but, in an artful passage, couched a rather pessimistic forecast in optimistic language: "We don't know how it is going to turn out next year when we don't have as much money. The future is going to depend on the success of the experiment. If the experiment is a success, there is not much doubt that future Congresses will continue the work."[18] Optimists concluded that the president was supporting a program to integrate youth into the nation through education, and predicting for it a long life. Pessimists could see that he was placing the burden for success on the NYA officials and putting the agency's fate at the mercy of Congress.

Some circles of American public education were hostile to the NYA, viewing it as the first step in the establishment of a federal education system competitive with the schools. George D. Strayer, professor of education at Columbia University's Teacher's College, initiated this opposition in July when he assailed the NYA at a Columbia-sponsored school administration conference. Strayer supported federal aid to education, provided control of that aid remained in the hands of local officials. Two months later, the *School Review*, a journal of the University of Chicago's Department of Education, charged the NYA with duplicating, wastefully and unconstitutionally, programs already existing in the schools. Through the work of the NYA, the journal declared, "federal agencies are actually at work controlling and administering public education within the states." The NYA was criticized for "passing over" the "regularly constituted educational authorities" at the local level.[19]

Faced with this pressure, Roosevelt described the NYA less and less as a reformist venture and more as a kind of junior WPA. When asked at a press conference in September to respond to growing criticism of the NYA, Roosevelt cautioned that "we have to bear in mind that the whole of it is a relief measure and that the major part goes to help boys and girls attending school and college where they otherwise would not be able to do so." While leaving the experimental work program unmentioned, he added that the lion's share of the money ($27 million) went to student aid.[20]

While Aubrey Williams and the Taussig group generally agreed on the nature of youth distress, the nuances of their respective analyses of the youth problem were to draw the NAC and the Washington office into conflict over its solution. On 16 October 1935 Williams declared that youth's fundamental need was equal opportunity for education. "These young people who have been unfortunate enough to come of age during the depression will be permanently handicapped. . . . The opportunities for advancement of the poor youth and the rich youth are by no means equal." The next day, Taussig sent the First Lady a copy of a speech he had just delivered before the American Federation of Labor. Every youth required the "thrill of a job," Taussig told the labor leaders; but he or she also required integration into the mainstream of American opportunity, the point Williams had made. "If we neglect them," Taussig explained, "if we exploit them, if we fail to make them a part of our social and economic life, we need not be surprised if they blast from our feet the very foundations of our society."[21]

The two sides differed greatly over the method of attack each considered necessary to the moment. Convinced that there were sufficient funds and presidential support only for relief, not reform, Williams emphasized the numbers of the problem, or, as he put it, the "5,000,000 to 8,000,000 young people [who] are wholly unoccupied" and the "3,000,000 young people . . . on relief." At the 16 October meeting of the New York City Welfare Council, Williams was distressed that the NYA had gotten off to a bad start in doing what it had to do: put young people back to work or keep them in school. He even wondered aloud whether he would emerge from his job with "his shirt" or any "character" intact.[22]

Those who shared Taussig's more expansive hopes for the agency included Braucher, Bethune, and Young on the NAC, and state directors S. Burns Weston of Ohio and Isaac Sutton of Pennsylvania. They were not distressed by the NYA's limited funding. Consistent with their desire for permanent reform, they believed that the placement of youths on work projects could await a period of less costly experimentation and analysis. In 1935 the NAC voted to conduct a census to measure youth unemployment before trying to do much about it. Other proposals reflected the philosophy that time had to be spent on experimentation before money could be spent on work projects. On 19 October Weston wrote Taussig of his desire to use NYA funds to plan "a state-wide vocational guidance and training program under the state Department of Education." He denied that the NYA's small appropriation need be a barrier to progress. "There are a vast number of possibilities of being helpful," he explained, "in ways that do not require the expenditure of money, by providing in the spirit indicated cooperative community thinking and action."[23]

FOR AUBREY WILLIAMS, the NYA's first objective was to provide training and hope to as many of the three million youths on relief as possible. For Charles Taussig, this objective was merely the means to a larger and more important end: eliminating the threat to democracy posed by large numbers of jobless young people. Williams thought that the NYA must first meet the material needs of the maximum number of idle youths before attempting to scale higher heights. At the same time, he fought hard to achieve, through organized action, broad reform of the nation's pattern of serving the poor. No less than Taussig, he knew that the youth problem was vast in scale. "We could find useful and necessary work [for youths] far beyond the boundaries of the present limited program," he wrote in January 1936. The problem was that the NYA's means of assistance were so limited. If he was of two minds toward the NYA's role, it was at least in part because of his own unusually varied personal experience as a young man. Although he had celebrated his twentieth birthday before receiving his high school diploma, Williams managed, in just a few more years, to receive graduate training at the Sorbonne and a master's degree in social work at the University of Cincinnati. With his personal understanding both of the pain of the individual and the reformer's impulse to experiment, Williams was at first uncertain about which problem the NYA should confront first. In the meantime, he worked hard to spread the NYA's out-of-school appropriation of $23 million to an ever-larger constituency.[24]

Taussig, a brain-truster, had spent his youth in the family business and had never gone to college. Nevertheless, he was the author of instructional books for young people (*Book of Radio* [1922] and *Book of Hobbies* [1924]) and was concerned about their social and political roles. As one of the "house intellectuals" whom Roosevelt liked to consult on the background of national problems (others included Columbia University professors Adolf Berle, Jr., and Rexford Tugwell, and Raymond Moley of Barnard College), Taussig was accustomed to viewing those problems broadly; he analyzed rather than personalized them. If both men agreed that youth unemployment merely illuminated the more intractable problem of an inadequate education system,[25] Taussig was less likely than Williams to be distracted from this problem by the heartrending dimensions of joblessness among the young. He believed it less important that the NYA put a few hundred thousand youths to work than that it establish a precedent for direct federal involvement in the education of the young. Even with its small first-year appropriation, the NYA could initiate the research and experimentation necessary before such a new form of education could be launched.

Taussig was convinced that young people who were consigned to years of idleness and cynicism would become ripe for the domestic demagogues arising in depression America. He believed that Americans, in each of the stages of their history, had successfully provided young people with both patriotic instruction and a social niche. First there was the birth and growth of free public education, then the emergence of the private, adult-supervised "character-building" organizations. The depression promised not only to end this history of society's continuously expanding hegemony over the development of young people's self-perception of life purpose but to throw the trend into reverse. With no job and no prospect of one, out-of-school youths were afflicted with the same nightmare that school youths, unable to afford additional education, faced: a period of forced idleness, sometimes five years long, in which no agency of society was superintending their education. These formed the elements of Taussig's conception of the youth problem. What prompted him to act was his belief that the problem was a nightmare for society as a whole; young people had to be inextricably interwoven into the fabric of American democracy. The entire social fabric would unravel if the strands of youth were allowed to slip away.[26]

The emergency was simply too great for Taussig to accept Brown's and Williams's belief that the NYA might last only one year.[27] Too many of the young lived in a limbo of despair. These limbo years, when young people were too young and unskilled for adult labor but too much in need of work to remain in school, defined the youth problem for Taussig. If American democracy was to remain vibrant, the NYA would have to fill the void for several years with the opportunities for social integration that the old social institutions (school, workplace, and family) had provided as a matter of course. On 27 February 1936 Taussig delivered a speech in St. Louis entitled "Youth and Democracy." Young people, he argued, "want jobs. They want more education and, in some cases, are critical of our present educational system. They want to be able to get married at a reasonable age . . . , have their own homes [and] to participate in government." Emphasizing the alienation of youth from society, he warned that "to ignore these young people as we have in the past" would lead many youths to "become thoroughly indoctrinated with subversive ideas." They would then "permanently set themselves apart as enemies of the very fundamentals of our country." The hour to achieve integration was not too late, provided that society could convince the young that "we mean to do well by them," and that it "discover the substitutes for the old pioneering opportunities that youth once had."[28]

In his St. Louis speech Taussig cast about broadly for solutions to the problem (he even implied that settlement in Alaska might be the way out for some youths). He came down to the one sure remedy: greater educational opportunities. If the period of education could be extended by four or five years, young people could be prepared for "enlightened citizenship," removed from the job market, and be given the discipline and moral regeneration they required in their present malleable and apathetic mood. With the new technologies of the airplane, the automobile, and the motion picture—and a younger generation unable to control these creations or resist their dangers—"the story of Frankenstein's monster may well become reality. . . . Here is a job for education, and I am not certain but that the major attack on the whole problem of youth does not lie in that realm." Convinced that youth required spiritual rebirth, educational opportunities sponsored by Washington, and a lesson in the nature of the new technologies, Taussig grew apocalyptic about the importance of the NYA's work.[29] His attitude mirrored that of Aubrey Williams only one year before and would do so again in the future. In early 1936, however, the Alabamian was not in step with Taussig's view. Williams believed that the NYA and WPA had great potential for reforming federal social service practices (particularly in the area of work relief), but that this promise was vitiated by the NYA's fiscal inability to address the needs of more than a fraction of the young people in distress.

In the next few months Taussig's position on the purposes of the NYA came nearer to becoming the policy of the agency as a whole. It was not strictly a personal triumph, for it did not result from mere powers of persuasion. Williams himself was concerned about the implications for American democracy of millions of jobless youths. By May 1936 the work program was operating much more smoothly. The NYA was assisting 390,000 students nationwide, while 210,000 out-of-school youths were working for the agency five months after that program began. Armed with the news that the NYA was helping 600,000 needy youths, Williams could go to Congress optimistic that the NYA would be greeted with enthusiasm by those considering new relief appropriations. With the need for relief being met, Williams could turn to other problems. The need to build a more solid foundation for democracy was one of them.[30]

The president was also leaning in favor of the Taussig approach by this time. There were multiple reasons for his change of heart. His portrayals of the program as a relief endeavor, designed in part to placate conservative educators, became rarer as more NAC members supported the planning-ideological approach of their chairman. With Aubrey Williams leaning the same way and Eleanor Roosevelt importuning FDR to listen to Taussig,[31] the NAC chairman had ample opportunities to make his case to the White House. Finally, Taussig's own pleading was persuasive.

The growing universality of the conviction that the NYA must engage in vocational education, planning, and research became more evident at the NAC's second conference, held on 28 and 29 April 1936. On the first day, Charles H. Judd, a psychologist and supporter of an enlarged role for the federal government in education (while serving as chairman of the University of Chicago's education department), reported the results of a subcommittee investigation into the idea of using NYA funds to conduct a nationwide census of the dimensions of youth unemployment. The NYA's executive order had merely suggested the idea as one possible NYA activity. After reading the draft, however, Roosevelt had replaced the word "could" with "should" in the sentence that raised the possibility of NYA involvement in such an investigation. Four meetings had been held in the intervening months to discuss the proposal; it was decided that the NYA should coordinate federal and private efforts to accomplish the effort. Shortly before the April conference, though, it was learned that the private American Council on Education and the USOE had already planned such a census, and Judd announced that a census would not be funded by the NYA. Nevertheless, the subcommittee report, by supporting the notion of an NYA youth census, had tacitly endorsed Taussig's experimental approach.[32]

What Taussig had said all along now became an oft-repeated theme at the NAC meeting: young people beyond the reach of the benign socializing institutions and unassisted by the New Deal might fall prey to alien creeds. Since federal education programs had no precedent prior to the New Deal, experimentation would be necessary to develop them.

Even those who had formerly argued that the real youth problem was the sheer numbers of those in distress, and who had opposed siphoning away funds from work relief to research, now emphasized the ideological approach. The NAC's youth representative, Thomas Neblett, had been president of the National Student Federation, an organization that had demanded of the NYA more jobs and less rhetoric. Now, however, Neblett suggested the need for long-range planning, pointing out the problems not of hard-pressed college students but of "exploited" European youths. "It is upon the backs of these disillusioned young people that strides toward dictatorship have been made," Neblett warned. "Certainly it is well to consider what can be done in America to protect freedom of conscience and thinking, and freedom of individual action."[33]

Aubrey Williams, while still convinced that work relief should share priority with citizenship training, was so cheered by the NYA's accomplishments that he agreed that both goals might now be pursued. He conceded that the out-of-school program, "the most difficult part of the job," had made him initially skeptical of the NYA's ability to do much for the young. It was difficult to establish worthwhile projects without spending too much on materials and personnel, thus leaving too little for the young people themselves. Make-work projects provided a cheap alternative, but Williams doubted that the American people would tolerate them. "We shall not start a lot of mushroom things that do not last," he insisted. The result had been a bottleneck still not fully cleared. Williams could not entirely shake his persistent gloom. As he admitted, "We certainly are far from what you might call optimistic about where we are going and how soon we shall arrive."

But Williams was hopeful that now, at least, the agency knew where it *wanted* to go. Now, with hundreds of thousands of youths laboring on work projects, the time had come to pursue more ambitious projects such as citizenship training. "I don't believe it is true that we labor under a sense of frustration," the NYA director explained. As a result of the last four months, "I am more hopeful that some answer can be found. That utter sense of folly that the problem was so tremendous and so immense that there was no use trying to do anything and that it was outside the bound of doing something about. I think that feeling has been somewhat dissipated, and that is probably one of the things that has been done, if really anything has been done in any fundamental way."[34] Perhaps more significant, Williams was now confident not only that the NYA would be extended for at least another year but that it could do more than give young people temporary places on work projects. "We have the opportunity to rearrange some fundamentals in this nation during the next few years," he declared, "and it can be done—it can be done."[35]

The NAC members were perhaps surprised when Taussig, faced with an opportunity to elaborate on his general analysis at the very moment his views were gaining currency, pointed instead to a specific problem: U.S. possessions and territories had been left out of the NYA. Surprise quickly disappeared, however, when it became clear that Taussig wished to discuss the problems of Puerto Rico and the Virgin Islands (not Alaska or Hawaii) with a view to showing how they constituted a laboratory for understanding the problems of democracy in the continental United States. Taussig identified the problem in Puerto Rico, "which is just short of revolt," as largely a youth problem. In connection with his work as president of the American Molasses Company and his sugar holdings on the island, he had recently visited Puerto Rico. There he had had ample opportunity to combine business with a more personal pursuit—analyzing the nature of radical youth movements. Puerto Rico's problems were considerably more complex than Taussig suggested,[36] but his interest in young people led him to focus on their peculiar needs.

Taussig told the NAC members that he was not interested in the independence question. He stressed the degree to which Puerto Rico served as a representative example of what might occur in the United States if the NYA did not seek a policy designed to safeguard democracy in the forty-eight states. The plight of mainland youth differed from that of their Puerto Rican peers only in the sense that the situation had been festering longer, and to a greater extreme, in the tropics. Puerto Rican youngsters had been longer without any form of adult supervision. They had no experience in what it meant to contribute to a benign cause (society) that was at one and the same time larger than themselves and an expression of themselves. The danger was that without experience in distinguishing between worthy and unworthy causes, they would align themselves behind the latter. Without school or work these young people had contact with no one but their peers. Consequently, they were creating a youth culture separate from the larger "American culture" to which they should have felt they belonged. Two out of five received no education at all. In fact, "the bulk of the young people . . . not only have no schools or schooling but have no jobs." The result was that "they stand around in the little towns of Puerto Rico all day and in the evenings . . . and these emissaries from the agitating groups come in and gradually win [other youths] around."[37]

Taussig's solution for Puerto Ricans was identical to his panacea for other young Americans. The NYA must reach youths who had no contact with the school and the workplace, the foremost conserving institutions of socialization. In outlining his prescription for Puerto Rico, Taussig was presenting, in a subtle but conscious way, his overall philosophy: the NYA must show society's concern for youth and prepare them for citizenship. This did not mean the NYA should engage in propaganda. It did mean that the agency would "give the youth an opportunity to do some work, and wherever possible to go to school, and . . . have the feeling that the government was giving some thought to them. . . . If we can do that, I frankly believe that we may approach this problem in an entirely new manner." [38]

Despite the conversion of Williams and many NAC members to his viewpoint, the president still needed persuading. Since Roosevelt was sensitive to the opposition to federal relief, especially in an election year, Taussig knew he would be harder to influence than the NAC. Two weeks after the April meeting, he wrote the president that he feared the NYA's work was far from finished, explaining that "we should not let our small success give us a false sense of security." He now argued that democracy was imperiled by the young on two fronts, not just one. To fulfill the task of integration Taussig recommended five-year local programs funded by the NYA, enlisting youths to build rural schoolhouses, libraries, manual training shops, or aviation fields, depending on a community's needs. The young would then gain a feeling of being valuable members of society. In order to "avert many of the troubles that seem to be looming ahead," he wrote, the NYA must "give . . . the youth of the country a sense of proprietorship in something tangible, no matter how small."

One of the looming troubles was more immediate than the problem of integration. "I have been in close contact with the youth problem and it is fraught with danger. The radical youth, many of whom belong to the Communist party, will not go along with us. . . . Nothing short of revolution will satisfy them. They concede that the National Youth Administration has ameliorated the lot of some 600,000 youths, but this only angers them, for they feel it delays their program." Taussig claimed that his proposed jobs program would neutralize the effectiveness of the radicals and, at no additional cost, eliminate the other peril to democracy, youth's alienation from society. Society had to give its "children some sort of perpetual proprietorship in the work they create with their own hands." Returning again to the theme of radicalism, Taussig wrote pointedly: "I would rather rely in a national emergency on a youth who, with his own hands, drove one nail in his local school building and who had a sense of personal pride in it, than in a youth who repeated an oath of allegiance three times a day." [39]

In both word and deed the president proved responsive to Taussig's argument. By mid-June he had approved both a one-year extension of the NYA and a substantial increase in its appropriation. (Until 1939, when the NYA was granted bureaucratic autonomy under the Federal Security Agency, it was granted funds via executive order, out of the funds allocated to the WPA; thereafter the NYA received its appropriation directly from Congress.) The agency would receive $71,250,000 for 1936–37, not enough, as Williams pointed out, to increase the number of youths assisted by the agency, but sufficient to produce a considerable expansion of NYA services. Formerly, out-of-school projects had been confined to the areas of recreation leadership, rural youth development, public service, and research. Now these restrictions could be dropped. The NYA could experiment in its efforts to provide "a wider variety of work [and] a more varied experience." The barriers blocking realization of Taussig's scheme to aid youth out of touch with the socialization institutions had effectively been overcome.[40]

Roosevelt endorsed Taussig's position that education and jobs were merely the means to achieving a greater goal—that of integrating youth and society for the benefit of democracy. On 26 June 1936, the first anniversary of the NYA's birth, Roosevelt explained to Williams that "no greater obligation faces the government than to justify the faith of its young people in the fundamental rightness of our democratic institutions and to preserve their strength, loyalty, and idealism against the time when they must assume the responsibilities of citizenship." Roosevelt praised the NYA's "splendid record" and pointed to 600,000 youths at work as "excellent testimony that our means of meeting that obligation are sound."[41]

Naturally, those NYA officials who had eschewed relief all along were jubilant at the course of events. In Ohio, S. Burns Weston rejoiced that "the whole NYA program is a great social experiment." He urged one private agency investigating youth problems, the American Youth Commission of the American Council on Education, to study the NYA in Ohio to better understand national changes on the youth front. "If it is defensible to 'sink sample shafts' into the needs of youth by using Maryland as a state, Dallas as a large city and Muncie as a small city, as the Commission is doing," Weston pondered, "it would seem defensible to sink a 'sample shaft' . . . by using NYA in Ohio as part of one great and important experiment."[42]

Williams too applauded the fact that the NYA would operate on an appropriation about 42 percent greater than that of the previous year. With the NYA's new ability to experiment with more ambitious projects of an educational nature, Williams promised to rectify what some regarded as "inadequate provisions for unemployed girls and young women." On the model of the old FERA program, he envisioned fifty camps—one or more in each state—for needy women certified for relief. "In addition to a light education routine, they will engage in some form of landscape and forestry work and raise and can vegetables for free distribution to relief families."[43]

Although Williams demonstrated a less than perfect understanding of the form of education dispensed by the women's centers (the women did not perform CCC-type labor), he did give an indication of the NYA's next priority. The resident center experiment would begin with an expansion of the women's program begun by Hilda Smith and taken over by the NYA in 1935. Resident centers increasingly seemed to be ideal places for the achievement of what, by June 1936, had become the NYA's number one priority: bringing youth together and in reach of the normal work and social opportunities of American life, for the benefit of American democracy. Insofar as NYA officials were concerned, the usefulness of Hilda Smith's resident program would depend on its success in meeting the task now applied to the overall program. If integration for democracy could not be achieved through the model of the resident centers for women, then NYA officials were fully prepared, by their first year's experience, to experiment with other models of residential living.

CHAPTER SEVEN

Resettling to Rescue

lthough the NYA always was, as James MacGregor Burns asserted, a
New Deal "experiment," its agenda continually paralleled that of
the White House. In 1937 and 1938, when FDR was seeking to
move the center of American politics leftward, the NYA's resident training
centers fittingly began to dot the bucolic countryside. These centers were
designed to provide labor education for blue-collar workingwomen and to
provide youth in rural areas with industrial training shops like those in
the cities. The women's centers represented the NYA's past perspective
toward workers' education: NYA education was to reflect local concerns
and, if necessary, local prejudices. Resident centers for rural youth, on the
other hand, were designed to realize the hopes for nationwide education
reform prevailing in the upper reaches of the NYA leadership and in the
White House. Rural youth would be relocated not to the city (where urban
problems existed along with industrial opportunities), but to rural camps
where group organization, fresh air, and industrial education would all be
present. Private educators would take notice and follow in the direction
the NYA pointed. No longer would urban youth enjoy an educational advantage over their country fellows in the procurement of skilled blue-collar
jobs, the jobs expected to be in greatest supply in the future.[1]

Beginning in 1938, however, the NYA began to reconvert the resident
centers to the needs of national defense as a more conservative White
House agenda began to alter their focus. European appeasement abroad
and electoral defeat at home encouraged Roosevelt to spend the last weeks
of 1938 groping for policies that would quiet, yet prepare, public opin-

ion for an American aid program for the European democracies. Seeking means of drawing Americans away from isolationism and of measuring its strength, Roosevelt saw the NYA as an instrument to test the limits of public readiness for collective security. Speaking in the very heart of isolationist America, Chicago, Roosevelt in 1937 demanded that international aggressors be "quarantined." In so doing, Roosevelt was showing his fondness for sending up trial balloons to distinguish politically feasible actions from those unacceptably controversial. The "experiments" of the NYA were often examples of such trial balloons. Providing the black cabinet with its highest bureaucratic perch within the New Deal, extending preferential treatment to black graduate students, and bringing urban educational opportunities to the countryside were all innovative steps of the NYA. They had value not just for the youth they assisted but also for a president concerned about domestic politics. The value of having the NYA undertake these activities was simple. So long as the public permitted such endeavors to take place, useful reform would result. If they touched too sensitive a public nerve, the Roosevelt administration could retreat undamaged with the excuse that excesses were understandable in the rush to aid youth.[2]

In another program unique for the New Deal, the NYA assisted European refugees fleeing from fascism. Although Roosevelt did liberalize the government's interpretation of the 1924 National Origins Act, thus helping refugees, the NYA was the only New Deal agency enlisted to that end. Roosevelt's primary objective may have been to involve the United States in one more international initiative, thereby readying the American public for still greater steps toward international cooperation. But refugee assistance was also in part a stalking horse to test the public's readiness for collective security generally. In preparing for this probing of public opinion, Roosevelt seems to have expected the NYA—that ever-active launching pad of trial balloons—to play a restricted but still important role. If Roosevelt's refugee initiatives were designed to measure public readiness for greater interventionist measures, the NYA was enlisted to probe the corpus of American opinion toward refugees. Roosevelt initially permitted the NYA to do what he told his own advisers he would not do: use public funds and New Deal agencies to resettle young refugees (otherwise supported by private funds) within the interior of the nation.

For Roosevelt, the success of this program hinged on its *not* becoming a public issue. The resulting public silence was truly golden to the administration, for it could be interpreted as a signal of public readiness for greater aid to the Allies. The NYA, meanwhile, had performed a function as "conservative" (confirming a decision to turn from matters domestic to matters international) as its role in establishing resident training centers had been "liberal." It had played a small but visible role in justifying Roosevelt's turn away from the New Deal and toward a preoccupation with launching national security initiatives. Both the resettlement of rural youth in training centers and the resettlement of refugee youth in American life shared one common feature. Each demonstrated that the NYA was no anomalous liberal maverick within the New Deal but an appendage and ancillary of Roosevelt's strategies for realizing public policy and triumphing in presidential politics.

AFTER JUNE 1936, NYA officials saw their special task as nothing less than ensuring social and political stability by reaching young people untutored in their social and political roles as citizens of a democracy. In 1937 at least 3,923,000 young people aged fifteen to twenty-four were still out of work, or about 16 percent of the total youth population of 23,487,000. In 1930 "only" 27.5 percent of all the unemployed in America were young people. By 1937, youth made up nearly 36 percent of the total unemployed.

In spite of these figures, student aid and work projects were considered sufficient for those American youths who had only recently left the school system or joined the unemployment lines. The New Dealers felt assured of these youths' fidelity to democracy. Most had already been socialized to their citizenship responsibilities and integrated into the workplace, if not by employment then by the schools. It was discovered, for instance, that the median age at which out-of-school NYA youths had left school was 17.7, only a few months shy of the age at which most would have departed the schools anyway. Nevertheless, many youths—mostly from rural areas—had not been socialized to their citizenship responsibilities or integrated into the work world. The American Youth Commission's 1937 survey of Maryland showed that 40–46 percent of those surveyed had been unemployed at least a year after leaving school before finding work. In addition, 72.7 percent of all NYA youths originating in counties of fewer

than twenty-five hundred people had never received private employment
before getting their NYA jobs, compared with 56.6 percent of those from
the nation's big cities. For the rural youth group, NYA officials agreed, the
agency had to provide a substitute socialization program involving work,
education, and citizenship training.[3]

The setting for this experiment in democracy was the resident training center program, begun in 1937 and expanded the following year. If
the NYA was to integrate alienated rural youths back into society, officials reasoned, it seemed appropriate to reach them en masse; that is, in a
residential setting. But these were not the first residential programs operated by the NYA. The program of resident schools and camps for jobless
women, launched in 1934 by the FERA's specialist in workers' education
(Hilda W. Smith) and transferred to the NYA in 1935, had provided group
education during the late summer and winter of 1935.[4]

Those who assembled the NYA's final report insisted that "the work
camps for unemployed young women were the forerunner of [the] resident
projects" of 1937 and 1938. Only in the most literal sense, however, was
this true. The women's camps preceded the resident center program, to
be sure, but their influence on the latter was not as great as the NYA's final
report and one historian have implied. While the earlier centers helped
young women as "women," training them for domestic roles as well as
providing "workers' education," the resident program generally assisted
women and men as representatives of a youth group susceptible to anomie. Unlike the resident center scheme, the women's program eschewed
a concern for large-group problems in order to focus on the needs of the
small group and the individual.[5]

By 1937 the NYA's purpose was to provide social integration and citizenship training to youths of both sexes. The desire to train women for
a sex-based role, while still present, was considered much less pressing. This fact was revealed by the continuing inability of Hilda Smith's
office to convince state and national NYA officials of the program's worth,
and by its failure to supply to more than a small number of youths the
"special training and educational advantages"—in civic education especially—that millions seemed to require. The women's program never
moved beyond the experimental stage, in both its educational initiatives
and in its programs for physical and emotional rehabilitation. It was a
measure of the distinctiveness of these two NYA resident programs that
the 1938 youth resident centers, by supplying programs considered defi-

cient in the women's camps, flourished where the earlier experiment had failed.[6]

WHEN THE NYA assumed authority over the FERA's resident schools and camps for women, it was the signal for a number of changes in policy. Consistent with the NYA policy of decentralization, the duplicated lines of authority (formerly controlled jointly—and confusingly—by both the specialist in workers' education and the state directors of women's work) now became even more tangled. Shortly after the NYA program began, each state director was given joint authority with eight workers' education field representatives to draft a program for the camps. As a result of the controversial nature of women's work and the climate of hostility toward the idea of women working in the 1930s, cooperation proved elusive.[7]

The workers' education curriculum was one of the New Deal's most original and daring innovations. It was an unusual program for the New Deal to undertake because it did not accord with Roosevelt's desire to sponsor programs that could be defended by pointing to precedent. The only precedent for workers' education was the example of Bryn Mawr a decade before. Designed as it was to encourage women to question existing social conditions, ponder matters of social justice, and comprehend their place as workers in a depression economy, workers' education could only have offended those who believed that the New Deal must send women workers back to home and nursery.[8]

The FERA program had so far escaped criticism because its small size had obscured its existence. Now, however, with the need for relief so widespread, many state directors were not prepared to support so bold a program of political and social education, especially for women. Susan Wladaver-Morgan has pointed out that some state directors influenced their camps to the point that young residents were taught not how to change society for the better but how to make the best of existing conditions. This was the message of Illinois NYA director William J. Campbell. Campbell, who had served five years as vice president of the Catholic Youth Organization he had helped create, not only forbade any mention of "trade unionism" but was quoted as saying: "What could these little girls be interested in social problems for, they get enough sadness at home. Give them lightness and cheer, good recreation, a little home economics— but let economics alone!"[9]

The women's resident program was characterized by more continuity than change under the NYA. Although all other NYA programs operated under the work principle (NYA youths had to perform a service for their checks), the resident program was financed by unexpended funds of the now-defunct FERA, and so continued to dispense education rather than work. Moreover, in May 1936, Hilda Smith herself denied that the state directors had created much of a problem. "Though the state directors were in charge of the states," she wrote, "the responsibility was usually delegated to a state emergency relief official of the Women's Division," an individual who "was frequently the same person who was in charge in 1934."[10]

Changes in the women's program under the NYA included increased funding after 1935, higher costs, continuously oscillating enrollment, and longer educational terms. Aubrey Williams initially approved a per capita operating cost of only $7.20 a week. This amounted to $374.40 a year, compared with $1000 in the CCC. This limit rapidly increased as the states proved unable to operate low-cost camps. Housed in small, deteriorating buildings, many of the schools helped too few women to benefit from economies of scale. The NYA practice of appropriating funds one term at a time prevented administrators from economizing through long-term planning. As late as October 1937, NYA officials were permitting camps to operate on a weekly per capita budget of $11.25.[11]

Enrollment and the length of terms in the camps also fluctuated after 1935. In August 1935, forty-seven camps began offering 3112 women a two-month term of camp living. By May 1936 a new summer term had begun, in which eleven camps had enrolled a total of 1400 girls in eighteen different sessions. As NYA officials became convinced that a different scheme might help more women more effectively, camp funding and enrollment plummeted. In December 1936 there were only 650 girls in eleven camps nationwide. It was a measure of the reduced priority given the program that, two summers after 1934, when 2800 women had been enrolled in over forty camps, the New Dealers could find funds for only eighteen camps and 1425 women. The one positive change lay in the area of length of term. The two-month term expanded to three and four months under the NYA, whole camp staffs (previously hired for one term at a time) were assured of wages covering a six-month "tour of duty." These new rules undoubtedly helped rationalize curriculum planning within the camps.[12]

If these were the changes wrought by the NYA, the continuities were more striking. The program remained consciously experimental, a fact indicated by the decision to undertake a winter camp program. The winter program did not begin until several months after the creation of the NYA. In August 1935, however, Smith directed state NYA leaders to organize summer camps immediately. While some state directors tried to alter the content of workers' education, others, such as Ohio's Weston, proved reluctant, so late in the summer, to sponsor camps at all. As Hilda Smith observed in May 1936, many of the state directors washed their hands of the program and delegated authority for its operation to the private sponsors and state relief administrators who had administered it all along. As a result, the women's resident program provided only a few indications of the concerns swaying NYA officials in the states and the National Advisory Committee. The latter was concerned with upholding youth's fidelity to democracy by demonstrating the oneness of young people and society. By contrast, the women's program forged ahead with its earlier reforms. These included helping women to understand economic forces, training them for domestic roles, and providing what by any measure was an impressive degree of racial integration in the camps. While some of these programs were daring for the 1930s, it is more significant that they were holdovers from the 1934 program and therefore did not address the concerns growing dominant within the NYA. As a result of this failure, NYA officials in 1937 and 1938 would seek to replace the women's camps with a different kind of residential program.[13]

Administrators of the women's program were certainly aware of the widespread concern with meeting young people's need for integration and training in democracy. They made an effort to provide a supplementary form of schooling for women who had abandoned the schools, aware that no other institution was so important in providing social involvement for this age group. As a 1936 report on the camp program revealed:

> At work, at home, and in social relations, every young man and young woman meets with problems for which there has been little preparation. The public schools can scarcely provide for these situations because they occur after the young people have left school. Persons in the insecure and low income group have little opportunity to continue their education in the variety of ways which would be necessary for understanding these problems. In their confusion, they become thwarted in the development of necessary social attitudes and skills. It is the lack of these which makes it difficult for them to hold

a job, build a home and to find a place in the community. . . . In the education
program of this country, there is no agency designed to serve adequately this
out of school, out of work young woman.[14]

With this assumption as one basis for the program, it is not surprising
that a high proportion of the young women helped by the agency were of
the age group that would normally have been in school (sixteen to nineteen). A survey of 1913 enrollees in June 1937 indicated that three out of
four were twenty years of age or younger and that 58 percent were under
nineteen, even though women were eligible up to twenty-five years of age.
Equally interesting, the administrators made an effort to help the rural
"outsiders" of concern to the NYA's reformers. About one-fourth of the
enrollees came from rural areas, and an additional 34 percent were from
villages of less than twenty-five hundred persons. Thus, nearly three-fifths
of the women in the FERA program were rural in origin, compared with
only 41 percent of the female population in the nation as a whole. Moreover, there were efforts to teach democracy, in both its modern form of
expression and in the hallowed forms of an older America. The 1936 report
observed that "in some camps elections followed the current American
political pattern with conventions, campaign speeches, nominations, and
secret balloting; in others, procedure resembled more nearly the early
New England pattern of government in America, with the town meeting
as its core."[15]

Although these programs anticipated the curriculum of the NYA's second resident program, administrators of the women's centers inaugurated
few changes in educational fare after 1935. One of the innovations of the
post-1938 NYA resident program was its combination of related study and
training. After working with industrial equipment in the morning or after-
noon, rural youths spent the rest of the day taking coursework related to
their on-the-job activities. In only one area of the women's resident program, training for work in the home, was there any anticipation of this
later NYA innovation. Hilda Smith noted in 1936 that "an effort was made
to interrelate classwork with the older daily activities." Thus, much of the
home management taught was

incidental to the daily routine of cleaning and caring for the camps. Classes
in arts and crafts . . . helped in the production of camp equipment. Dramat-
ics, trips, picnics, evening programs and singing were frequently correlated
with regular class work. . . . It was hoped that through discussion and infor-

mal class work, the girls would be stimulated to a real and lasting interest in community and social problems.[16]

The officials of the women's program regarded job training as an appropriate means of improving women's domestic skills. Education, however, was to stimulate "interest" only and was not oriented toward helping women find nondomestic jobs or initiating other changes in the modern world. The integrative aspect of workers' education, designed as it originally was to encourage workers to understand and involve themselves in the correction of existing social ills, was downplayed at the very moment that the NAC proposed to bring young people into the day-to-day activities of American society.

In 1934 only nine of the twenty-eight camps offered a pure program of workers' education (four offered domestic training, and nine of the remaining fifteen provided a related curriculum of health, recreation, and job training). After 1935, however, workers' education had to share class time in every camp with vocational guidance, household management, health education, arts and crafts, and recreation. In addition, the "work" in workers' education—the emphasis on job training—declined in 1935, when Smith's office decided to discontinue vocational education classes. The previous year, 20 percent of the enrollees had been placed in jobs. But program officials believed that this only encouraged many women to expect that job training was the purpose of the camps. It was thought better to discontinue this aspect of the program rather than raise expectations that could not be realized.[17]

The result was that after 1935, workers' education became a less practical affair; indeed, it turned into something of an intellectual exercise. Its purpose shifted from helping women to take their place in, and change, the work world to helping them understand present conditions. Discussion classes were held into "the causes, results, and suggested cures for unemployment." The degree to which this education failed to provide a place in community life varied from one woman to the next, for each had different needs. Rural women faced the greatest barriers to involvement in American urban-industrial life. Barred by distance from professional work and educational opportunities, these women required job skills, not a discussion of Sherwood Anderson's *Puzzled America* (a book used occasionally at the resident schools) or "pump-priming" economics. Yet, according to the program report, discussions were conducted "on the problems of agricultural workers, on what is happening to land and crops and the people who gain a living through growing crops." Afterward, the women doubt-less gained somewhat greater insight into the problems of their people, but no greater understanding of the way out of their own more personal plight.[18]

A different form of residential experience seemed to be called for. From the standpoint of achieving social integration, the women's program seemed to be doing more harm than good. Many of its students were drawn from the groups most seriously in need of a form of integrative edu-cation. Each passing year seemed to witness the enrollment in the camps of a group of women more acutely in need of education than the previ-ous. More than half (730) of the 1378 camp women surveyed during the first year (1934) had completed their high school education, while only 26 percent of the 2000 women interviewed in the 1936–37 camp period had completed the twelfth grade. A nearly equal number (28 percent) had been out of school since at least the eighth grade. These women in par-ticular seemed peculiarly susceptible to the anomie NYA officials hoped to avoid. As the NYA's secretary, Thelma McKelvey, wrote in April 1937, the program was designed to ward off discouragement by reaching young women "who have been unemployed and unable to find their place in community life."[19]

The women's program achieved in some camps what the CCC dared to permit in only the rarest cases: racial integration. "From the first," John Salmond wrote, CCC officials permitted "the mixing of the races . . . only in those regions where Negro enrollment was so slight that no Negro com-pany could be formed. Elsewhere, Negroes were usually assigned to all-Negro camps." Wladaver-Morgan pointed out that Pennsylvania, Illinois, and Wyoming had racially integrated women's camps. Smith's successor as director of the program, Dorothea de Schweinetz (daughter of Paul de Schweinetz, a bishop and longtime treasurer of the Moravian church), de-creed that "Negro and White teachers should receive the same salaries for the same kind of work." The South remained rigidly segregated, in the women's programs as in nearly every other social program, public or pri-vate. While the CCC aided blacks in proportion to their numbers in the general (not the relief) population, the women's centers struck a somewhat fairer balance. In the summer of 1937, 1583 of the women surveyed, or 82 percent, were white, while 308 (16 percent) were black, Indian, or some other minority.[20]

By 1 October 1937 about eight thousand women had received some form of education in the centers. In the previous year alone the centers had provided a total of fifty-nine terms of operation. Despite this achievement, NYA officials hoped for a more broadly based form of education for integration than that offered to the young women, one not limited to a single sex. Meanwhile, however, they were still recovering from cuts in the relief budget in June, which reduced the total NYA student appropriation from $24,287,000 in 1936 to $19,598,000 in 1937. In August it had been decided to discontinue the "she, she, she" on the first of October. With per capita costs rising to $45 per month, the financial burden was particularly acute. In explaining the decision, NYA officials released a statement that "because of the drastic curtailment in funds available to the NYA, and because of the relatively high per capita costs of operating the camps," they were "curtailed at the end of the fiscal year."[21]

It was not the resident center concept that appeared to lack cost-effectiveness but the particular form it had taken in the women's camps. NYA officials remained committed to the idea that resident centers, for men as well as women, would speed the way to social integration. The women's camps had to be closed, Eleanor Roosevelt wrote, because "more could be done for a larger number of girls with the same money used in some other kind of project." On 3 August 1937, accordingly, the NAC recommended that a few inexpensive resident centers be continued. The committee urged that these develop further the concept of combined work and study, with on-the-job training offered in tandem with related courses. The NAC was willing to fund these centers at a maximum monthly per capita cost of $32.[22]

The resident concept still seemed viable, especially for the rural and "outsider" young women in need of socialization. Five experimental camps were slated for operation: two in South Dakota and one each in New Mexico, Kansas, and Alabama. In addition, for the important rural group, the Department of Agriculture was approached to train Maryland girls as domestic workers and laboratory assistants.[23] Thus there was a curious flurry of activity on the resident center front even as the "she, she, she" program was dying. Education for "social understanding" was giving way to the overall NYA strategy of education for social integration.

EVEN BEFORE 1937, NYA leaders had acknowledged that rural young men might benefit as much as young women from a residential setting of group living and education. The year before, a variety of New Deal agencies had collaborated at Southwestern Louisiana Institute to bring relief to the rural youth group. The WPA built the housing for the enrollees at the college (which specialized in engineering, teaching, and agricultural courses), while the Department of Agriculture purchased land on which the youths could work and grow crops, which were then distributed to families on relief. This endeavor reflected the NYA's priority during its first year: the relief of unemployment.[24]

In December 1936 the NYA set up handicraft workshops at Southwestern. Six months later the NAC recommended that the Agriculture Department continue this work by administering a center in Maryland. Thus was born a recognition that rural youths were too isolated to take advantage of existing opportunities for relief. Nevertheless, these early residence centers were viewed as a means of bringing relief to rural youngsters, not a means to integrate the youth into urban patterns of living.[25]

Beginning in 1937, a changed conception was evident. As one historian has noted, "by 1937, the NYA began setting up industrial projects as well, ideally as close to new employment opportunities as possible, so that businesses could have a hand in training youths and youths could have ready access to jobs."[26] As the NYA's own historians noted: "the youth employed at resident projects spent a given number of hours each week working under the supervision of competent foremen and utilizing modern production methods similar to those which prevailed in private industry." Education now took a more specific form. It was no longer oriented toward workers' education but instead toward subjects that "had a direct bearing on the type of work they were doing." After working in an automobile shop, an NYA youth attended classes on the theory of the internal combustion engine. Classes in other subjects, too, were designed to train youths for industrial work. Business English was offered, and "shop mathematics" became standard fare at the new centers of 1937 and 1938.[27]

Beginning in 1938, the resident centers were enlisted in the NYA's overall objective, integrating youth into the mainstream concerns and activities of society as a whole. In practical terms that meant "industrializing" large numbers of those (usually rural) youths who were out of touch with these concerns and activities. If a substantial number of isolated youths could be provided with industrial vocations, ran the justification for the centers, the NYA would better serve democracy. This industrialization would not only heighten social integration but also would add new recruits to the defense industries. The resident centers were now to serve the practical, and less experimental, purpose of shielding a democracy under siege.

In contrast to the women's program, whose camps housed an average of twenty-five women each, the new program could be successful only if it rescued an increasingly large number of youths from isolation. Thus the size of the centers began to grow, with some housing 250 or more young people. Usually these centers were located at colleges and universities, in dormitories either modified or supplemented by special housing constructed by the NYA. Costs for room, board, and medical care were deducted from the enrollee's monthly income, while an arrangement with the colleges allowed the NYA to provide college-level education at no cost to the federal government. Some centers were built as camps in woodland settings, but even here training was oriented toward merging youth into the pathways of an industrial, not an agrarian, America.[28]

The resident program underwent a change in direction that paralleled the shift in NYA policy from a relief strategy to one designed to serve the security needs of the nation. The shift is evident in the history of three centers, each begun before the relief approach was abandoned and each expanded after the NAC and the Washington office concurred with Taussig's plan for a form of integrative education. The first, an NYA women's center that opened in late 1936 in Weiser, Idaho, had followed the pattern of such camps by training women in homemaking, painting, and "cleaning and furnishing the dormitories." After the autumn of 1937, however, the camp became coeducational and instruction was divided between work and related training. Though rural youths were taught agricultural skills such as dairying and farm business, the camps also offered workshop experience in steam heating, plumbing, cabinetmaking, auto mechanics, sheet metal, and welding. A "commercial foods division" provided instruction in culinary arts. Clerical and homemaking courses continued to be offered to the women.[29]

At the resident centers of Shakopee, Minnesota, and Leesville, Ohio, a similar trend was in evidence. After an attempt merely to keep youths busy and on relief, the directors of these centers displayed an interest in training the young men to fill the jobs and meet the concerns of a technologically complex society. While it operated under FERA and WPA funds (until April 1938), the Shakopee center avoided job-training courses and attempted instead to "better qualify young men for home and community life." One highly symbolic activity, occupying the labor of 100 youths, was the restoration and conversion of an old gristmill and tavern into a museum. NYA officials hailed the preservation of these "landmarks of pioneer days."

Within three years, however, the center's projects demonstrated a greater concern for the contemporary economy, providing training in drafting, aviation, woodworking, radio, and welding.[30]

The Leesville center was actually called the Muskingum Resident Project, and for good reason: it was designed not to aid a town but to assist in harnessing the waters and natural resource potential of the Muskingum River valley in Ohio, a region approximately the size of Massachusetts. The NYA project was but a small episode in the history of the Muskingum Watershed Conservancy District (MWCD), an organizational rather than a geographic entity created by court decree on 3 June 1933. The MWCD's purpose was to engage in planning and creating fourteen reservoirs to stem the flooding and soil erosion then plaguing eighteen counties in northeastern Ohio (about one-fifth of the state). In addition to flood and soil control, the district members hoped to develop a new recreation area and achieve "the integration of the whole into a complete demonstration of all branches of conservation."[31]

Bryce Browning, secretary-treasurer of the MWCD, sought to facilitate these efforts by utilizing low-cost youth labor in the lake area. Partly through his initiative, the district offered to sponsor an NYA resident center. The MWCD's generosity made it a difficult offer to refuse. The district offered a site on Leesville Lake at no charge and permitted the NYA the use of farm buildings in the area. The NYA was granted access to the district's supply of seedlings, sand, lumber, and surveying equipment. An agreement was worked out whereby camp buildings constructed by the NYA would become MWCD property, "to be used for youth education in conservation" after the NYA abandoned the site.[32]

The MWCD promised to hire only "scattered and isolated" rural youths; in other words, those who had no other opportunity for federal relief. Nevertheless, the district showed little ingenuity in project proposals, suggesting such CCC-like activities as "cutting trails . . . , building cabins and ski runs, toboggan slides and other winter sports activities." The center was to operate on a series of four-month terms and house 250 youths at a time. Over 180 of these were to be engaged in "field" work (construction). Each would earn 35.5 cents per hour, work seventy hours a month, and receive directly $5 of their average monthly income of $24.85. The remainder, as in the CCC, went home to the enrollee's family.[33]

Had NYA officials accepted the MWCD's project recommendations, the resident center would have been virtually indistinguishable from a CCC camp. The young men would have been engaged not in industrial training but in hard, physical, out-of-doors labor. But NYA officials made sure that the Muskingum center bore little resemblance to the CCC. State Director S. Burns Weston approved the proposal only after the MWCD promised that NYA youths (engaged in constructing reservoirs) would be involved in a "full-time [combined] work-educational program." When J. W. Davis, a CCC selection agent in Ohio, wrote Weston that some regarded Muskingum as a CCC camp, the NYA director replied that the center's varied activities rendered the comparison inappropriate.

The NYA's chief planner of resident projects, David R. Williams, insisted to Weston that Muskingum's enrollment should not exceed 150 persons precisely because it was *not* a CCC camp. "Maybe we could go up to 150," he conceded over the telephone, "but this is not like a CCC camp. If we tried to make it like one, we would get in trouble." Finally, Joseph Penfold (the NYA's liaison to the MWCD) wrote that the enrollees were neighbors of the camp, rural youth who had "their lives and background in the Muskingum watershed," not the city boys of the CCC. As a result, wrote Weston, Muskingum would not copy the past but would point the way toward the future, through a program of "broad social significance."

The Muskingum center was designed to involve youth in the life and concerns of the surrounding community, and the MWCD worked to raise as well as restore the quality of life. It hoped to "make available to the people of Ohio and the nation the boundless recreation resources created by the conservation pools." The MWCD planners expected to show young people that as partners in planning they were also partners in democracy. "Techniques of Agriculture and Industry are developing at a terrific pace," they explained.

It is evident that the welfare of the nation and its people will be in direct proportion to the ability of the people to plan these developments and pursue them to their logical conclusions. To this end, youth must be provided the opportunity to develop its abilities in planning. . . . Youth must be given the opportunity to discover that the individual is not one butting his head against the world, but that he is contributing towards [the] development and progress of plans he helped to formulate. . . .

He will discover that the successful, happy hod carrier is the one who pictures in his mind the completed structure and realizes that his contribution is an essential part of it. He will learn that cooperative effort carries with it a self-imposed discipline essential to success.[34]

Through the Muskingum center, young people were to become disciplined members of society. These expressions summed up what had become overall NYA policy by 1938: integration for democracy. The likening of rural youth to hod carriers may suggest an NYA desire for social control; and indeed, NYA officials were sometimes less than discreet in their choice of words to explain their objectives. For example, in 1940 H. V. Gilson, an NYA resident center regional supervisor, claimed that resident youth must be "indoctrinated with democracy," although they were to learn democratic procedure on their own, and through their own efforts. Gilson's explanation revealed that a humanitarian concern with improving youth's place in America (rather than a selfish desire for social control) had merged in the minds of NYA planners with a concern for the future:

> If democracy is going to survive, these youth, as citizens, are going to be compelled to put some effort into it.
> One way to put this lesson across is to give our NYA youth an opportunity to practice the business of self-government. Our resident center programs offer a splendid opportunity to do this very thing, because they are, to a large extent, communities within themselves. Many of the problems of living at a resident center are very similar to those faced by people living in a small town.[35]

The resident center program represented both an end and a beginning for the NYA. It marked the culmination of efforts to provide out-of-school youths desperately in need of education an experimental alternative to the public schools. It was easy to argue that a society with more adult workers than jobs would have to return idle youths to the classroom. A more sophisticated solution was needed, however, when the young refused to go, and set themselves apart from others at a time when national unity was becoming a national imperative. Moreover, many rural youths living in isolated places had never had the opportunity to learn about their society or what being an American meant. In 1938 Palmer O. Johnson, charged with studying the NYA for the President's Advisory Committee on Education (PACE), considered the rural group when he wrote to his coauthor, Oswald L. Harvey: "You may . . . appear oversanguine in the expectation of solving the [youth] problem by more education, especially by existing educational agencies. Certain sores developed during the . . . nineteenth century are not likely to be cured by education under present conditions."[36]

The resident center program was not an "existing educational agency." The National Advisory Committee met at St. Paul, Minnesota, on 31 October and 1 November 1938 and released a report that summed up the program's purpose. The centers "set up for the boy and girl who have left school another type of school which doesn't fit into the usual classification of elementary school, high school and college." The program had been born out of a recognition that the young required a different kind of schooling to eliminate a different kind of ignorance. To be sure, youth lacked the basic job skills indispensable to achieving employment in a depression economy. The resident centers would provide this, but they would do more. They would transform youth from outsider to insider, from the alienated to the initiated, and replace anomie with a desire to serve others and society.[37]

These hopes for American youth were never to be realized. The 1939 conversion of the resident centers to training centers for national defense cost the NYA its emphasis on job training in the interests of the enrollees themselves. But before that happened, one population of young people was targeted for assistance to ease their transition from outsiders to insiders. Surprisingly, at the outset of this special program these young people were not Americans at all. For, by November 1938, the NYA policy of acting to preserve democracy had come full circle. That month the agency began enrolling refugees from fascism in the resident centers as a means of measuring public opinion and conditioning the public to support Roosevelt's collective security policies. Not since 1933 and 1934 had NYA planners, to so great an extent, had Hitler on their minds. This time, however, NYA leaders knew that they would not have to forestall the coming of a "domestic führer." This time the danger was more indirect, symbolized not by the lure of fascism to young minds but by the prospect that the continuing strength of American isolationism might breed national paralysis in the face of Nazi expansion. Resettlement of refugees, under the auspices of the NYA resident centers, was to be one of the instrumentalities by which the president hoped to measure that strength as a prelude to diminishing it.

CHAPTER EIGHT

An Agency Without Borders

he escape hatches available to refugees in flight from fascism were rapidly closing in 1938. A number of factors were responsible for this. Perhaps most important (save for German policy itself) was the attitude of the receiving nations. During the first five years of Nazi rule, international resistance to receiving refugees was not as strong as it later became. Before 1938 the German government had enhanced the possibility that the unfortunates would be welcomed abroad by confiscating only a fraction of their property. During these early years many Jews and so-called non-Aryans, unaware of what the future held and hopeful that persecution would eventually abate, took no steps to leave. Consequently, because the refugee flow seemed manageable, France, Spain, South America, and other potential hosts were all relatively generous in their initial refugee policies. The British maintained a virtual "open door" into Palestine. But all of this was before 1938. Where Nazi efforts at forcing Jewish emigration had previously been limited to economic persecution, in 1938 the tactics of Nazi oppression began to include violence and terror. After the Austrian *Anschluss*, many were anxious to leave. The receiving nations, though, had never wanted any of the refugees and now came to fear them all. In the face of this refugee crisis, virtually all the nations of the world, including the United States, tightened their borders. Only a tiny trickle of this wave of suffering humanity ever glimpsed the Statue of Liberty.[1]

In terms of domestic politics, Franklin Roosevelt had much to lose and virtually nothing to gain by opening America's borders to the refugees.

Anti-Semitism was on the rise in America and would not peak until 1944. Of course, the refugee problem was a crisis for all humanity, not just Jews, but few Americans perceived this at the time. To be sure, an esti- mated eight in ten of the refugees were Jews. But as columnist Dorothy Thompson noted, failure to succor them threatened to devalue the moral currency of Christian ideals in the minds of men of all faiths, convert- ing those ideals into little more than lip service. This was undoubtedly a moral truth. But most voters voted their politics, their prejudices, and their economic calculations before their moral principles.[2]

When he confronted the refugee crisis, Roosevelt had to reckon with the reality of nativistic prejudice in a time of depression. "Nativistic national- ism," as David Wyman called it, was an old, seldom dormant, and easily awakened American tradition. The argument that refugees took jobs from native-born Americans had special cogency in the 1930s, especially during the severe "Roosevelt recession" of 1938. In vain did advocates of rescue argue that refugees were consumers, too. Clarence E. Pickett, secretary of the American Friends Service Committee (AFSC), explained that "every pair of hands that comes to this country bring along a mouth to feed." But the argument that refugees would stimulate rather than depress the economy, while true enough, hardly dented the wall of prejudice. The refugees had many American friends in the form of powerful religious, humanitarian, and labor organizations, including the AFSC, the Ameri- can Jewish Congress, the American Federation of Labor, the International Ladies' Garment Workers Union, and the Federal Council of Churches. But the patriotic and veterans' organizations that fiercely opposed *any* efforts to help refugees had one major advantage. Action by Roosevelt on their behalf appeared to be indispensable to retaining their electoral sup- port, whereas it is difficult to conceive how Roosevelt, with the record of an enlightened administration behind him, could have lost Jewish and labor support for his party no matter how callous his refugee policy.[3]

Although in an absolute sense Roosevelt did lamentably little to assist refugees between 1938 and 1941, he did more than any other Western leader. Historians have since speculated why, in April 1938, he called on all Western nations to meet at the French town of Evian-les-Bains that summer to explore means of speeding the transfer of refugees from Ger- many to the receiving nations. The question is compounded by the fact that Roosevelt simultaneously convened a national committee of his own, the President's Advisory Committee on Political Refugees (PAC), not only to coordinate private and governmental efforts on behalf of refugees but to advise the administration on how best to proceed with such assistance. It seems certain that Roosevelt had no plans to go much further than his helpful but inadequate action in combining the German and Austrian quotas. Nor did he have any intention of asking Congress to "mortgage" quotas or otherwise alter existing American immigration legislation. One is therefore forced to ask what results Roosevelt expected from the Evian conference and the PAC. One possible answer may help explain why Roosevelt permitted the NYA to assist the PAC in taking practical measures to increase the numbers of refugees finding safe haven in America.[4]

A mixture of humanitarianism and collective security fears help explain Roosevelt's call for an international rescue effort. The evidence suggests that while Roosevelt felt genuine sympathy for the refugees, the political opposition to aid would have stayed his hand had facts other than humanitarianism not argued for action. These other factors seem to be threefold. First, Roosevelt needed continually to test and retest the strength of isolationism as a prelude to determining his next projected step toward collective security. A refugee program, by eliciting public reaction to an effort at international cooperation, would provide such a gauge. Second, the president may have perceived that aid to refugee youth would be less dangerous politically than aid to adults. Third, the pogroms organized by the Nazis in November 1938 and later characterized under the rubric *Kristallnacht* briefly muted public criticism of refugee assistance and possibly emboldened FDR to continue preexisting rescue efforts. One of these preexisting efforts was a quiet NYA program designed to break down resistance to rescue by transforming refugees in the American mind from an amorphous mass of aliens to individuals soon to become Americans. The vehicle for accomplishing this objective was the resettlement of a fortunate handful of refugees recently arrived in New York City into the rural interior of America, or, more specifically, their placement in NYA resident centers. In any event, the most that can be said about the influence of *Kristallnacht* on the NYA refugee program is that the pogroms prevented shelving of the program. The number of youth slated for aid before *Kristallnacht* did not increase afterward, but without the "night of broken glass" the NYA program might not have moved forward at all.[5]

At first Roosevelt seemed willing to consider enlisting the New Deal agencies behind the rescue effort. This feeling, however, did not last. In April Roosevelt called on nine prominent Americans to meet him later that

month and form themselves into a committee to coordinate private rescue efforts and advise him on an appropriate governmental response. This
became the PAC. Conceivably Roosevelt's instructions might have led to
the direct injection of resources by other federal programs into the rescue
effort. But after Under Secretary of State Sumner Welles warned him that
the public might regard a New Deal for the refugees as a prelude to the
revision of immigration legislation, Roosevelt retreated. At the first meeting of the PAC, Roosevelt said that he "felt that at least for the present it
would be unwise to put forward any proposal which would occasion public
dispute and controversy such as a change in the immigration quotas or
appropriations or loans from public funds." This position would seem to
have immediately blocked any New Deal agency from assisting refugees,
for federal funds would have been involved in any such effort. Moreover, at Evian, the Western nations agreed to form the Inter-governmental
Committee on Refugees (IGC) to facilitate refugee resettlement. Public
reaction to the formation of the IGC could only have solidified Roosevelt's
reluctance to change his mind on the segregation of rescue efforts and
New Deal funds. Several of the patriotic organizations erupted in protest,
and restrictionists in Congress warned darkly of an administration plan to
revise the quota system.[6]

On the other hand, Roosevelt was clearly dissatisfied with the results
of the Evian conference. Most nations regarded it as either a threat or a
vehicle for public relations. The conference was barren of immediate ac-
complishment. The creation of the IGC was the sole glimmer of hope to
come out of Evian, in the sense that the committee held out the prospect
of possible future results. Undaunted, the president cast about for ways of
resettling refugees in isolated corners of the globe, places where refugees
would be "welcomed," if only because there would be no inhabitants to
oppose them! Roosevelt's efforts on behalf of such exploration and recon-
naissance would appear "political" and self-serving if they had not been
so indefatigable. In 1938 and 1939 he initiated or encouraged investiga-
tions into the prospects for refugee resettlement in Ethiopia, Venezuela,
northern Africa, and Alaska.

At the same time Roosevelt was seeking ways of determining the limits
of public support for collective security. Before the European war he never
really found this support, and so he withheld from public knowledge and
scrutiny his view that aid to victims of aggression must include arms one
way or another. In January 1939 he declared ambiguously, "There are

many methods short of war, but stronger and more effective than mere words, of bringing home to aggressor governments the aggregate sentiments of our own people." But when Senator Elbert D. Thomas of Utah proposed amending neutrality legislation to permit the president to aid victims of aggression using the smoke screen of cash-and-carry, Roosevelt made no comment. He did not even make clear his support for the politically safer cash-and-carry until 28 May 1939, and then only in the lower-profile medium of a message to Congress by Secretary of State Cordell Hull. Always uncertain about the distance between his leadership and public support, Roosevelt looked back on his foreign policy for indications of its effects not only on foreign leaders but also on American public opinion.[7]

American refugee policy was in part an instrument of FDR's foreign policy. Newsweek regarded Evian as a purposeful rebuke to the March 1938 Nazi annexation of Austria.[8] In addition, however, such assistance to refugees would measure American public support for further involvement by their government in international affairs. In view of restrictionist sentiment, however, such a test must be made by a New Deal agency outside the limelight, one that had "gotten away with" aid to unpopular minorities in the past. The obvious choice was the NYA.

But there was another reason why the NYA was a desirable vehicle, politically, to assist refugees. Vigorous private youth-serving agencies had been in the field of refugee assistance since 1933. Of all the New Deal agencies, the NYA, because it was a youth agency, could best draw on these organizations, and they in turn could absorb much of the public criticism, if criticism there was, by providing affidavits of support, funding, and placement expertise. A broad array of American colleges and universities had collected funds and assembled affidavits of support, a precondition for the issuance of student visas. In December 1938 the IGC established the Intercollegiate Committee to Aid Student Refugees, whose purpose was to solicit contributions from American college students and faculty to bring to America "those young students who are the victims of racial and religious persecution in fascist countries." In the words of Dorothy Thompson, although Americans "could be much more generous . . . in admitting children and young people," private action to speed the flow of such refugees "indicated a generous spirit and a positive democracy." Undoubtedly Roosevelt counted on that generosity to enable him to ascertain "the aggregate sentiments of our people" without unduly irritating residual American nativism and anti-Semitism.[9]

THE BEGINNINGS of the NYA program for refugees in May 1938 indicate that agency officials, not just FDR, had undoubted sympathies for the plight of the "unwanted." But by November 1939, when NYA refugee aid ceased, few refugees had been assisted (and none quickly). It appears that the program, once under way, was not designed to aid many refugees. Those most concerned had envisioned the program as a lifeline to hundreds or possibly thousands of desperate youths. But the Roosevelt administration, by its pace and procedure in setting the program into motion, indicated that it disagreed. The White House wanted the refugee program to aid only a few refugees in order to probe public opinion and prepare the public for a much more extensive effort at another time. Because of the intervening European war, however, that time never came. The months when the NYA program was operational turned out to be the administration's last chance for large-scale refugee assistance. According to Wyman, this was a time when "American immigration policy was more liberal than at any other time between 1931 and 1946." The Roosevelt administration used these months to try to reduce opposition to rescue and test public support for collective security.[10]

The idea for NYA involvement in the rescue effort came from Rabbi David de Sola Pool, an original member of the agency's National Advisory Committee. His recommendations indicated considerable familiarity with the nature of existing efforts on behalf of refugee youth. For years the national committees of refugee assistance in Europe and the United States had agreed that retraining refugees was a fundamental precondition for successful rescue. Many young refugees had trained for professional employment in urban areas that was unavailable in depression America. Given the U.S. visa policy, which required that all immigrants produce affidavits of financial support within the United States, evidence of monetary support was required to open the gates to America. A retraining program within the United States would drastically reduce the period for which private groups would be required to assist each new refugee. Private groups could withdraw aid from a retrained and self-supporting refugee once he no longer required it, and transfer it to one still seeking safe haven. The evidence indicates that de Sola Pool presented such an argument as this when, over lunch, he discussed refugee matters with Taussig in late April or early May 1938.[11]

A receptive Taussig moved energetically on this proposal. What he said at the luncheon is not clear, but based on the actions he took immediately afterward, he probably told de Sola Pool that NYA resettlement of refugees in rural areas was the best response that the NYA could make to their plight. Private groups could pay the wages of NYA refugee youths while NYA supervisors trained them in manual skills, such as automobile mechanics and engineering, suited to employment in small towns and cities. Located in rural areas where the refugees would be out of sight of big-city newspapers and publicity, the resident centers could offer the manual skills refugees needed. As de Sola Pool understood the resident centers (and he understood them quite well), they were places where rural youths learned manual skills in preparation for entry into the urban work force. He therefore seems to have assumed that only refugees from rural Germany and Austria would be eligible. This might work against Jews, most of whom lived in cities. But that was a risk which, for the sake of rescue, he was prepared to take. "It is my thought," he explained, "that through the cooperation of such offices as those in Berlin and Vienna, a selection could be made of youth adapted for settlement in rural communities or small towns in the United States." The NYA's role would be to place and retrain them. The religious and ethnic background of the refugees made no difference to him, he added, as long as some were saved. At any rate, the rabbi must have been delighted that Taussig spoke of refugees primarily as a problem of rescue, and not primarily as a problem of domestic politics.[12]

Between the luncheon and 14 May, when Taussig replied to de Sola Pool, the NAC chairman discussed the concept of an NYA refugee effort with Under Secretary of State Sumner Welles, Aubrey Williams, and PAC chairman James G. McDonald. McDonald, former high commissioner for refugees of the League of Nations, said that he believed the NYA could "be of great service along the lines" discussed by Taussig and de Sola Pool. Williams and Eleanor Roosevelt both reacted positively to the proposal. Williams immediately scheduled a meeting of eight state directors on 19 May to determine a more precise procedure for facilitating refugee assistance under NYA auspices. At the meeting Taussig instructed the state directors to "quietly put out some feelers in suitable communities" to ascertain the extent to which private groups would fund the retraining and salaries of refugee students. In addition, Taussig ordered planning for the program to commence under an NYA subcommittee consisting of himself, de Sola Pool, Father Edward Roberts Moore of the Catholic Archdiocese of New York, and General Electric president (and NAC member) Owen D. Young.

In a revealing reply, de Sola Pool indicated that he believed the new program would be structured with an eye to the crisis in Europe, not public opinion at home. Explaining how moved he was that Taussig was acting so speedily, de Sola Pool praised him for going "a long way toward realizing what was but a vision some days ago. The possibility of rescuing at least the youth well nigh strangled in Central Europe seems now very real."[13] Reacting to Taussig's letter of 14 May (which overflowed with enthusiasm for refugee assistance), de Sola Pool nurtured a hope that ultimately proved unjustified. Taussig's subsequent experience with the state directors, his dependence on McDonald, and perhaps the intervention of FDR himself not only slowed the pace of rescue but altered the original objectives of the plan. The state directors acted slowly when they acted at all. Only two of the eight state directors, Karl D. Hesley of New York and Burns Weston of Ohio, appear to have replied to Williams's directive by letter. Each indicated that they had apprised themselves of the private organizations active on the refugee front. Hesley's one specific offer was to establish a fund, sustained by contributions of the New York NYA staff, "to support one youth refugee for one year in New York State." Other state directors indicated what was already known, that private groups possessed the requisite desire and financial ability to buoy any placement initiative that the federal government chose to launch.[14]

Certain that enthusiasm within the state offices was limited, Taussig and Williams also knew that the White House wanted any program to take politics into account. Accordingly, the NYA subcommittee for refugee assistance introduced conditions for that assistance that rendered the program largely symbolic and experimental. A report on the program probably submitted to FDR in 1940 explained that during the initial month of planning

it was decided that a refugee youth aid program could be carried out: (1) if there was sufficient local interest and support; (2) if the youth's wages were paid out of private funds; (3) if little or no publicity was given to the enterprise, especially at first; and (4) if emphasis was placed on the fact that the youth were coming here under regularly existing quotas and would, in time, become American citizens.[15]

   These four conditions were obviously designed not to facilitate the transfer of refugees from private assistance to self-support but to help the administration sell its program politically. They were also designed to slow the program's pace (it was already well known that sufficient local interest existed in most states) and even to conceal the existence of the program from the full glare of publicity. These were peculiar conditions indeed if the purpose was to galvanize local support quickly and arouse a nation to action. But these same conditions melded well with a program designed to measure the depths of public readiness for refugee assistance at minimal political risk. The latter objective seems to have guided NYA planning after mid-May 1938. Given such political pressures, any chance that the program would be designed to rescue as many refugees as possible (and to speed their assimilation into the American economy) required a heavier role in planning for McDonald, de Sola Pool, and other highly energetic and concerned spokesmen for refugee interests. Such a development also required a reorientation of priorities, away from the stress on politics and toward an emphasis on the needs of the refugees themselves.

   Partly because McDonald was out of the country during the summer of 1938, caution and hesitation continued to delay finalization of the NYA refugee program. But had the White House desired, there could have been quick action. Private committees, eager to assist the NYA, had been active in the field of refugee relief. Before he left for Europe, McDonald introduced NYA officials to the National Coordinating Committee for Aid to Refugees and Emigrants Coming from Germany (NCCARE), soon to change its name to the National Refugee Service (NRS). This was a committee vitally concerned with breaking down American anti-Semitism and preparing public opinion for broader assistance efforts. In other words, the goals of NCCARE dovetailed with White House objectives, which were to use refugee assistance as a gauge of public opinion and to neutralize resistance to future refugee campaigns. As David Wyman explained,

   The National Refugee Service worked hard at resettling newcomers in communities away from the east coast. Among several reasons for this program was the wish to avoid concentration of refugees in such areas as New York

City. There the inclination to form enclaves fed stories of an alien flood, and
their employment in noticeable numbers led to agitation against the immigrants as an economic threat.[16]

Whether or not McDonald selected NCCARE to work with the NYA
because of their shared objectives, the fact was that the NYA subcommittee did not act until McDonald returned from Europe to coordinate
NYA-NCCARE efforts. On 23 August McDonald met with NYA officials at
NCCARE headquarters in New York to discuss a plan by Thacher Winslow
of the NYA's national office for a working procedure that would be acceptable to both NCCARE and the state directors of the NYA. (Winslow had
studied the effects of unemployment on European youth in his book *Youth:
A World Problem* [1937].) Among those present at the meeting were
Cecelia Razovsky, executive director of NCCARE; S. C. Kohs, national
field director of the committee; the Reverend Joseph W. Osterman, director of the Committee for Catholic Refugees from Germany; and Winslow.
It is easy to see why Winslow's plan won the approval of the prorefu-
gee NCCARE. The procedure would have required the NYA to place in
resident centers practically all those young people whose transportation,
wages, and residential costs could be borne by NCCARE or local groups
affiliated with it.

Speaking before the state directors on 7 September, Razovsky and Kohs
made it clear that the NYA could place hundreds of refugees in its resident centers if it wanted to do so. They announced that they would send
Winslow a list of between eighty and one hundred cities where committees affiliated with the National Coordinating Committee were active.
Each of these cities possessed the funds to support at least some young
people in the NYA resident centers. But the meeting of the state directors
also revealed a fact that evidently disturbed the White House. The state
directors seemed divided between those who had already independently
contacted groups willing and able to aid refugees and those who professed
complete indifference toward (and even ignorance of) the program. A brief
excerpt from Winslow's firsthand account of the meeting reveals that some
directors were enthusiastic about mobilizing local groups for action on the
refugee front.

Mr. [Dillard] Lasseter [state director of Georgia] revealed that he had just
learned of a Jewish group which had raised $100,000 in order to start a farm

training school for refugee youth. Since Mr. Lasseter was one of those who had already known of the proposed NYA plan, he went to this group and explained to its members how the NYA could take care of at least 150 refugees on already existing resident agricultural training units. This group promptly decided to abandon its plan and use its funds to pay the wages of refugee youth on NYA projects. Mr. Newman of Virginia—who had not known of the NYA proposal before—stated that a Jewish group was also planning to start a similar project in his state and suggested that he might go to this group, as Mr. Lasseter had done, and offer NYA assistance. Mr. Selke of Minnesota said that about $8,000 had, to his knowledge, been raised in his State and that this sum was about to be sent to New York because they did not know how to use it. Mr. Selke believed that he could get some of this fund to assist youth refugees while on Minnesota resident projects.[17]

It is difficult to believe that all of the directors who professed ignorance of the NYA refugee plan were genuinely innocent of knowledge, as Newman and Selke obviously were. Three quarters of the directors claimed that they had never heard of the concept of NYA refugee assistance, an idea about which eight had been asked to prepare careful reports months earlier. Weeks earlier, Winslow had spoken personally with state directors as far geographically from the refugee concern as California, Oregon, Utah, and Colorado. At least one director, Utah's, not only knew of the refugee proposal but was, at the very least, unenthusiastic about the idea.[18]

President Roosevelt knew about this curious division among the state directors—between those eager to assist refugees and those uninterested or even hostile to the idea. More important, the president appears to have been concerned about the division. Perhaps he feared that the disparity between the energy of some and the inactivity of others might draw adverse attention to the effort. It might provoke and direct anti-Semitic fury toward the activist group and, toward the inactive, the anger of those seeking rescue. At any rate, it appears that the president intervened immediately and decisively.

After meeting in New York City on 7 September, the state directors traveled to Roosevelt's Hyde Park estate for further discussions. Significantly, the president was at Hyde Park and made a brief unscheduled appearance at the meeting. Roosevelt's words were not recorded. After the meeting, however, there was a sudden unanimity of opinion regarding how the refugee program should proceed that was at no time evident before the Hyde Park session. All sides now agreed that the NYA would enroll only a tiny fraction of the figure mentioned by Razovsky and Kohs. Winslow asked each state director to "let him know of any definite openings for one or more youth of a certain type on a specified project in a stated locality." Twenty-six states reported interest, but only two (Georgia and Illinois) committed themselves to aiding more than fifteen refugees. What NCCARE leaders saw as a kind of underground railroad to rescue hundreds had suddenly been reduced at Hyde Park to a token enterprise designed to lay the groundwork for more substantive future action. It seems probable that the newfound consensus for token action on the NYA refugee front was imposed by the president.[19]

Although the documentary evidence is spotty, the subsequent work of the NYA indicated a prior decision (probably made at this Hyde Park session) to limit refugee assistance to a handful of refugees per state. Not until February 1939 were any refugees placed by the NYA. By November 1939, the month that the program ended, only eighty-five had been assisted nationwide. No state assisted more than they committed themselves to help in September 1938. That initial commitment was not, after all, the start of an ongoing campaign but a modest experiment that began and ended with the maiden sample. Thus the decision to reduce the level of assistance to a token few was a bottleneck that was never meant to be broken. It was a bottleneck consciously incorporated into the plan.[20]

The NYA's ability to rescue refugees was hampered by other factors, including the administration's passion for anonymity, its obsession with "Americanization," and its focus on public opinion to the exclusion of the needs of the refugees. Focusing on the receivers rather than on those received, the men and women around Roosevelt felt compelled to assist only the number of young refugees necessary to test public readiness for rescue—and no more. The needs of those to be rescued would have to await the cultivation of the American people. The fact that the refugees had no time to wait is perhaps clearer in hindsight than it was in 1938.

Taussig expressed the administration's concern for secrecy in October 1938. In two seemingly contradictory sentences he wrote that "the program for handling refugees is now complete and I look forward to the National Youth Administration being of assistance in this field. It has been decided, until we are able to point to some concrete results, that we will avoid any publicity to this program." In the wake of the *Kristallnacht* persecutions (9–10 November 1938), American public opinion was outraged at Nazi barbarism. The Roosevelt administration, however, was now even more concerned with maintaining a low profile for its refugee activities. Secretary of Labor Frances Perkins said that "a cautious approach is necessary to be certain we are doing the right thing and that the American people will cooperate." In its effort to maintain secrecy the NYA achieved total success. Not one word about the program appeared in the *New York Times* or any national newsweekly in 1938 or 1939. Undoubtedly secrecy would have been a greater impediment to rescue had the administration not already decided to limit rescue to a token few.[21]

The emphasis on "Americanization" laid bare the true purpose of the program. Roosevelt officials stressed that the refugees were at "loose ends" in New York City and needed help adjusting to American life. Undoubtedly they did. But according to the NYA's own final summation of the refugee program, "Americanization" meant assimilation for the refugees' own good. "The major purpose of the NYA's program," the final report concluded, "is thus to assist in getting these youth out of New York City and send them to various parts of the country where they can be more readily assimilated and Americanized. The young persons, of course, come to the United States under existing immigration quotas. Eventually, they will become American citizens. The problem is, therefore, to see that they are Americanized as soon as possible." Yet it should be remembered that NCCARE (now NSF) wanted to get the youths out of New York City not so much for their own good as for the sake of the public image of refugee relief. The desire was to neutralize restrictionist sentiment and public opposition to rescue. If successful, future refugees would benefit, so long as there was time to keep the pipeline open. In the meantime, the Roosevelt administration would surely benefit from having immunized itself from public criticism.[22]

The stress on Americanization for the good of the refugees was disingenuous in a way that could not be concealed. Rabbi de Sola Pool had expected the NYA to send rural refugee youths to the resident centers, which were all geared to meet the needs of rural youngsters. But since the desire was to relieve New York City of a portion of its population of young refugees, most of those sent to the centers were of urban origin. Given the fact that the resident centers often taught rural skills as well as industrial training, it was an open question how these urban youth could possibly have benefited from some of the education provided there. The NYA's final report had an answer. "The NYA, through its system of work projects, was the desirable organization to put them to work, to get them distributed throughout the country, and to help their adjustments with American youth—thus enabling them to learn the English language and customs easier and quicker." But it was specious to argue that the English language could be learned with greater facility in Georgia than in New York City. Moreover, the final report noted that the young refugees "all had far more educational background than the NYA youth with whom they lived and worked. . . . [T]he majority of them spoke and wrote English."[23]

None of this should detract, however, from the fact that restrictionist sentiment *was* strong and *did* require attention and defusing. In addition, the NYA was well structured to the task of funneling youth into the American mainstream cheaply. The problem was that although the structures existed to accomplish these objectives, these potentialities were never realized. Assisting many refugees would dent the problem of rescue, while assisting only a few would address solely the problem of public opinion. The administration decided that the NYA would aid only a few. Thus, little care was taken to select young people who could have benefited most from the rural setting, because the program was focused primarily on the American reception, not on the European refugees. Even some of the lucky few who received NYA assistance were disappointed when they confronted this reality.

How the big-city refugees reacted to rural education and the isolation of the American interior (made more lonesome by the secrecy of the program) can in most cases only be surmised. Four refugees sent to Georgia left a written record of their experiences in 1939, indicating that they had expected and been promised more. All four reflected on the program and contributed their thoughts to a letter written by twenty-four-year-old Leo Erber to one of their private sponsors. Erber, the son of a concentration camp inmate, carefully expressed his gratitude along with his confusion about the gap between the NYA's stated goals and its actual performance. On their arrival in Atlanta ("a wonderful town") the refugees were whisked away to Monroe seventy-five miles to the east. Owing to a lack of publicity, none of the Jewish sponsors was present ("We felt a little shamed and disappointed . . ."). The NYA sponsors did give them "a splendid reception, which made us feeling [*sic*] at home, from the very beginning." But the rush of reporters was overwhelming since "nobody of the community was present."

Then came the routine of work and schooling. For these young people it was anything but routine. From Monday through Wednesday these refugees, late of New York City, performed eight hours of farm work daily. On each of the remaining two days, an additional hour of farm work was prescribed, as well as two hours of auto mechanics and ninety minutes of English. As Erber wrote cautiously, "You will see, that this program is different in many points from the informations you got, and you told us. Our actual work is not in that line, we ought to learn, and we are a little bit worried, if we can really get the experience in the trade, we need for further advance. The following weeks will show the result."

Erber also wrote that the four had been startled by "the unexpected hole in our purse" occasioned by the news that providing work clothing and bedding was the responsibility of the enrollees. Prices were 20 percent higher in Georgia than in New York, he added. Plumbing in the barracks had not been completed, and "space is very limited." Erber added that the four expected to "get used to these condition" soon and concluded: "We ask you, not to misunderstand these lines, which are no complaint, and only represent an information for your further work in this respect."[24]

Whether the experience of these four youths was typical of the Georgia program or that of the nation at large is uncertain. In a sense, the makeshift character and haphazard nature of work and education under the NYA refugee program were both planned and unanticipated. Each was a predictable by-product of a program whose carefully concealed purpose, as chartered in Washington and New York, had been fulfilled before the youth had reached the red earth of Georgia.

THE RESIDENT CENTERS had both a broad and a narrow educational agenda. They trained young people for a specific job, and also for a more general place in society. As the NAC report stated:

> The NYA provides a greater recognition of the type of education that trains primarily for living. It teaches youth how to get along with people; it teaches them a philosophy of life [which] they can use . . . in the interest of the greater good for the greater number. They are enabled to learn a bit of . . . cooperative-mindedness. Having been taught such things, they will . . . learn to work with the fellow who lives across the road as well as to understand some of the forces beyond the home line fences that affect their everyday welfare.[25]

The resident centers represented the end of the peacetime program of the NYA. Within a year Europe would be engulfed in war and the resident centers would undertake an allied, but somewhat different, endeavor: furnishing the material (not merely the spirit) required to help defend America from attack. This would be a new venture indeed, for the NYA had hitherto attempted to train youth for home defense, the defense of an idea (democracy) embattled by economic depression. The change was signaled on 12 August 1938, when Louis Johnson, assistant secretary of war, wrote FDR that existing apprenticeship sources were "inadequate for building up a reserve of skilled work men and airplane mechanics." Johnson asked that the CCC and NYA be reoriented to perform this service. Well before Pearl Harbor, this wish would be fulfilled.[26]

Between 1939 and 1943, first in the defense program and then in war production, there occurred a shift in the nature of NYA activities, from work intended to supply benefits to the enrollees (relief, education, and integration) to work of immediate value to the nation (defense work). There was much irony in this change. As the nation had moved away from a preoccupation with the alienation of its youth, NYA officials focused their concern on the growing threat from abroad. The shift meant that a promise to depression youth would go unredeemed by the NYA; specifically, the hope that the nation as a whole could teach youth the value of self-government. Perhaps the unity of a nation girding for war would henceforth supply those lessons unassisted. Whether NYA leaders might also abandon their other objective, supplementing the nation's educational sources, was less certain in 1939. The NYA was turning away from internal social experimentation. In the end, the war that derailed NYA efforts to teach youth about an ideology also blunted efforts to educate young people in a new way.

It is appropriate to close the story of the New Dealers' depression-era plans for youth in 1939. Thereafter, NYA history was not shaped so much by the policies of its officials as by the intentions of Congress and the rapid disappearance of the youth unemployment problem. The stage for these events was set in April 1939, when, in a major government reorganization effort, Roosevelt asked that the NYA be placed in the new Federal Security Agency (FSA). There it would receive appropriations directly from Congress (not the WPA), be granted greater autonomy, and move away from a relief approach to one of national defense, education, and training. Congress approved in July 1939, when it allocated $100 million to the NYA.[27]

If Congress influenced the NYA by directing it to expand its training programs, the legislative branch was merely signaling that henceforth NYA history would be determined by rising youth employment in the private sector and a worsening international situation. A November 1937 census of unemployment disclosed that 3,923,000 Americans aged fifteen to twenty-four were out of work. Three years later, the nation's sixteenth census listed 2,648,000 youths in this category. Rising levels of defense spending in mid-1940, and then passage of the Selective Service Act later in the year, continued to reduce this total.[28]

Thereafter, President Roosevelt experienced even greater success in convincing the public that the nation needed to rearm. As America's factories retooled for war and Europe faced the fascist onslaught, the NYA was forced to abandon its reformist plans. The Lend-Lease Act passed in March 1941 permitted the nation to loan arms to the Allies, and so to expand its defense output. Americans had abundant reasons to expect that this output would eventually be used to protect their own fighting men. Earlier in the year Hitler had renewed the bombing of London. On 22 June Germany invaded the Soviet Union. From the summer of 1940 on, the U.S. Navy became more and more involved in an undeclared war in the Atlantic and Caribbean. By October 1941, 68 percent of Americans polled indicated that they favored all-out aid to Great Britain even at the risk of entry into the war.[29]

One congressional response to the changed situation in the arena of unemployment, public opinion, and national security was to steer the NYA away from its depression-era path. Between 1941 and 1942, NYA funds for student aid and work projects were reduced from $95,984,000 to $85,984,000. In June 1942 the graduate student aid program was terminated and remaining student aid funds were slashed by two-thirds, from $15,963,520 to $5,829,379. Meanwhile, the House passed supplementary spending bills in 1941 and 1942 that allotted the NYA specially earmarked funds for its defense programs.[30]

Ultimately, even the resident center program—the NYA scheme most oriented toward addressing young people's personal need for social integration and employment—was reorganized to help the nation win the war. Average monthly enrollment in the 595 operating centers in 1940 was 27,685, or approximately 1 in 10 NYA youths nationwide. In the two fiscal years beginning in July 1941 and July 1942, resident youths totaled 33,531 and 38,607, respectively. No fewer than 24,074 of the residents in the second year were being trained for war work; they represented 28.2 percent of all young people in the NYA defense program. Shortly thereafter, all project youths were enrolled in the defense effort. Those resident centers not equipped to supply this form of training were forced to shut down.[31]

After 1939 the NYA dwindled in significance as a dramatic and daring force for social cohesion. If a sense of community was thought to be lacking in young people during the 1930s, and if in the depression decade the NYA was virtually the only agency supplying such an awareness, the same was not true of the war years. During the years 1939 to 1945, young people were enlisted in a national effort as never before, but it was the war, not the NYA, that was doing the enlisting. Should the NYA cease to exist, all knew that the munitions factories and the various branches of the armed services had plenty of openings for young people, openings more than sufficient to supply youth with an understanding of what a "common cause" was all about. Aubrey Williams and Charles Taussig, who predicted a postwar need for an agency such as the NYA,[32] knew that continued emphasis on integration as an ideal would only supply ammunition for the congressmen seeking its discontinuation. So long as the NYA's officials continued to pursue their old depression ideal of a patriotic resurgence, now achieved by other agencies, it would appear superfluous to the war effort.

In order to make a case for the NYA's continuing importance, then, Williams led an effort not only to channel as many youths as possible into war production programs but also to increase enrollment as well. One result of this strategy was the closing of the most innovative chapter in NYA history, the story of its purpose in ending disaffection among the young. Williams made few attempts after 1939 to reach the young people who, because of ethnic or geographic origin, faced the most barriers to inclusion in the social mainstream.

Before America's entry into the war, Williams had balanced extremely well the NYA's need to do something for the defense effort and its commitment to New Deal democratic values. After the Munich crisis in 1938, he instructed state directors to train young people for defense work. Masterfully, he explained that this decision represented a reaffirmation of the NYA's strategy of providing youth a lesson in democracy, not a rejection of it. If the army assumed control of youth-training programs, he explained, young people's democratic values might be imperiled. The NYA would take on the job precisely in order to prevent this occurrence. While war is "repulsive to me," Williams explained, "I am absolutely convinced that we have an opportunity here to participate in a program affecting national defense in a manner that should be acceptable to us and to the state of feeling which is part of our bringing up and part of our whole background."[33]

Through such adroit strategy and salesmanship Williams countered critics who contended that the NYA was doing nothing for national defense. At the same time, he mollified the idealists within the agency who wanted no compromise of the NYA's status as an experiment in democracy. The monument to his efforts was the fact that the NYA, alone among the New Deal relief agencies, saw its funding expand rather than shrink between 1938 and 1941. In this period NYA appropriations grew 60.5 percent, from $74,245,000 to $119,150,000. Meanwhile, CCC funds declined 32.4 percent, from $230,318,000 to $155,604,000. But without additional compromises, an agency so committed to democratic values and the alleviation of youth's personal problems could never have survived a war in which centralization of authority and sacrifice of personal interests were regarded as patriotic and essential for the duration. Williams was temperamentally able to make the compromises. Indeed, as the war progressed, the survival of the NYA became for him almost as much an end as a useful tool in his effort to enlarge the scope of liberal reform. Thus it was worth considerable sacrifice of principle on his part to see it survive. Yet, for educational reformers such as Charles Judd, and for Taussig—who saw the NYA as a means of revitalizing democracy and instructing young people about politics—the NYA's value was inseparable from its democratic orientation.[34]

As defense, and later war, expenditures rose, many in Congress sought ways to pare all nonessential federal spending. Through three courses of action Williams hoped to shield the NYA from their cutting knives. In 1940 he attempted to neutralize the growing suspicion among educators that the NYA was the opening salvo in a campaign to destroy local control of education. In June he signed an agreement with Commissioner of Education John W. Studebaker giving state educators full control over off-the-job training of NYA youths. Doubtless Williams believed that the NYA's growing involvement in defense work (on-the-job training) would allow the agency to continue to provide training within the spirit of the agreement. By mid-1941 he had made his second move, unveiling a plan for defense work that proposed training, in just one year, 380,000 youths for jobs in machine shop, sheet metal, and welding fields.[35]

Williams's third compromise was to withdraw from a commitment made to S. Burns Weston, whom he had appointed director of the National Advisory Committee. Williams had given Weston authority to revitalize the relationship between communities and the federal government in the NYA program. In John Salmond's words, Weston believed that "maintaining community involvement in defense planning was the best safeguard for the preservation of democracy in the United States." Later, however, Williams grew convinced that the NYA could no longer afford to divert funds from the vital task of increasing enrollment to other concerns, such as community relations. He believed that defense training could proceed without such community involvement, and therefore slashed Weston's budget by 70 percent.[36]

These decisions revealed just how wide was the gap between Williams's point of view and that of the NYA idealists, who valued the NYA primarily as a new form of education. Judd resigned from the National Advisory Committee over the issue of Williams's agreement with Studebaker, while Taussig responded by writing letters of concern to the First Lady (who herself confessed to being disturbed by the news). It was symbolic that Taussig soon moved from one agency (the NYA), just as it was abandoning its experimental planning approach, in order to take over the cochairmanship of another planning board, the Anglo-American Caribbean Commission. This body was charged with drafting proposals to lessen the poverty of the Caribbean islands controlled jointly by the United States and Great Britain by reforming their economies. It was no less a commentary on the changed nature of the NYA that in 1942 yet another former ardent champion of the agency, Weston, joined his friend Taussig on that commission panel.[37]

The irony was that Williams lost so much support from within the NYA without appreciably reducing congressional and other external hostility to the agency. The Joint Committee on the Reduction of Non-Essential Expenditures investigated the NYA in 1941 and called for the abandonment of all nondefense programs under its jurisdiction. Some committee members, including Virginia senators Harry Byrd (chairman) and Carter Glass, and Representative John Taber of New York, were fiscal conservatives and extreme anti–New Dealers, and so it was clear that the battle would not end with Williams's acquiescence to their decision. Another NYA opponent,

Senator Kenneth McKellar of Tennessee, led a southern contingent of his own against the agency. McKellar's animus against the New Deal hinged on its role in race relations, his disagreement over Tennessee Valley Authority policy, and simple personal pique toward the president. McKellar flailed away at any New Deal agency within reach of his withering rhetoric. In 1942 it was the CCC. The following year McKellar convened hearings that would consign the NYA to oblivion. Although one purpose of the hearings would be to sentence the NYA to death, McKellar also wanted a soapbox from which to broadcast his view that the war was revolutionizing southern race relations. Meanwhile, McKellar's witnesses fought hard to see that the NYA's historic meaning would not also be lost in the course of the hearings.[38]

IN THE SPRING OF 1942 the Senate Committee on Education and Labor agreed to Senator McKellar's request for hearings to consider terminating both the CCC and the NYA. The president lobbied vigorously against the bill. "Now at the present time NYA is training about [400,000] boys and girls each year to go into industry," he remarked at his 14 April press conference. "All right. Now, if we abolish NYA we have to set up something else to train [400,000] people. Query: Where is the economy?" On the other side of the debate, McKellar argued that under the CCC and NYA, "we are making what President Roosevelt once described as molly-coddles out of our young people." Each agency, he explained, had multiple disadvantages. Not only were they escape hatches through which cowards eluded the draft, but each spent money needlessly at a time when "Japan and Germany have combined against us and we need our money, all our money."[39]

But it was the passions of each side that were being spent needlessly in 1942. The NYA's fate was being determined outside the hearing room, by an unemployment problem rapidly reduced to near invisibility by the war and a growing conservatism in Congress soon to be strengthened in the midterm election of 1942. The McKellar bill never passed, but exactly one year later Congress did terminate the NYA. In the meantime, hearings provided conservatives with an opportunity to parade witnesses hostile to the NYA before the committee and provoke NYA supporters to angry rebuttal.

One supporter was an NYA worker named Roberta Gaulden, a young woman employed in both the student aid and out-of-school programs. Almost certainly she followed the charges and countercharges that April through the newspapers. Her observations became participation after the comments of one witness, Governor Leon Phillips of Oklahoma, moved her to write in wrath to committee chairman Elbert D. Thomas of Utah. Although Phillips admitted to having brought no evidence to support his claims, he stated unequivocally that "theft is one of the first by-products of a former enrollee of the CCC camps." The CCC, he explained, convinced enrollees that government would "take care of them, and if they do not readily find something easy, a great percentage of them go into the car-stealing business. . . . [A] great majority of the young fellows that are in the Granite Reformatory . . . are former enrollees of the CCC camps." As for the NYA, "of course, anybody can get on NYA that [sic] wants to," and the NYA supervisors were not that much better. "I have two of them now in the penitentiary. They go from idleness to drinking and from there to the pen."

Gaulden wrote Thomas of her ten-month experience in the NYA, chiefly "to correct the Governor's mistaken opinion" of the agency. It was no job for loafers. "I worked so hard in that first [stenographic] job that I was too exhausted each night to do anything but go to bed." After eight months she took a college aid job with the NYA, a position that still failed to supply the funds she needed to stay in school. After dropping out, "I became so despondent over the loss of my college education that at times I could easily have persuaded myself to jump off a bridge." But again the National Youth Administration came to the rescue. The NYA found her a secretarial job that taught her the skills needed to pass a civil service exam and land a government job at $120 a month. She vowed someday to return to college. "And this time I'm not going to stop until I've earned at least six degrees." Her verdict: "National Youth Administration has made everything possible for me; National Youth Administration is the best friend I have."[40]

The perspectives of Phillips and Gaulden were just two shades in the spectrum of views Americans held toward the NYA in 1942. Their evaluations were determined more by their relationship to unemployment than by the agency's own intrinsic merits or demerits. Where that relationship was personal and direct, NYA was regarded uncritically; to those Americans for whom joblessness was a social, not a personal, problem, the NYA was regarded abstractly. As such, like colors in a prism, the views of conservative educators, politicians, and fervent supporters of the NYA were

TABLE 1. Appropriations given to the Civilian
Conservation Corps and the National Youth
Administration, 1935–43.

Year	CCC	NYA
1935	$332,851,000	$ 6,364,000
1936	292,397,000	55,212,000
1937	245,756,000	56,951,000
1938	230,318,000	61,158,000
1939	230,513,000	74,245,000
1940	215,846,000	92,075,000
1941	155,604,000	119,150,000
1942	34,030,000	43,337,000
1943	—	3,794,000

Source: U.S. Bureau of the Census, *Historical Statistics of the United States: Colonial Times to the Present* (Washington, D.C.: U.S. Government Printing Office, 1975), 357.

refracted through perspective and a personal lens. Because they represented only the views of those committed to placing their names in public print, they constitute the personal testimonies of only a tiny minority of the NYA's beneficiaries and critics.

While it can be demonstrated that a majority of Oklahoma's prison population were not graduates of the CCC, it is an arid endeavor to determine the degree to which the NYA was youth's best friend. That was a verdict the NYA youths, individually, had to make for themselves. The question that is historically answerable, and that this book has explored, is not what the NYA accomplished but what its architects sought to accomplish. A brief comparison of the fiscal year appropriations awarded the CCC and NYA, respectively, will serve to highlight the relative limitations that prevented the agency from fully achieving the reformist objectives that New Deal planners envisioned for it in 1935 (see Table 1).

Appropriations initially modest and subsequently curtailed were among the problems blocking fruition of the NYA's plans. The emergency of a world careening toward war imposed its own changes, producing an agency its planners had not at all anticipated or desired. "The war's the thing," S. Burns Weston and the NYA's National Advisory Committee de-

clared to Congress in 1942. That point was both a plea for future funding—
a statement designed to convince critics that the NYA had retooled itself
completely to meet the needs of national defense—and an admission that
young people's depression-bred tendency toward political disaffection and
anomie had all been superseded as an object of agency concern by the war.
The goal of turning out planes, tanks, guns, and the trained manpower to
produce them would henceforth receive primacy.[41]

By the beginning of 1943, however, an agency now billed as a supplier
of war materiél to industry could demonstrate no postwar need. Uncere-
monial abolition followed. After 1943 the NYA's friends and critics alike
were left with the task of assessing what place, if any, the NYA approach
to education and citizenship had in the nation's future. Answers to that
question would come only through a look backward, to the NYA's place in
the New Deal past.

CHAPTER NINE

New Deal Youth
in the American Memory

N   ew Deal historiography has drawn a distinction between those
         Roosevelt programs that recalled the World War I experience
         or were the culmination of long planning (Social Security, relief,
industrial self-regulation) and those that forecast the future by attacking
ad hoc problems that would be central to the agenda of later generations
of reformers (segregation, poverty, and war). Generally, most mainstream
historians have focused on the former type of program, allowing them to
show Roosevelt not only clearly in command of the New Deal but also
in the forefront of their stories.[1] Historians more critical of the New Deal
chronicle smaller ventures inspired or initiated by the Roosevelt administration, such as the Resettlement Administration, the FSA, the Southern
Conference for Human Welfare, and the NYA. Their purpose seems often
to be to expose the heartfelt hopes of lower-echelon but highly idealistic
New Dealers behind the throne, their momentary yet significant successes
as well as their ultimate frustration and failure.[2] The implication is that
these New Dealers had little but their passion to aid them in their assaults
on poverty and race prejudice. Their labors were largely symbolic, first,
because they were anticipatory of the ferment of the 1960s, and, second,
because they were puny in the face of Rooseveltian apathy and the enor-
mity of 1930s racism and poverty. In these accounts, moreover, Roosevelt
plays no leading role because he is considered largely uninterested in the

reformist activities of his underlings. Thus the New Deal's "programs from the heart," real and imagined, have been left to a small wing of the profession to analyze, a wing interested less in the relationship of these programs to Roosevelt and the rest of the New Deal than to the pageant of postwar reform. This fact has seldom occasioned much comment or criticism from the profession because of an assumption that the programs so analyzed really were from the New Deal's unrepresentative side; that is, from its rare sentimental proclivities.[3]

The NYA defies easy characterization, although that has been its historiographic lot. With the exception of John Salmond's fine biography of Aubrey Williams, all of the published histories that treat the NYA at length have tried to locate its central thrust in some solitary commitment, whether it be to racial equality, relief, or compassion politics. The result has been the erroneous notion that the agency's chief purpose was a simplistic one. Earlier historians traced the NYA to the ideas of the First Lady, not surprising since such a view had been cultivated by NYA administrators in the 1930s.[4] NYA officials found it useful to exaggerate Eleanor Roosevelt's role in the agency's origins precisely because she played an indispensable role in publicizing the agency and lobbying Congress for appropriations. One of ER's friends remembered that "both Harry Hopkins and Aubrey Williams, without my even asking them, told me emphatically that Mrs. Roosevelt was responsible for the creation of the NYA." As three of the NYA's best friends, Hopkins, Williams, and ER herself knew that her image as "mother of the NYA," false though it was, made the NYA appear to be unadulterated humanitarianism and a worthwhile charity for congressional tithing. It would not be the first time that Eleanor Roosevelt, one of the savviest of New Deal politicians, found it conducive to the cause of reform to cultivate a self-image of naïveté.[5]

Far from being a maverick experiment foreshadowing the future, the NYA was symptomatic of the success of the New Deal's political style and the poverty of its long-term vision. At a time when many wondered whether democracy was up to the task of lifting the nation out of the depression, the genius of the New Deal lay in its ability to convince the majority of the public, rightly or wrongly, that it could be done rapidly and economically. Amazingly adept at responding to interest group pressure, the Roosevelt administration realized in 1935 that five different but powerful political players demanded federal oversight of the problem of youth and education, a problem almost wholly unaddressed by the Civilian

Conservation Corps. Those whose political pressure was responsible for
the NYA included the Roosevelt administration itself (with FDR himself in
the lead), social scientists worried about rapid technological change and its
implications for American culture, school superintendents, college presidents, and radical students. Except for FDR, none of these ingredients
in the recipe that became the NYA was more important than the others:
each by turns convinced FDR at an important moment that such an agency
would be politically wise.

   Starting with only $50 million, the New Deal created a program that
paid uncanny homage to traditions of social service, cultural concerns of
the moment, the immediate political needs of the New Deal, and the
ultimately untenable prediction that the economy of the American future
would resemble that of the present. Not least on Roosevelt's mind was the
realization that a program such as the NYA would conjure in the public
mind an equation between the future of American youth and the future of
the NYA and New Deal.

   In part the NYA reflected a redefinition of what social scientists had
always called "the youth problem," the problem of guaranteeing youth,
for the nation's sake, a smooth transition from adolescence to adulthood.
Turn-of-the-century prescriptions had proposed physical conditioning and
back-to-nature schemes under the stewardship of private groups, but such
laissez-faire notions seemed insufficient in the depression decade, when
attitudinal problems of adjustment, anomie, and political apathy struck
many Americans as clear and present national dangers. While reformers in
the vanguard of social science and education sought to end the unwritten
prohibition of federal participation in education, most other Americans
were suspicious, in a time of rapid social change, of further assaults on
tradition. The New Deal seldom wished to publicize these idealistic purposes. Although such concerns were widely shared in the 1930s, their federal expression might have raised questions of the propriety of the federal
government serving as a social laboratory, with youth as the guinea pigs.
"Mother of the NYA" scanned better, and safer. Nor did the New Deal
desire to publicize the controversial cast of characters that had inspired
the NYA, which included college presidents and radical leftist youth pres-
suring the Roosevelt administration to inaugurate the first federal student
aid program in American history. In addition, the NYA's intellectual heritage included advisers who urged a youth movement as a counter to the
Hitler Youth.[6]

There was as well a separate, cultural tributary to the NYA, a tributary of thought flowing into the New Deal and antedating it by years. Federal planners attuned to the social science of Margaret Mead and Ruth Benedict argued that youth culture and American culture were interdependent entities, though susceptible to development at cross-purposes. The two required effective and vigorous federal management if they were to achieve successful symbiosis. The alternative was anomie, the alienation of youth from the rest of society. The cultural perspective played an important if peripheral role in encouraging the New Deal to aid hundreds of thousands of youth in the middle years of the Great Depression.[7]

Although all of these competing constituencies were eager in 1935 to invest the NYA with a philosophy, its existence and subsequent evolution owed themselves largely to the political assessments of the president of the United States. Had FDR done nothing to establish an NYA, the intellectuals, college presidents, and social scientists could not have threatened his reelection. Had compassion alone argued for a New Deal agency to educate the unskilled, the NYA would have gone the way of such unrealized dreams of the 1930s as the antilynching bill and a racially nondiscriminatory CCC. The deep intellectual taproots from which the NYA sprouted guaranteed the agency a constituency of support without which Roosevelt probably never would have considered the idea. But political factors convinced FDR to go beyond consideration and give his approval. The NYA figured prominently in FDR's plan to win reelection in 1936 and to seek dramatic party realignment thereafter. In 1935, when the agency began, Roosevelt probably envisioned a tenure for the agency numbering in months rather than years. But fired in the inferno of politics, the NYA continued to burn brightly for four years, changing in alloy and nature because of the changing direction and heat of 1930s policies. Strangely enough, by serving the Roosevelt administration's political needs so well during its first four years (the most left-leaning of all the New Deal years), the NYA remained at once central to the political calculus of the New Deal and radically progressive, one of the Roosevelt administration's instruments for political realignment and ombudsman to the powerless. Wedded to politics rather than principle, the NYA's effort to help the previously ignored was as brief as it was dramatic, a casualty to the watershed changes of 1939–41.[8]

At every stage in the NYA's life course, from conception to death, the NYA might have been shelved had FDR's changing political needs not repeatedly surprised him with the agency's continuing political utility. To say this, however, is not enough unless one realizes that a federal agency's administrative direction often veers independently of its political rationale. In a time when the national winds were constantly changing, as in the 1930s, only continued support and oversight by the president would have made possible the achievement of the political ends for which the NYA was the means. Roosevelt was continuously involved in NYA planning, and responsible both for its initial structure and subsequent changes. At a time when federal attention to such problems as racial injustice, unequal educational opportunity, and the scarcity of vocationalism in American education was all but nonexistent, the NYA, in grappling with these problems, acted from a political calculus originating in the White House.

From the start Roosevelt realized the political factors that argued for an NYA. As early as 1933 he directed that the concept be studied in the event future events warranted its realization. Until December 1933 FDR merely promised moral support for college presidents and educators anxious for federal student aid. At heart an economic conservative, Roosevelt resisted the idea that the U.S. Treasury should be open to "raids" by special-interest groups. For generations, nearly everyone had regarded youth as a national "interest" more "special" than others, and therefore requiring social oversight. Such views exacerbated the anxiety that some Roosevelt advisers felt as they watched European youth enlist in pacifist or fascist youth organizations. Initially Roosevelt was fearful of charges of regimentation. Always optimistic about American youth, he preferred to encourage grass-roots organizations rather than organize young people from above. The dangers of 1933, as he saw it, were excessive federal spending and, more distantly, anomie. Even when radical communist and socialist student groups met in Washington in December 1933 and talked of the possibility of confederation, Roosevelt regarded such activism as more a sign of health in the body politic than illness. Radical youth seemed to be fighting the battle against anomie, too.

So long as radical students chanted their appeals for economic reform, there was little danger that they would lead a mass movement of students, most of whom were concerned about foreign wars rather than domestic reform. By the end of 1934, however, Roosevelt's political fortunes had grown cloudy. The American Right was drawing conservatives of both parties into an anti-Roosevelt organization, the American Liberty League. Also garnering support were "voices of protest" on the left represented by the "Radio Priest" Father Charles E. Coughlin, "Share the Wealth" Senator Huey P. Long of Louisiana, and the radical redistributionist Francis Townsend. At this juncture, student radicalism represented for Roosevelt both a serious threat and a rare opportunity. By December 1934 radicals had persuaded millions of students to cut classes in support of a one-day Student Strike Against War, although the motivation behind most of the participants was peace, not ideology. By this date Roosevelt was at open war against the Nye Committee and worried about the isolationism that the radical students were abetting. But by focusing the attention of the nation on students, and that of students on themselves, radicals had spared Roosevelt the need to risk charges of regimentation by organizing his own youth movement—they had themselves created a kind of youth movement ripe for cooptation. By providing a milder version of the radical proposal most likely to solve other White House problems (student aid), Roosevelt hoped to reduce the strength of a student movement dangerous largely because of its pacifism. By January 1935, when senators began urging him to do something for jobless youth, Roosevelt was prepared to act. Roosevelt viewed the NYA as insurance for 1936, insurance he thought probably unnecessary but possibly useful. Its long-term usefulness, of course, would depend on political currents after 1936.

Because Roosevelt's interest in the NYA at first was largely political, he did not block NYA executive director Aubrey Williams's effort to demonstrate a more democratic approach to education. The NYA's very existence served FDR's objectives, and so he was little concerned at first with its direction. Given the NYA's paltry funding, Williams's reform hopes for the agency were largely quixotic, and Williams knew it. But the NYA's purely political phase proved to be nothing but an interlude. By creating a powerful conservative coalition against the New Deal, Roosevelt's attempt to "pack" the Supreme Court in 1937 backfired and left him searching for liberal allies. That turn of events provided the NYA with a new lease on life and a radically changed mandate. Having determined to wage war on Democratic party conservatives and launch the New Deal in a more leftward direction, Roosevelt looked favorably on Williams's reformist ventures in the area of race, refugee assistance, education, and relief. Concurrently, Roosevelt's need for left-liberal support in his battle to replace the banished conservatives with New Deal candidates gave him new reason not only to retain the New Deal but to expand its functions. Such a course was logical in view of the Popular Front mentality that was transforming moderates and radicals alike into strong supporters of the New Deal. An expanded NYA would solidify an alignment vital to Democratic politics in the post–Court reform, prewar phase of the 1930s. The severe economic recession (really depression) of 1937–38 also argued for an expanded NYA. Thus the real reforms sought and achieved by the NYA after 1936 were, as before, largely made possible by, and dependent on, politics. The late summer of 1939, with the coming of the Nazi-Soviet alliance, the end of the Popular Front, and the beginning of the European war, vastly weakened the argument for an expanded NYA. The accompanying reemployment in the defense industries eventually left the agency politically isolated in its plea for permanence, a battle it lost in 1943.

Although the NYA was continuously recast to meet the needs of a society lurching from depression to war, its metamorphosis in the American imagination was determined by influences postdating the New Deal. The contrast between the ways Americans remembered the other New Deal youth agency, the Civilian Conservation Corps, and the ways they recalled the NYA provides insights into the ingredients of public memory. Begun without fanfare in a season of intense politics, the NYA lacked the national consensus that the CCC possessed. The CCC's image was fixed in a moment of crisis, 1933, enabling it to draw on a seemingly inexhaustible well of national gratitude never available to the NYA.[9]

Within months of its creation in March 1933, the CCC achieved immense prominence in the public mind. From the beginning, journalists described it as a kind of "forest army" enlisted in the war against the depression. That summer, as the first enrollees were just entering the camps, one writer exclaimed that the CCC "gives every sign of successful conclusion." Cloaking the New Deal's first youth agency in conservative garb, writers described the CCC as a latter-day American Expeditionary Force, an armada against want. Roosevelt called it "a vast army of [the] unemployed [sent] into healthful surroundings." *Newsweek* described the men as "the administration's expeditionary force against unemployment." To the *Literary Digest* they were "the doughboys of 1933." *Newsweek* published a photograph of smiling CCC youths waving from a departing train (eerily reminiscent of 1914 photographs of French troops entraining for the Western Front) with the caption "Youths Off for the War Against Unemployment in the Conservation Corps." The CCC's army image, instilling awe in the American public, combined with its constructive (rather than destructive) purpose virtually to ensure that, alone of all the New Deal agencies, it would be impervious to criticism on fiscal grounds. As with any army, the CCC's success was judged in terms of its ability to turn out strong, healthy citizens and make the nation secure. "All you have to do is to look at the boys themselves to see that the camps . . . are a success," FDR noted later that year. *Newsweek* doubted that the CCC contained "the seeds of fascism," adding, "whatever it contains, it will rid American streets of 300,000 hungry men this winter." The CCC, as Harrison Doty noted, was indeed a "curious war. . . . The advance brings order and construction. The enemy is not a nation, but a condition. . . . The condition is the Depression."[10]

Two years after the CCC appeared, the Roosevelt administration could not hope to duplicate its success in selling the CCC by employing similar salesmanship techniques with the NYA. Exaggerated claims that a national emergency warranted the NYA would only have raised embarrassing questions as to why earlier New Deal initiatives had not already reduced the emergency to self-extinguishing proportions. In fact, FDR was arguing by 1935 that "happy days" had returned. The president promised that through the NYA, the remnant of jobless youth not assisted by recovery or the CCC would be removed from the job market for their own (and the nation's) benefit.[11]

What Roosevelt could not do was advertise the NYA as a weapon in a depression war, for that war was (at least during the period before the president's sober second inaugural address) being described in Roosevelt's speeches as all but won. Nor could he frankly admit to a Congress increasingly breeding a hornet's nest of conservatives that the NYA would serve as a model effort to explore the potential for educational reform, or that it might become not a junior WPA but a reform agent all its own—if it could win congressional funding for a sufficient duration.

The historiographic portraiture of the NYA has thus been the product of two unexpected influences. First, the nature of American politics in the agency's birth year, 1935, determined that the agency would become grist for the mills of New Deal friends and foes alike. Unlike the CCC, the context within which it would be shaped was not a period of New Deal ascendancy but the year before a presidential election and, subsequently, eight years of declining domestic fortunes for the administration. Accordingly, political exigencies encouraged politicians and reporters to explore the NYA experience for evidence corroborating their preconceived views of the administration in general and the president in particular. For ex-

ample, Charles P. Taft, Jr., son of the twenty-seventh president, argued
in 1936 that the New Deal had imposed programs on local America. He
refused to comment on the NYA, he wrote, for fear that "I will lose my
temper." The very decentralization of the agency, which should have ex-
empted it from charges of regimentation, denied the NYA any single controlling object, permitting the suspicious to accuse the New Dealers of
harboring all manner of nefarious designs. Mrs. Eugene Meyer, wife of
the publisher of the *Washington Post*, professed to believe that "if we do
not get rid of the WPA, including the National Youth Administration, and
turn back relief to local control and administration, God help America."
Like many innocent objects of suspicion in our history, such as German
Americans in World War I and Japanese Americans a generation later, the
NYA attracted the enmity of the paranoid because its (nonexistent) plan
to subvert the established order seemed so carefully concealed. The first
chroniclers of the NYA, Ernest and Betty Lindley, puzzled that "for three
years NYA has flourished with scant national publicity," but hit on a probable explanation: the utter absence of overt drama in the agency's outward
approach. "NYA youths wear no uniform, no distinguishing insignia. The
NYA work programs are made up of thousands of small units—a boy here
and a girl there, fifteen boys here and twenty girls there, rarely as many
as 100 workers in the same place at the same task. Shaped by a multitude
of local and individual needs and facilities. . . , these units are diverse in
character."[12] To the end of the New Deal, the reforms of 1935 and after
stirred up controversies that had not attended the Roosevelt measures
of 1933.

After the war, the NYA's changing image was viewed through a second
lens: the prism of an embattled American liberalism. Just as turn-of-the-
century war and prosperity eliminated both the appeal and the existence
of the Populists as America's first modern reformers, in the same way
the cold war and post–World War II prosperity blurred a precise understanding of the New Deal. The attractions of the ideology of consensus,
in a world where "the end of ideology" seemed at hand, were too obvious for many to put in perspective. Liberalism underwent a sea change in
the 1940s and 1950s, wherein most of the friends of reform argued that
the progressive cause would best be served by a conservative surcease
of agitation. To validate their liberal credentials in the wake of such a
stance, writers portrayed true Progressives as conservatives at heart. The
Populists, whose redistributive goals could not be softened, emerged in

historical writing as deluded malcontents rather than constructive reformers. Nor could the postwar consensus digest the class-conscious rhetoric of the New Deal, so often full of declarations about forgotten men and economic royalists. Richard Hofstadter and George Mowry wrote of the New Deal's social democratic orientation and its methodology of swelling government power in the interests of the laboring classes. The New Deal seemed to them an unprecedented break from the American reform tradition of battling concentrated economic power in the interests of an aspiring entrepreneurial class.[13]

Even the army-directed CCC seemed to some in the 1940s and 1950s to be a red flag signaling the New Deal's flirtation with communism. Politicians and journalists wondered during the war whether the once-popular "tree army" was a haven for draft dodgers and (inconsistently in view of the Soviet-American alliance) Communists. The NYA could hardly escape an image even more harsh, since it was well known that many of the left-leaning New Dealers had lavished much of their attention on the agency. Still, most professional historians tended simply to ignore the NYA, dismissing it as a tiny shoot of the WPA that never quite developed into a bud worth examining. Memories of the NYA were left mainly in the custody of journalists, politicians, and old New Dealers, who brought to their tasks separate agendas that did not include the desire to understand the agency's significance to the depression generation.[14]

Beginning with the onset of the cold war, anger over the left-liberalism of the NYA bubbled over in Congress. In 1945 the Senate rejected the nomination of Aubrey Williams, former executive director of the NYA, to become head of the Rural Electrification Administration. Senate conservatives, disturbed by Williams's race liberalism and desire for an expanded New Deal, argued that Williams was a key link in a chain binding the NYA and international communism. After Tennessee Democrat Kenneth E. McKellar accused the NYA of channeling $155 million to Communists or "fellow travelers," one of Williams's few southern supporters, Allen Ellender of Louisiana, countered in disgust: "Mr. Williams stands indicted, among other things, as a communist, a falsifier of records, while serving as NYA Administrator, a man who sabotaged the war effort and one who conducted the NYA as a communist organization."[15]

A liberal activist after 1945, Williams drew continual criticism with each cause he championed and unwittingly carried the NYA's reputation through every public firestorm he encountered. As late as 1954, when

McCarthyism's political usefulness was distinctly in decline (but not among southern Democrats), Williams was still the target of red-baiting. When a Senate committee subpoenaed Williams to testify regarding alleged communist influence in an interracial group he headed, Senator James O. Eastland of Mississippi brought up the NYA's association with leftist liberals as the sine qua non of the agency's purpose.[16] Long before 1954, accusations of the NYA's alleged radical designs on democracy had crowded out any interest in, much less knowledge of, the NYA's ideological origins as a defender of democracy and antidote to radicalism.

So widespread was the NYA's image as a vaguely radical episode that, before the 1960s, it attracted scholarly attention only among those concerned with the American radical tradition. In 1957 George P. Rawick wrote the most thorough and well-reasoned history of the NYA up to that time. Rawick was the first historian to assess the relationship between the NYA and the leading representatives of the public schools. But even Rawick accepted the scholarly judgment that the NYA's roots lay in the immediate political turmoil of the New Deal, concluding that the creation of the NYA lacked purpose or plan beyond relief of unemployment. The NYA, he wrote, "grew out of a series of uncoordinated programs under the FERA in 1933 and 1934, developing *ad hoc* because no one knew how long the emergency would last."[17]

Ironically, during the early postwar years, surviving New Dealers assisted in the oversimplification of the NYA's origins. Perhaps wishing to correct the caricature of an overadministered, compassionless agency formed to serve the interests of its administrators, many memoirists portrayed the NYA as a reflection of an equally oversimplified humanitarianism on the part of the president and his wife. Some believed that the NYA was the creature of the First Lady's maternal instincts, while others insisted FDR supplied its soul.[18] In the process, all did the agency's memory considerably more harm than good, buttressing the foundation of the myth that the NYA was more the spontaneous product of two people's compassion than a symptom of important ideas in American life. Many of the former New Dealers (including the First Lady herself) implied that Mrs. Roosevelt's sheer persistence convinced a reluctant president to support the NYA idea. Eleanor Roosevelt's autobiography, *This I Remember*, revealed that Harry Hopkins and Aubrey Williams were reluctant to press the idea on FDR. They hesitated because others in the administration had warned the president that any federal youth program would inspire charges that he was attempting to regiment youth. But when the First Lady conveyed the idea to him, Roosevelt simply asked her whether she thought it was the right thing to do. *This I Remember* left the distinct impression that her affirmative reply persuaded him to set aside any remaining objections that he may have had. FDR merely responded that "I guess our young people cannot be regimented in this way or any other way."

It is quite likely that such a conversation did take place. What is problematic about the accounts of New Deal memoirists such as Mrs. Roosevelt is their failure to add that inside and outside the administration other conversations were taking place between lobbyists equally concerned with the youth problem. Although individually less powerful than the residents of the White House, collectively the adherents of a federal response to youth unemployment were rendering the NYA idea politically unstoppable. Some accounts distort history by implying that the president was completely unsympathetic toward FERA plans to assist young people in 1933 and 1934. He is supposed to have said on one occasion that the depression was the problem of the whole people, and individual groups such as youth did not deserve special attention. The writer Fulton Oursler listened as FDR teased the First Lady at dinner about her support for a federal youth program. But when she pointed out that every one of the young people would soon vote, the president paused and agreed that there was much wisdom in what she was saying.[19]

ROOSEVELT'S MOTIVES for supporting the NYA were perhaps more political and possibly more shadowy than those of the First Lady. But this fact only makes more puzzling repeated assertions by the memoirists of the New Deal that Eleanor Roosevelt, more than her husband, was responsible for the NYA's genesis. A close reading of the historical record suggests instead that he was philosophically predisposed toward some such program as the NYA long before it was conceived by FERA planners, but that Eleanor Roosevelt helped hasten his understanding of its appropriateness to the political situation existing in 1934 and 1935. Rather than convert him, Eleanor Roosevelt sped his acceptance of a proposition toward which he was already gravitating. This hypothesis explains why men who knew well the roles of both Roosevelts in the NYA's evolution, such as Aubrey Williams, could maintain that the First Lady was the NYA's principal creator. Such a verdict was correct—and incorrect. Eleanor Roosevelt's

actions helped shape the timing of the NYA's establishment, not the fact
of its existence. The NYA was the product of a political momentum that
was almost, if not quite, self-generating.

Some scholars have agreed with the memoirists' position that New Deal
ventures were often the expression of one mind. Describing the advent
of the New Deal as the chronicle of "how the American people began
in the first presidential term of Franklin D. Roosevelt to respond to the
crisis" of depression, Arthur M. Schlesinger, Jr., nevertheless simplified
that story by portraying Roosevelt as a man who himself personally em-
bodied the aspirations of the American people rushing toward fulfillment.
Schlesinger's perspective originated from the 1930s awareness that conflict
between economic groups had continuously recurred throughout American history, finding expression in the actions of dominant personality types.
The Age of Roosevelt (1958) substituted a twentieth-century variant for
the hero of *The Age of Jackson* (1945) but found in the spirit of the New
Deal the apotheosis of Old Hickory. Schlesinger portrayed the CCC as
the instrument of the whole people acting through the heart of one man.
Little notice was paid the NYA, which had issued from the ideas of many
men and women and did not prefigure a New Deal originating from the
Olympian decisions of a small circle of giants. Schlesinger mentioned the
NYA in *The Politics of Upheaval* (1960) but did not include a descrip-
tion of its mandate and function. He insisted, however, that FDR was
as committed to the NYA as Eleanor Roosevelt, repeating Mary McLeod
Bethune's memory of the president's personal commitment to the agency.[20]

Others who distorted the origins of the NYA through good intentions
were the architects of Lyndon Johnson's Great Society reforms and the
biographers of Eleanor Roosevelt. To the planners of LBJ's war on poverty,
the NYA was an agency of substantial political significance, but not an example to follow. The NYA was important to President Johnson, who had
served as a Texas state director in the 1930s and who lovingly invoked
its memory as the spiritual ancestor of the Job Corps, Upward Bound,
and other Great Society ventures. Spokesmen for the Great Society also
thought it important to link their cause to the NYA as a means of selling the Johnson reforms to the millions who still remembered FDR with
reverence. But unlike the Roosevelt administration, the Johnson planners believed that the poverty problem required a surgical solution, not
the assault on a broad front preferred by the New Deal. Some of those
who participated in the Great Society defined their problem as how "to

engineer a series of precisely measured modifications of the physical and psychological environment of the poor that, essentially, would cause them to act as if they were middle-class." The solution would not be complicated or expensive but would require commitment and resources. "The limiting factor is not what can be done," explained John Kenneth Galbraith. It was a question less of "feasibility than of will." [21]

Whether or not the NYA's approach to youth was more effective than the Great Society's, LBJ's planners recognized at the time that it was not the approach they preferred. NYA officials had believed it worthwhile to attempt the rescue of a young underclass whether or not the larger society ultimately supported the effort. They were not at all deterred by their pessimism regarding their prospects for success, a pessimism the designers of the Great Society did not share. The latter insisted that they ought not even try without the will to succeed, and never doubted of success if the will was present. Nor did the men around Johnson ever doubt that they were reaching the people who really represented the core of the poverty problem. Under the pressure of politics and the glare of publicity, the Johnson administration devoted the bulk of its resources in the War on Poverty to the problem of providing job training to young blacks in the inner cities. NYA officials borrowed extensively from ideas of the past for their more vaunted objectives of providing an education in democratic values and reordering the priorities of the American public school system. The "can-do" spirit of the Johnson reformers bore little resemblance to what might be called the utopian pessimism of the New Dealers: determined to try, come what may, but uncertain of success. [22]

During the 1960s, therefore, the NYA was discussed rather condescendingly as a well-meaning exercise in organized compassion, but lacking the expert understanding of the sociological and psychological roots of poverty that the Great Society intended to supply. The NYA was portrayed as the product of New Deal sentimentalism rather than a reflection of current ideas. Eleanor Roosevelt seemed in 1960s biographies a woman of iron will, breaking through the political barricades on behalf of a heartrending cause. According to Alfred Steinberg, when even such hardened politicians as Harry Hopkins "got tongue-tied at the thought of sitting down with Franklin and convincing him of the need to offer work projects to help high school and college students stay in school," Mrs. Roosevelt did the job for them. Her motivation was her compassion: the youth were "such mixed-up creatures they called out the mother in her." Writing in 1964,

Joseph Lash, a friend of the First Lady who had been a student activist in the 1930s, wrote: "We did not know it then [in 1935] but the idea for an NYA had come from Mrs. Roosevelt."[23]

Tamara Hareven in 1968 agreed that Mrs. Roosevelt lent the agency more moral support than intellectual advice, a contribution that seemed important to Americans in search of a similar moral commitment for their own turbulent times. The First Lady, she wrote, "had hand-holding sessions with NYA State Directors when spirits were low . . . and gave 'pep' conferences followed by picnics at Hyde Park. Working calmly on her knitting, she listened to descriptions of projects and future plans."[24] Only when the "Great Society" grew tarnished from the storms of the Vietnam War, and the search for commitment lost its insistence, did the contemporary concerns of those who founded the NYA receive more attention. Joseph R. Kearney, also in 1968, wrote of the First Lady's reasoned analysis of youth problems and her conviction that relief was a stopgap. At the outset she hoped that the NYA would evolve from a program that offered little more than relief to one that provided sophisticated forms of education and training. To her delight, the history of the NYA reflected these developments. "From stressing unemployment relief in 1935–1936, from conferring more attention upon recreational aspects and unskilled clerical training in 1937–1938, the agency, by 1939, was concentrating upon 'outdoor labor, metal and woodworking shops for boys, and sewing workshops for girls.' It therefore seems entirely possible that, given Mrs. Roosevelt's position within the orbit of NYA policy, these shifts of policy were more than coincidental."[25] Joseph Lash's best-selling 1971 biography, *Eleanor and Franklin*, disseminated to a far wider audience the concept that there would have been no NYA without the intervention of the First Lady. Her idea to enlist unemployed young people for two years in community service at federal expense, Lash wrote, "was the germ of the National Youth Administration. But Harry Hopkins and Aubrey Williams had to be sold on it, Franklin had to be persuaded, public opinion had to be educated."[26]

Since the 1960s, writers have added little new to the traditional portraiture of the New Deal for youth, although the tone has grown increasingly favorable. Old participants in the New Deal drama often replicated recent historiography in relating their memories, suggesting that they were recalling recent books rather than their more distant experiences. At the same time, the 1970s and 1980s witnessed the proliferation of histories that portrayed the New Deal as a reform program of ambiguous accomplishments. Charles Trout, Lyle Dorsett, and others argued that Roosevelt's policies were ambitious and anticipatory of future federal reform measures, yet often ineffective at state and municipal levels. According to historians of the New Deal youth and education programs, if the New Left had been right in charging that Roosevelt's contributions to young people were limited by his sense of the politically possible, 1960s writers underestimated the depths of his humanitarian commitment to underprivileged youth.[27]

As always, the CCC's evergreen image as a battalion of soil soldiers battling human as well as soil erosion served that agency well in the 1970s and 1980s—even if the image continued to be encumbered with myths. By the second year of the Reagan administration, congressmen were seriously discussing a restoration (on a much smaller scale) of the agency. In March 1983, a few days before the fiftieth anniversary of the launching of the New Deal, 70 Republicans joined 231 Democrats in voting for creation of an American Conservation Corps, to employ up to 100,000 youths in CCC-type labor. The CCC's memory became so popular that some advocates of new youth programs defended their schemes by comparing them with the CCC, even when the comparison was, at best, forced. One correspondent to the *New York Times* said that a Brooklyn program to teach young people clerical skills and cooking techniques in a "residential vocational and educational program"—a program very similar to the unmentioned and forgotten NYA—was "fashioned after the Civilian Conservation Corps of the 1930s."[28]

Five decades of myths regarding the New Deal youth programs appeared to harden rather than remove the layering of misinterpretation first applied by their contemporaries. By a curious alchemy, these myths began to alter the memory even of those who had observed firsthand the unfolding of the Roosevelt programs. When Katie Loucheim, wife of an SEC official during the 1930s, resolved in 1977 to "find all those New Deal friends and acquaintances who were still around and persuade them to tell their stories," the storytellers she found at times relied not so much on their own memories as on the histories written in the 1950s and 1960s— the period of perhaps greatest misperception of the NYA's significance. Speaking to Loucheim, Lady Bird Johnson, for example, remembered the NYA as a time of high spirits ("one of the happiest times of our lives") and hard lessons ("a cram course in education for me"). Yet one of her stories about the NYA was a story already told—indeed, by her husband. "A generation after the New Deal," she related, "when we dedicated a job-training corps . . . in San Marcos, I looked around the platform at the people who were doing the introductions." Her remarks suggested that she had consulted the text of her husband's 1967 address to a delegation of women in politics to refresh her memory of an era nearly fifty years old. "There was a judge who handled the guest of honor, the governor, and on up to the President. All of them had been with the National Youth Administration."[29]

In 1982 and 1983 two books were published, one that illustrated the pitfalls, the other the promises, inherent in any attempt to discuss the myth-ridden topic of the New Deal and youth. The first, *The Path to Power*, Robert Caro's introductory volume of *The Years of Lyndon Johnson*, included an assessment of Johnson's old employer, the NYA. Caro did not cite, and evidently did not use, Rawick's account; he appears to have drawn most of his information on the NYA's birth from *Eleanor and Franklin*. He quoted Lash extensively and provided much the same interpretation. "The National Youth Administration," he wrote, "was the inspiration not of Franklin Roosevelt, but of his wife."[30] The following year, John Salmond published a book originally envisioned as a full-scale treatment of the NYA, but which in the end became a biography of Aubrey Williams. In *A Southern Rebel* Salmond provided valuable antidotes to two old myths. He denied that educators had always been hostile to the NYA, claiming that this opposition had originated with the agency's conversion to a work-training program for national defense (after 1939). Salmond left unstated an important fact: well before the period of mobilization for war, the NYA operated education and training programs for youth beyond the reach of the schools. Like Rawick, Salmond demonstrated that the NYA was the product of many minds and of political forces FDR could not ignore. Specifically, Salmond attacked the "notion that Eleanor Roosevelt 'sold' the NYA to a reluctant Roosevelt." "No doubt Mrs. Roosevelt was important in educating her husband on the dimensions of youth distress, yet by the time the final Williams-Hopkins blueprint had been approved, he had long been persuaded of the need to expand activities in that area. By June, 1935, to have advocated this to him would have been preaching to the converted."[31]

These two books leave many questions about the NYA unanswered. If Roosevelt and the New Dealers, no less than Mrs. Roosevelt, gave form to the NYA, what programs and policies did they develop in the FERA period (1933–35) to demonstrate this commitment? In 1983, the fiftieth anniversary of the launching of the New Deal, much remained uncertain and misunderstood about the significance of the National Youth Administration.

Emerging from an intellectual milieu supportive of training for lower-level service jobs and owing its existence to the political exigencies of the Roosevelt administration, the NYA was forgotten, perhaps because it seemed a panacea whose time had passed. But for the growing proportion of Americans living slightly above or below the poverty line, this judgment may be too hasty. Too often ill-prepared to go to college, living in an age of shrinking federal student aid outlays and an economy of increasing service jobs, poor and middle-class young people might find a federal dollar spent in job-oriented training a panacea meant for the present. The New Deal prediction may simply have been delayed, not mistaken.

The progressive reforms of the NYA remain as memories proving that the hardened heart of the federal government can be moved to support dramatic reform in the arenas of race, education, and poverty. Perhaps the NYA's legacy suggests that the approach to the federal government's "heart," however, can only succeed through politics, the New Deal's principal motive force. The history of the Roosevelt administration demonstrates that two problems subsequently resolved unhappily or incompletely—student pacifism and youth unemployment—can at least be profitably engaged, in Irving Bernstein's words, through "a caring society" rather than a combative one. The differing approaches to youth disaffection represented by presidential action in the 1930s and the 1960s could not be more instructive. Roosevelt's at least partial success at consensus building in a crisis time was a lesson that might have been learned with profit in the 1960s and, perhaps, today as well. Above all, the story of the NYA provides considerable insight into the mind and politics of the 1930s. That alone justifies the rescue of the story from collective national amnesia and from the mistaken myth that the New Deal for youth was an anomalous and accidental episode of the Roosevelt administration.

Notes

Introduction

1. Books that exemplify or critique this point of view include David Tyack, Robert Lowe and Elizabeth Hansot, *Public Schools in Hard Times: The Great Depression and Recent Years* (Cambridge: Harvard University Press, 1984), 106–29; Porter Sargent, *Between Two Wars: The Failure of Education, 1920–1940* (Boston, 1945); Harry V. Barnard and John H. Best, "Growing Federal Involvement in American Education, 1918–1945," *Current History* 62 (June 1972): 290–92, 308; S. Alexander Rippa, "Retrenchment in a Period of Defensive Opposition to the New Deal: The Business Community and the Public Schools, 1932–1934," *History of Education Quarterly* 2 (June 1962): 76–82.

2. Harvard Sitkoff, *A New Deal for Blacks: The Emergence of Civil Rights as a National Issue: The Depression Decade* (New York: Oxford University Press, 1978), 65–110; Nancy J. Weiss, *Farewell to the Party of Lincoln: Black Politics in the Age of FDR* (Princeton: Princeton University Press, 1983), 143–53.

3. Tyack et al., *Public Schools in Hard Times*, 132–38.

4. Nathan Miller, *FDR, An Intimate History* (Garden City, N.Y.: Doubleday, 1983), 368–69; Weiss, *Farewell to the Party of Lincoln*, 143–44; John A. Salmond, *A Southern Rebel: The Life and Times of Aubrey Willis Williams, 1890–1965* (Chapel Hill: University of North Carolina Press, 1983), 126–27, 135, 170–72.

5. U.S. Federal Security Agency, *Final Report of the National Youth Administration: Fiscal Years 1936 to 1943* (Washington, D.C.: U.S. Government Printing Office, 1944), 10–15; Tyack et al., *Public Schools in Hard Times*, 95–103.

6. Anthony J. Badger, *The New Deal: The Depression Years, 1933–1940* (New York: Hill and Wang, 1988), 305–6.

7. The only published chronicle of the NYA's administrative history is Salmond's brief survey in *A Southern Rebel*, 72–85, 127–78. Two dissertations on the NYA are

George P. Rawick, "The New Deal and Youth: The Civilian Conservation Corps, National Youth Administration and American Youth Congress" (Ph.D. diss., University of Wisconsin, 1957); and Richard A. Reiman, "Planning the National Youth Administration: Citizenship and Community in New Deal Thought" (Ph.D. diss., University of Cincinnati, 1984).

8. For these questions see Salmond, *A Southern Rebel*, 121–31, 158–59.

9. C. A. Bowers discussed this conflict in "Social Reconstructionism: Views from the Left and the Right, 1932–1942," *History of Education Quarterly* 10 (Spring 1970): 22–52. See also Tyack et al., *Public Schools in Hard Times*, 18–27.

10. Tyack et al., *Public Schools in Hard Times*, 92–95, 132–38.

11. Reiman, "Planning the National Youth Administration," passim.

12. Joseph Kett, *Rites of Passage: Adolescence in America, 1790 to the Present* (New York: Basic Books, 1977), 215–36; John Demos and Virginia Demos, "Adolescence in Historical Perspective," *Journal of Marriage and the Family* 31 (November 1969): 632–38.

13. Three books that explore the image of youth-as-problem in three different eras are Thacher Winslow, *Youth: A World Problem* (Washington, D.C.: Works Progress Administration, 1937), 30–45; Simon Frith, *Sound Effects: Youth, Leisure, and the Politics of Rock and Roll* (New York: Pantheon, 1981); and Theodore Roszak, *The Making of a Counterculture: Reflections on a Technocratic Society and Its Youthful Opposition* (Garden City, N.Y.: Doubleday, 1969), 1–41.

14. The German example of ideological education is discussed in Peter D. Stachura, *The German Youth Movement, 1900–1945: An Interpretative and Documentary History* (New York: St. Martin's Press, 1981), 144–58; Theda Skocpol and Kenneth Finegold, "State Capacity and Economic Intervention in the Early New Deal," *Political Science Quarterly* 97 (Summer 1982); Bonnie Fox Schwartz, *The Civil Works Administration: The Business of Employment during the New Deal* (Princeton: Princeton University Press, 1983).

15. For the suggestion that unemployment relief for youth emerged from a "politics of youth" in the White House, see Joseph P. Lash, *Eleanor Roosevelt: A Friend's Memoir* (Garden City, N.Y.: Doubleday, 1964); Tyack et al., *Public Schools in Hard Times*, 103–12. Eleanor Roosevelt is quoted by Lash, *Eleanor and Franklin: The Story of Their Relationship* (New York: W. W. Norton, 1971), 536–37.

One. The Old Deal Defines the New

1. Presidential press conference of 16 August 1933, National Historical Publications Commission, *The Press Conferences of Franklin D. Roosevelt, 1933–1945* (Hyde Park, N.Y.: Franklin D. Roosevelt Library, 1957), R1–2:189–91.

2. The New Deal's conservative style in its early economic recovery efforts is traced by Ellis W. Hawley, *The New Deal and the Problem of Monopoly: A Study in Economic Ambivalence* (Princeton: Princeton University Press, 1966), 53–59; Graham J. White, *FDR and the Press* (Chicago: University of Chicago Press, 1965), 55; press conference of Franklin D. Roosevelt, 16 August 1933, *Press Conferences.*

3. The New Dealers' propensity to disregard established wisdom in a variety of professions is sketched by Schwartz, *The Civil Works Administration*, 24–36; among the better overall analyses of the different purposes of New Deal relief programs are Donald Howard, *The WPA and Federal Relief Policy* (New York: Russell Sage Foundation, 1943), 25–34, 105–57, 775–826; Josephine C. Brown, *Public Relief, 1929–1939* (New York: Henry Holt, 1940), 230–42; and Edward A. Williams, *Federal Aid for Relief* (New York: Columbia University Press, 1939), 87–149.

4. William E. Leuchtenburg, *Franklin D. Roosevelt and the New Deal, 1932–1940* (New York: Harper and Row, 1963), 87–93, 165; Leuchtenburg, "The New Deal and the Analogue of War," in *Change and Continuity in Twentieth-Century America*, ed. John Braeman, Robert H. Bremner, and Everett Walters (Columbus: Ohio State University Press, 1964), 81–43.

5. The curious irony about public and private efforts to organize youth before the New Deal was that they aimed both to shepherd youth to maturity and also to shield them from the cares and concerns of adulthood. The young, it was thought, must be preserved in their youth during the stage appropriate to their age, but must be guided within those bounds to a level of maturity preparatory for adulthood. Reformers were eager to support solutions to societal ills consistent with their sincere concern for the needs of young people. Psychologist G. Stanley Hall posited a time of developmental "storm and stress" carrying promises and risks for the child. After 1904, when they appeared, Hall's ideas were often reconsidered for their implications to the larger society, but his view of youth's nature and needs became that of the society at large. Social control policies, to the extent that they require a cynical awareness on the part of policymakers that their plans sacrifice the needs of one element of society to those of another, do not accurately describe the youth programs and conferences of early twentieth-century America. Those policies reflected instead a sincere conviction that what was good for American youth was good for the nation, not the other way around. See Kett, *Rites of Passage*, 215–36; Robert H. Bremner, ed., *Children and Youth in America: A Documentary History, 1866–1932*, 3 vols. (Cambridge: Harvard University Press, 1971), 2:357–69, 410.

6. Demos and Demos, "Adolescence in Historical Perspective," 632–38. Not only were rural Americans increasingly deserting the countryside for the city, but the image of the country as a no-man's-land of demoralization was, by the early 1900s, fast supplanting the romantic image that had coursed through the speeches of William Jennings Bryan and the Populists. Some progressives, George E.

Mowry wrote, even "saw the city as a place of refuge from an ugly countryside." Others created what Mowry termed a "national nostalgia" for the land, and Richard Hofstadter labeled an agrarian "myth." Few romanticized the agrarian present. See Mowry, *The Era of Theodore Roosevelt, 1900–1912* (New York: Harper, 1958), 90–92; Richard Hofstadter, *The Age of Reform: From Bryan to FDR* (New York: Basic Books, 1977), 215–20.

7. Demos and Demos, "Adolescence in Historical Perspective," 635–36; G. Stanley Hall, *Adolescence: Its Psychology and Its Relations to Physiology, Anthropology, Sociology, Sex, Crime, Religion, and Education* (New York: D. Appleton, 1904); Kett, *Rites of Passage*, 215–20.

8. Kett, *Rites of Passage*, 219, 224–27; Jane Addams, *The Spirit of Youth and the City Streets* (New York: Macmillan, 1909), 107.

9. Wald and Kelly are quoted in Bremner, *Children and Youth in America*, 2:757, 776–77.

10. Clarke A. Chambers, *A Seedtime for Reform: American Social Service and Social Action* (Minneapolis: University of Minnesota Press, 1963), 48–49, 50–57.

11. U.S. Department of Labor, Children's Bureau, *Standards of Child Welfare*, Bureau Publication 60 (Washington, D.C.: U.S. Government Printing Office, 1919), 7, 11–12.

12. Ibid.

13. U.S. Children's Bureau, *Unemployment and Child Welfare*, Bureau Publication 125 (Washington, D.C.: U.S. Government Printing Office, 1923), 3–4; Chambers, *Seedtime*, 56.

14. Paula S. Fass, *The Damned and the Beautiful: American Youth in the 1920s* (New York: Oxford University Press, 1977), 6–7, 20–25.

15. In 1924, 54,908 graduates of four-year professional or baccalaureate programs (or 66.4 percent of the total number of such graduates) were male, and 27,875 (33.6 percent) were female. Ten years later, the ratio was 82,875 (or 60.5 percent) male graduates to 53,815 (39.5 percent) female graduates. See U.S. Bureau of the Census, *Historical Statistics of the United States*, 1:134, 386; Kett, *Rites of Passage*, 223–24.

16. Fass, *The Damned and the Beautiful*, 15; "Is Modern Youth Going to the Devil?" *Sunset* 56 (March 1926); "Motors and Morality," *Survey* 55 (15 October 1925); "This Wicked Young Generation," *Women's Citizen* 11 (May 1927); "They Are Hell Bent," *American Mercury* 105 (June 1928); "Youth's Pagan Religion," *Literary Digest* 92 (8 January 1927); "Has Youth Deteriorated?" *Forum* 76 (July 1926).

17. Robert S. Lynd and Helen M. Lynd, *Middletown: A Study in Contemporary American Culture* (New York: Harcourt, Brace, 1929), 138–39; Kett, *Rites of Passage*, 263.

18. Arthur S. Link, "What Happened to the Progressive Movement in the 1920s?" *American Historical Review* 64 (1959): 833–51.

19. Kett, *Rites of Passage*, 235–39.

20. Herbert Hoover's press conference, 2 July 1929, in U.S. Office of the Federal Register, *Public Papers of the Presidents of the United States: Herbert Hoover* (Washington, D.C.: U.S. Government Printing Office, 1974), 1:206–9.

21. Herbert Hoover, "Statement on Plans for a White House Conference on Child Health and Protection," 2 July 1929, *Public Papers: Herbert Hoover*, 1:211; Hoover, "Address to the White House Conference on Child Health and Protection," 19 November 1930, ibid., 2:495.

22. William F. Ogburn, *Social Change* (New York: B. W. Heubsch, 1922). Hoover's attachment to the ideas of "cultural lag" was evident when he convened his own committee, the President's Research Committee on Recent Social Trends, to study the implications of the concept in all areas of American social life. Ogburn headed the committee. See President's Research Committee on Recent Social Trends, *Recent Social Trends in the United States* (New York: McGraw-Hill, 1933), introduction.

23. Herbert Hoover, "Address Commemorating the Twentieth Anniversary of the Boy Scouts of America," 10 March 1930, *Public Papers: Herbert Hoover*, 1:211, 2:87–89.

24. Ibid.; and "Message to the National Education Association," *Public Papers: Herbert Hoover*, 2:269.

25. Ibid., 2:87–89; Herbert Hoover, "Address to the White House Conference on Child Health and Protection," 19 November 1930, *Public Papers: Herbert Hoover*, 2:494–95.

26. Herbert Hoover, *Further Addresses upon the American Road, 1938–1940* (New York: Charles Scribner's Sons, 1940), 3–20, 79–80.

27. David Burner, *Herbert Hoover: A Public Life* (New York: Alfred A. Knopf, 1979), 329; Albert U. Romasco, *The Poverty of Abundance: Hoover, the Nation and the Depression* (New York: Oxford University Press, 1965), passim; Hoover, *Further Addresses*, 55.

28. *New York Times*, 4 March 1923, sec. 7, p. 11; 8 September 1927, 44; 9 April 1932, 15.

29. David Burner, *The Politics of Provincialism: The Democratic Party in Transition, 1918–1932* (New York: Alfred A. Knopf, 1968), 147; Frank Freidel, *Franklin D. Roosevelt: The Ordeal* (Boston: Little, Brown, 1954), 97, 106–21.

30. Hugh G. Gallagher, *FDR's Splendid Deception* (New York: Dodd, Mead, 1985), 122–24, 53–58.

31. Frank Freidel, *Franklin D. Roosevelt: Launching the New Deal* (Boston: Little, Brown, 1973), 257; John Morton Blum, *From the Morgenthau Diaries: Years of Crisis, 1928–1938* (Boston: Houghton Mifflin, 1959), 26–27; Edgar B. Nixon, comp. and ed., *Franklin D. Roosevelt and Conservation* (Hyde Park, N.Y.: National Archives and Record Service, 1957), 123.

32. Thomas K. McCraw, "The New Deal and the Mixed Economy," in *Fifty Years Later: The New Deal Evaluated*, ed. Harvard Sitkoff (New York: Alfred A. Knopf, 1985), 37–67.

33. Ibid., 57.

Two. Schooling for Democracy, 1933–1934

1. Many sources document the New Deal's criticism of existing forms of education and its determination to offer job training to low-income students. Among the most revealing are Aubrey Williams to Joseph K. Hart, 13 March 1934, box 10, file "Education General, H–M," Records of the FERA and WPA Emergency Education Program, in Records of the Work Projects Administration (hereinafter FERA Papers), Record Group 69, National Archives (hereinafter NA); Hilda W. Smith, "Resident Schools and Camps for Unemployed Women" (Washington, D.C.: FERA mimeograph, 1934), introduction; "Memorandum on Plans and Organizations Proposed for Youth: 1934," box 32, Records of the Emergency Education Program, 1933–1934, FERA Papers, NA; and Tyack et al., *Public Schools in Hard Times*, 111–29.

2. Salmond, *A Southern Rebel*, 83–84; Rawick, "The New Deal and Youth," 173–89; "Charles W. Taussig," *National Cyclopedia of American Biography* (New York: James T. White, 1950), 36:78–79.

3. Edward Filene to Roosevelt, 7 September 1933, box 1, file "Youth, 1933–1935," President's Official File (hereinafter OF) 58, Franklin D. Roosevelt Library (hereinafter FDRL); "Suggestions with Regard to the Aiding of Youth, Disadvantaged by the Depression," 9 June 1934, box 34, Aubrey Williams Papers, FDRL.

4. "Division of Student Work," file "College Student Mortality," box 82, Papers of the National Youth Administration, Record Group 119, NA; U.S. Federal Security Agency, *Final Report of the NYA*, 11–24; John A. Salmond, *The Civilian Conservation Corps, 1933–1942: A New Deal Case Study* (Durham: Duke University Press, 1967), 4–5.

5. Robert H. Bremner, ed., *Children and Youth*, 2:761–62; U.S. Department of Labor, *Standards of Child Welfare*, 7, 11–20.

6. Kenneth Holland, "Work Camps for Youth," in *American Youth: An Enforced Renaissance*, ed. Thacher Winslow and Frank P. Davidson (Cambridge: Harvard University Press, 1940), 84; Holland, *Youth in European Labor Camps* (Washington, D.C.: American Council on Education, 1939), 51–68, 130–46, 206–21, 147–79; Winslow, *Youth: A World Problem*, 30–48, 53–58, 126–38.

7. Stachura, *The German Youth Movement*, 113–17, 131–36.

8. Robert Dallek, *Democrat and Diplomat: The Life of William E. Dodd* (New

York: Oxford University Press, 1968), 76–77, 316–17; Filene to Roosevelt, 7 September 1933, OF 58, FDRL; Taussig, "Memorandum on the Proposed Educational Activities of the Administration," December 1933, box 91, file "Taussig Speeches, 1933–1934," FDRL (hereinafter Taussig, "Memorandum").

9. Dallek, *Democrat and Diplomat*, 316–17; Dodd to Roosevelt, 30 July 1933; Roosevelt to Dodd, 13 November 1933; Dodd to R. Walton Moore, 5 November 1934; all in Edgar B. Nixon, *Franklin D. Roosevelt and Foreign Affairs*, 3 vols. (Cambridge: Harvard University Press, 1969), 1:336, 484–85, 2:275–77.

10. Sidney Fine, *The Automobile under the Blue Eagle: Labor, Management and the Automobile Manufacturing Code* (Ann Arbor: University of Michigan Press, 1963), 78–79.

11. Filene to Roosevelt, 7 September 1933, OF 58, FDRL.

12. Ibid.

13. Ibid.

14. Early to Filene, 21 September 1933, box 1, file "Youth, 1933–1935," OF 58, FDRL.

15. Rawick, "The New Deal and Youth," 173–89.

16. "Charles W. Taussig," *National Cyclopedia of American Biography*, 36:78–79; Rexford G. Tugwell, *The Brains Trust* (New York: Viking Press, 1968), 201, 475–76, 479. Taussig died in Bay Shore, New York, on 9 May 1948.

17. Taussig, "Memorandum"; Ralph S. Brax, *The First Student Movement: Student Activism in the United States during the 1930s* (Port Washington, N.Y.: Kennikat Press, 1981), 31–37, 70–71.

18. Taussig, "Memorandum"; George Wolfskill and John A. Hudson, *All but the People: Franklin D. Roosevelt and His Critics, 1933–1939* (New York: Macmillan, 1969), 159–66.

19. Taussig, "Memorandum."

20. Ibid.

21. Ibid.

22. Rawick, "The New Deal and Youth," 172–88.

23. "American Youth Congress," Division of Student Work: Office of the Director, box 1, General Files, 1936–1941, NYA Papers, NA; Rawick, "The New Deal and Youth," 172–85.

24. Rawick, "The New Deal and Youth," 172–88.

25. S. Burns Weston to Taussig, 24 August 1934, box 17, file "S. Burns Weston, 1934–1935," Charles Taussig Papers, FDRL.

26. Weston to Taussig, 28 August 1934, ibid.

27. Hopkins to FDR, 14 August 1933, box 10, FERA Papers, FDRL; "Roosevelt Acts with Johnson and Hopkins to Coordinate Codes, Works and Relief," *New York Times*, 15 August 1933.

28. Searle Charles, *Minister of Relief: Harry Hopkins and the Great Depres-*

sion (Syracuse: Syracuse University Press, 1963), 60–65, 74, 91; Hilda W. Smith, "Resident Schools and Camps for Unemployed Women," introduction; Salmond, *A Southern Rebel,* 18–19.

29. Robert Sherwood, *Roosevelt and Hopkins: The Story of Their Relationship* (Boston: Houghton Mifflin, 1948), 21–22.

30. Irving Bernstein, *A Caring Society: The New Deal, the Worker and the Great Depression* (Boston: Houghton Mifflin, 1985), 25–28.

31. For a complete list of those within the New Deal who contributed draft proposals for a new FERA program for youth, see "Memorandum on Plans and Organizations Proposed for Youth: 1934," box 32, Records of the Emergency Education Program, FERA Papers, NA.

32. "Aubrey Williams Personal History," box 36, file "Williams Biographical Data," Aubrey Williams Papers, FDRL; Salmond, *A Southern Rebel,* 10–15, 28–30, 37–42, 97–101; Williams to Joseph K. Hart, 13 March 1934, box 10, file "Education: H–M," FERA Papers, NA.

33. Tyack et al., *Public Schools in Hard Times,* 111–29, see especially the chapter entitled "A New Deal in Education?"

34. A brief Zook biography is in *School Life* 18 (June 1933): 183; Mann's comment is in *New York Times,* 19 May 1934, 13; Eunice Fuller Barnard, *New York Times,* 16 July 1933.

35. According to Arthur Schlesinger, Jr., nothing "attracted Roosevelt less than rigid intellectual systems. . . . Rejecting the platonic distinction between 'capitalism' and 'socialism,' he led the way toward a new society which took elements from each and rendered both obsolescent." See Schlesinger, *The Age of Roosevelt: The Politics of Upheaval* (Boston: Houghton Mifflin, 1960), 649–51; Studebaker's early years are discussed in *New York Times,* 23 May 1934, 5; and *School Life* 19 (June 1934): 207; Studebaker's article on the Des Moines public forums experiment is in *School Life* 18 (18 May 1933): 175.

36. The New Deal as schoolhouse is discussed in Tyack et al., *Public Schools in Hard Times,* 114–15. Concerning the principle of local control of education, Roosevelt in 1936 insisted to members of the National Education Association that "I am not in disagreement with it." If any New Deal programs appeared to violate this principle, it was only because "these activities have not concerned education alone. Always there has been the element of relief." FDR's "Greeting to the National Education Association," 4 February 1936, in Samuel I. Rosenman, comp., *The Public Papers and Addresses of Franklin D. Roosevelt,* 13 vols. (New York: Random House, 1938), 4:78.

37. Quoted in Tyack et al., *Public Schools in Hard Times,* 21–22.

38. Ibid., 18–24.

39. Joy Elmer Morgan, "The Schools and the Present Crisis," *NEA Journal* 22 (March 1933): 71; Willard E. Givens, article in National Education Association of

the United States, *Proceedings of the Seventy-first Annual Meeting Held at Chicago, Illinois, July 1–7, 1933* (Washington, D.C.: National Education Association, 1933), 71–78.

40. S. A. Courtis, "A Philosophy of Reconstruction in Public Education," *The Nation's Schools* 13 (June 1934): 20–22; Milton C. Potter, "The School's Role in the New Era Is Theme for Convention," *The Nation's Schools* 11 (January 1933): 52.

41. Tyack et al., *Public Schools in Hard Times*, 62–67.

42. FDR's "Radio Address on State's Rights," 2 March 1930, in Rosenman, *Public Papers of FDR*, 1:569–70.

43. FDR's "Extemporaneous Speech at Washington College, Chestertown, Md.," 21 October 1933, in Rosenman, *Public Papers of FDR*, 2:417–20; FDR to George F. Arps, 27 March 1934, in ibid., 3:171–72; Roosevelt's press conference of 23 November 1934, in ibid., 3:475.

44. FDR to Arps, 27 March 1934; and Roosevelt's press conference of 23 November 1934; both in ibid.; Franklin D. Roosevelt Library, *Complete Presidential Press Conferences of Franklin D. Roosevelt*, 25 vols. (New York: Da Capo Press, 1972), 4:204–32, 6:205–7; Rosenman, *Public Papers of FDR*, 4:418–19, 496–99.

Three. The Entering Wedge of College Student Aid

1. William Dow Boutwell, "The Emergency Agencies and Education," *Congressional Digest* 2 (February 1934): 39, 64.

2. For letters expressing independently the view that all New Deal agencies affecting youth must coordinate their efforts, see Alderman to Hopkins, 25 June 1934, box 32, file "Memos and Plans," FERA Papers, Record Group 69, NA; and George F. Zook, U.S. commissioner of education, invitation to "Conference on Youth Problems," 11 April 1934, box 8, file 106, Records of the U.S. Office of Education (hereinafter USOE Papers), Record Group 12, NA; and John H. Millar to Jacob Baker, 14 June 1934, box 32, "Emergency Education Program, 1933–1939," FERA Papers, NA.

3. FERA, *Monthly Report of the Federal Emergency Relief Administration* (Washington, D.C., December 1933), 8–9, 39; May 1934, 8; April 1934, 11.

4. "Statistics of the Emergency Education Program," box 30, file "March, 1934," FERA Papers, NA.

5. U.S. Bureau of Labor Statistics, *Monthly Labor Review* 38 (May 1934): 1120–23; Lewis R. Alderman, "The Emergency Education Program," *School Life* 19 (June 1934): 216–17.

6. Russell T. Sharpe, "College and the Poor Boy," *Atlantic Monthly* 151 (June 1933): 703–5.

7. U.S. Bureau of the Census, *Historical Statistics of the United States: Colonial Times to 1970* (Washington, D.C.: U.S. Government Printing Office, 1975), 383; "Division of Student Work," box 82, file "College Student Mortality," NYA Papers, NA; U.S. Federal Security Agency, *Final Report of the NYA*, 11–24.

8. James E. Pollard, *The History of the Ohio State University: Its First Seventy-five Years, 1873–1948* (Columbus: Ohio State University Press, 1952), 302–10.

9. Aubrey Williams to Tilla Durr, 7 May 1957, Aubrey Williams Papers, FDRL.

10. "George F. Zook," in *Who's Who in America, 1934–1935* (Chicago: A. N. Marquis, 1934), 18:2623; Zook to Hopkins, 12 August 1933; "Conference on August 8, 1933, Called by the US Commissioner of Education to Consider Possible Methods of Cooperation Between Educators and the FERA"; both in box 10, file "Education General, A–C," FERA Papers, NA.

11. "Conference on August 8, 1933, Called by the US Commissioner of Education," box 10, FERA Papers, NA.

12. Leuchtenburg, *FDR and the New Deal*, 338–39; Freidel, *FDR: Launching the New Deal*, 340; U.S. Federal Security Agency, *Youth on the Student Work Program* (Washington, D.C.: U.S. Government Printing Office, 1940), 63.

13. Hopkins to state relief administrators, 28 September 1933, box 1, file "September–December, 1933," OF 444, FDRL; Bellush, *The Failure of the NRA* (New York: Norton, 1975), 4–5, 127.

14. Betty Lindley and Ernest K. Lindley, *A New Deal for Youth: The Story of the National Youth Administration* (New York: Viking Press, 1938), 193–96; Hopkins to state relief administrators, 28 September 1933, box 1, OF 444, FDRL.

15. *New York Times*, 13 August 1933, p. 2, col. 6; and 15 August 1933, p. 13, col. 2; Hopkins to FDR, 14 August 1933, on "Educational Training for the Unemployed," box 10, file "Education, N–Z," FERA Papers, NA.

16. Hopkins to FDR, 14 August 1933, box 10, FERA Papers, NA.

17. Ibid.; another copy is in file "FERA January–August, 1933," box 1, OF 444, FDRL.

18. The 1932 figure for the proportion of college-age Americans pursuing higher education was 7.4 percent, a figure that dropped to 6.6 percent in 1934. In 1978, by comparison, 32.1 percent of Americans aged eighteen to twenty-four attended some form of institution of higher education. See *Historical Statistics of the United States*, 1:383. The New Deal's emphasis on helping the poorest constituents of the nation's schools is discussed in Tyack et al., *Public Schools in Hard Times*, 103–12.

19. "Roosevelt Acts with Johnson and Hopkins to Coordinate Codes, Works and Relief," *New York Times*, 15 August 1933; Robert L. Kelly to Hopkins, 16 August 1933; Richard S. Burington to FDR, 31 August 1933; both in box 10, file "Education General, A–C," FERA Papers; and John H. Lang to Hopkins, 15 August 1933, box 10, file "N–Z," FERA Papers, NA.

20. *New York Times*, 19 October 1933, p. 21, col. 2; 31 October 1933, p. 4, col. 5.

21. FERA press release, 2 February 1934, "FERA to Help Needy College Students," box 1, file "January–March, 1934," OF 444, FDRL.

22. Hopkins to FDR, 14 August 1933, box 10, FERA Papers, NA.

23. Ibid.

24. Sexson E. Humphreys to FDR, 5 January 1935; Hopkins to Early, 11 January 1935; both in box 9, "Education," file "Education General," FERA Papers, NA; Rosenman, *Public Papers of FDR*, 4:476, 5:162–64.

25. Memo, FDR to Hopkins, 30 May 1935, file "March–May, 1935," OF 444, FDRL; Memo, FDR to Williams, 12 December 1935, box 18, OF 444-d, FDRL.

26. U.S. Federal Security Agency, *Final Report of the NYA*, 46–47.

27. "NYA Student Work Program, June, 1940," box 14, file "NYA General," Aubrey Williams Papers, FDRL; Alderman to Charles Spencer, 30 March 1934, box 30, file "March, 1934"; and Alderman to L. W. Boe, president of St. Olaf College (Minn.), 27 February 1934, box 30, file "January–February, 1934," both in FERA Papers, NA.

28. "Lewis R. Alderman," in *Who's Who in America, 1934–1935*, 18:159–60; a Klinefelter biography and photograph are in *School Life* (May 1937); see also *School Life* 22 (September 1936): 1–3.

29. Lang to Bookman, 12 September 1933; Leah V. Barr to Lang, 13 September 1933; both in box 10, file "Education, H–M," FERA Papers; an article on Olson's August 1933 visit to Washington in search of student aid funds is in *New York Times*, 4 August 1933, p. 3, col. 2; for Olson's October request and Alderman's reply, see Alderman to Bookman, 27 October 1933, box 10, file "Education General, Memorandums," FERA Papers, NA.

30. U.S. Federal Security Agency, *Final Report of the NYA*, 46–47; FERA press release, 2 February 1934, box 1, OF 444, FDRL.

31. For the expenditures and regulations outlined in the announcement of the student aid program, see *New York Times*, 3 February 1934, p. 2., col. 2; and FERA press release, 2 February 1934, OF 444, FDRL.

32. FERA press release, 2 February 1934.

33. Alderman to J. W. Cammack, president of Averett College (Va.), no date, box 30, file "April–May, 1934," FERA Papers, NA.

34. Hopkins to Early, 11 January 1935, box 9, file "Education General," FERA Papers, NA.

Four. The Inner War over Youth Policy

1. National Education Association, *Proceedings: Chicago*, 951; Tyack et al., *Public Schools in Hard Times*, 98–101, 108–10.

2. Williams to Joseph K. Hart, 13 March 1934, box 10, file "Education, H–M," FERA Papers, NA.

3. Ibid.; Tyack et al., *Public Schools in Hard Times*, 108–9. Hopkins, quoted in Tyack et al., ibid.

4. Again and again Minehan warned of the social costs of apathy toward youth unemployment. "American cities may be overrun with groups of hoodlums. . . . Street beggars, hideous, deformed, and depressing may swarm our land and deface our cities and again many of them will be graduate city tramps." Such a life-style was "opposed to all concepts of society not only as we know it but as it must be in the future if we are to progress." Minehan regarded work camps as an expedient to buy time, not itself a solution. "Unless we are to become a militaristic or monastic nation, we cannot confine our youth permanently in camps. The camps will save the boys on the road today, but tomorrow we must have other and more comprehensive programs" (Thomas Minehan, *Boy and Girl Tramps of America* [New York: Farrar and Rinehart, 1934], 240–45).

5. According to Lubove, for men of Hopkins's generation, "Organization was the key to efficient philanthropy." "Believing that social problems were subject to rational analysis and control, but also that their scope and complexity were too vast to be handled by the impulses of benevolent individuals," reformers created "an immense network of welfare organizations." The result was an emphasis on bureaucratization: "Function instead of cause; administrator instead of charismatic leader; rational organization and centralized machinery of control instead of individual impulse and village neighborliness" (Roy Lubove, *The Professional Altruist: The Emergence of Social Work as a Career* [Cambridge: Harvard University Press, 1965], 157–58). For a discussion of Hopkins's 1934 appearances before Congress and his European tour (taken on the advice of the president), see Charles, *Minister of Relief*, 60–65, 74, 91.

6. A contemporary account of the process by which Hilda W. Smith established the women's resident school program (often dubbed the "she, she, she") is Smith, "Resident Schools and Camps for Unemployed Women"; Smith's introduction to the New Deal is illuminated by her 1933 request for a meeting with Eleanor Roosevelt. See Smith to Eleanor Roosevelt, 30 September 1933, box 10, file "Education General, A–C," FERA papers, NA.

7. Joseph K. Hart to Williams, 13 March 1934, box 10, file "Education, H–M" FERA papers, NA.

8. Williams to Hart, 13 March 1934, box 10, file "Education General, H–M," FERA papers, NA. At his 13 February 1942 press conference Roosevelt charac-

terized budget-cutting opponents of federal programs as "glib" boys. He meant the term to apply to "the bright boys who say you can curtail all of the Federal expenditures." The problem with these people, FDR added, is that they have no answer when asked where to start cutting. "You take dozens and dozens of bureaus here in Washington," he explained. "Your glib boy says, 'Oh, cut them all out. Cut them all down.'" Following the conference, Aubrey Williams wrote a congratulatory letter to the president, praising his invention of "a wonderful cognomen," the "Glib Boys." See Franklin D. Roosevelt Library, *Complete Presidential Press Conferences of Franklin D. Roosevelt*, vols. 19–20: 1942 (New York: Da Capo Press, 1972), 19:137–40; Williams to FDR, 17 February 1942, box 4, file "White House," Aubrey Williams Papers, FDRL; Williams's April 1934 article is in *New York Times*, 1 April 1934, sec. 9, 1; Williams's 1937 and 1940 comments on education are quoted in Harry Zeitlin, "Federal Relations in American Education, 1933–1943: A Study of New Deal Efforts and Innovations" (Ph.D. diss., Columbia University, 1958), 202–3.

9. *New York Times*, 1 April 1934, sec. 9.

10. George F. Zook to members of the Conference on Youth Problems, 11 April 1934, "Report of Conference on Youth Problems, June 1–2, 1934," box 12, "Emergency Education Program, Miscellaneous Files," FERA Papers, NA.

11. Ibid.; Zook to M. M. Proffitt, 17 May 1934, box 12, "Emergency Education Program, Miscellaneous Files," FERA Papers, NA.

12. Reiman, "Planning the National Youth Administration," 258–98; Hilda W. Smith to Eleanor Roosevelt, 30 September 1933, box 10, "Emergency Education Program, Miscellaneous Files," FERA Papers, NA.

13. Hilda W. Smith, "Memorandum for the FERA," September 1933, box 32, "Emergency Education Program, Miscellaneous Files," FERA Papers, NA.

14. John H. Millar to William Haber, 21 April 1934, box 30, "Emergency Education Program, Miscellaneous Files," FERA Papers, NA.

15. Millar's ideas were presented in four important letters during the spring of 1934: to Haber, 21 April 1934, ibid.; Millar, "Confidential Inquiry," mailed to 140 federal and education officials, 26 April 1934; Millar to Nels Anderson, 24 April 1934; and Millar to Jacob Baker, 14 June 1934; all in box 32, "Emergency Education Program, Miscellaneous Files," FERA Papers, NA.

16. Millar to Haber, 21 April 1934, box 30, "Old Series," FERA Papers; Millar, "Confidential Inquiry"; Zeitlin, "Federal Relations in American Education, 1933–1943," 192.

17. "Suggestions with Regards to the Aiding of Youth, Disadvantaged by the Depression," 9 June 1934, box 13, Aubrey Williams Papers, FDRL.

18. Haber to Williams, 12 April 1934; Millar to Haber, 21 April 1934; both in box 30, "Emergency Education Program, Miscellaneous Files," FERA Papers, NA.

19. Millar, "Confidential Inquiry."

20. Nels Anderson to Millar, 26 April 1934; Millar to Fred J. Kelly, 31 May 1934; both in box 32, "Emergency Education Program, Miscellaneous Files," FERA Papers, NA.

21. Millar to Nels Anderson, 24 April 1934, box 32, "Emergency Education Program, Miscellaneous Files," FERA Papers, NA; Millar, "Confidential Inquiry."

22. Viola Ilma to Millar, 6 June 1934; Millar to Robert Lansdale, 4 May 1934; both in box 32, "Emergency Education Program, Miscellaneous Files," FERA Papers, NA.

23. C. R. Mann to Millar, 28 May 1934; Millar to Jacob Baker, 14 June 1934; Millar, "Confidential Inquiry," 26 April 1934; all in box 32, "Emergency Education Program, Miscellaneous Files," FERA Papers, NA.

24. "Civil Scholarships, 1934," "Civil Training Corps," box 13, Aubrey Williams Papers, FDRL.

25. Millar to Jacob Baker, 14 June 1934, box 32, "Emergency Education Program, Miscellaneous Files," FERA Papers, NA.

26. Viola Ilma to Millar, 6 June 1934, box 32; Jacob Baker, "General History" of FERA, 3 July 1935, box 2; both in "Emergency Education Program, Miscellaneous Files," FERA Papers, NA.

27. Zook to M. M. Proffitt, 17 May 1934, box 12; "Suggestions with Regards to the Aiding of Youth," 9 June 1934, box 9; both in "Emergency Education Program, Miscellaneous Files," FERA Papers, NA.

28. Zook to Hopkins, 7 June 1934, box 32, "Emergency Education Program, Miscellaneous Files," FERA Papers, NA.

29. "Suggestions with Regards to the Aiding of Youth," 9 June 1934, box 9, "Emergency Education Program, Miscellaneous Files," FERA Papers, NA.

30. Ibid.

31. Lansdale to Williams, 9 June 1934, box 13, Williams Papers, FDRL.

32. Millar to Alderman, 12 July 1934, box 32; "Report of Conference on Youth Problems, June 1–2, 1934," box 12; both in "Emergency Education Program, Miscellaneous Files," FERA Papers, NA.

33. Memo, Williams to Baker, 10 July 1934; memo, Baker to Goldschmidt, 10 July 1934 (written on Williams to Baker memo), box 32, "Emergency Education Program, Miscellaneous Files," FERA Papers, NA; Katie Loucheim, *The Making of the New Deal: The Insiders Speak* (Cambridge: Harvard University Press, 1983), 187–94, 320.

34. While the authorship of this document remains somewhat obscure, hand-written notations on the draft permit more than tentative, if not certain, attributions. It was signed at the bottom by Goldschmidt, and at the top, in a different handwriting, by "J. B." (Baker). Next to the latter's initials are the words "Return—anything else with this?" Since the draft was inspired in the first place by a Williams memo, it seems reasonable to conclude that the instructions were intended

for Williams's notice. Inasmuch as the most extensive handwritten revisions on the draft were in a handwriting different from Baker's, most likely the revisions were Kramer's. "Unemployed Youth" (undated, ca. summer 1934), box 32, "Emergency Education Program, Miscellaneous Files," FERA Papers, NA.

35. Ibid.

36. Ibid.

37. Ibid.

38. The reminiscences of Robert Gard, quoted in Studs Terkel, *Hard Times: An Oral History of the Great Depression* (New York: Pantheon, 1986) 347.

Five. The Battle Won: The NYA Takes Shape

1. "A Program for Unemployed Youth," Hopkins to state relief administrators, 28 November 1934, box 50, file "Youth Program-Planning Division," Hopkins MSS; Fred J. Kelly to Williams, 7 November 1934, box 13, file "NYA Early Conferences, etc.," Williams MSS.

2. Williams's apprenticeship program, which emphasized education rather than work relief, stood in sharp contrast to the CCC. The educational program of the latter was a disappointment as far as job training was concerned. See Salmond, *The CCC*, 49–50.

3. "Unemployed Youth" (undated, ca. summer 1934), box 50, file "Youth Program-Planning Division," Hopkins Papers, FDRL.

4. Lansdale to Williams, 9 June 1934, box 13, Williams Papers, FDRL.

5. That FERA officials believed further revision was required is indicated by the presentation the following month of a new youth program, attributed to Aubrey Williams. Williams's plan offered greater decentralization, civic education, and job training. Fred J. Kelly to Williams, 7 November 1934, box 13, Williams Papers, FDRL; "Program for Youth" ("prepared by A. W."), undated (ca. November 1934), file "Youth Program-Planning Division," FDRL.

6. John A. Lang, "A Service for Youth," *New York Times*, 28 October 1934, sec. 8.

7. Hopkins to state relief administrators, 28 November 1934, box 50, file "Youth Program-Planning Division," Hopkins Papers, FDRL.

8. These were months when New Deal relief officials and those outside the administration arrived independently at the same conclusion: that real work would more effectively eliminate the despair and political demoralization of the young. Journalists, politicians, and educators all thought a democracy could expect young people's continued support only so long as it could supply them work, not merely education.

Following the November 1934 elections (in which the Democrats gained thirteen House seats and nine in the Senate), the New Dealers had another reason
to call for work projects for young people: the chance it would offer to revive the
Civil Works Administration. The CWA had been discontinued earlier in the year,
in part because of a fear that conservatives would convince the public that the
endeavor represented an unjustifiable break with tradition. See Charles, *Minister
of Relief*, 60–65.

9. "Youth Held Victim of Changed World," *New York Times*, 17 September
1934, p. 19, col. 5.

10. "Youth Today," *New York Times*, 31 October 1934, p. 18, col. 3.

11. "Youth Held Victim of Changed World"; Benedict S. Alper and George E.
Lodgen, "Youth Without Work," *Survey* 70 (September 1934): 285–86.

12. "Youth Held Victim of Changed World"; "Youth Today."

13. For a discussion of the circumstances surrounding the introduction of the
Lang plan in June 1934, see chapter 5 in this volume; Lang, "A Service for Youth."
The authorship of the Civil Training Corps idea, discussed in chapter 4 of this
volume, remains unclear.

14. The remarks of Chase, Cowley, Kelly, and Graham are quoted in Lang, "A
Service for Youth."

15. Lang, "A Service for Youth."

16. Hopkins to state relief administrators, 1–3 October 1934, box 13, file "NYA
Early Conferences, etc.," Williams Papers, FDRL.

17. Hopkins to state relief administrators, 3 October 1934, Williams Papers,
FDRL.

18. Hopkins to state relief administrators, 1 October 1934, Williams Papers,
FDRL; Hopkins also considered calling the state programs "Youth Work Guilds."
See Hopkins to state administrators, 1 October 1934, box 13, file "NYA Early
Conferences, etc.," Williams Papers, FDRL.

19. The nine officials were, in addition to Baker and Haber, Georgia relief director Gay Shepperson, John Colt, Conrad van Hyning, L. R. Alderman, Robert Lansdale, Josephine Brown, and Arthur Goldschmidt. Jacob Baker to Hopkins, 16 October 1934, box 13, file "NYA Early Conferences, etc.," Williams Papers, FDRL.

20. Charles, *Minister of Relief*, 30, 129; Doris McLaughlin, "Putting Michigan
Back to Work," *Michigan History* 66.1 (1982): 30–37; Baker to Hopkins, 16 October
1934, Williams Papers, FDRL.

21. Circumstantial evidence points to the conclusion that Williams was the
author of the November draft. In November, an officer of the USOE, Fred J. Kelly,
referred to the draft in a letter to Williams as "your" plan. One copy of the plan,
found by George Rawick in the Hopkins papers, had a hand-penciled notation,
"prepared by A. W." Moreover, Williams's biographer, John Salmond, attributed

the November draft to the Alabamian and said that Hopkins gave him the assignment of producing it. See Kelly to Williams, 7 November 1934, box 13, file "NYA Early Conferences, etc.," Williams Papers, FDRL; Rawick, "The New Deal and Youth," 176; "Program for Youth" ("prepared by A. W."), undated (ca. November 1934), file "Youth Program-Planning Division," FDRL; Hopkins to state relief administrators, 28 November 1934, Hopkins Papers, FDRL; Salmond, *A Southern Rebel*, 76.

22. Hopkins to state relief administrators, 28 November 1934; and "A Program for Youth"; both in Hopkins Papers, FDRL.

23. The Williams quotes are drawn from his memorandum "A Program for Youth," Hopkins Papers, FDRL.

24. Kelly to Williams, 7 November 1934, Williams Papers, FDRL.

25. Ibid.; Kelly to Studebaker, 7 November 1934, Education files, FERA Papers, Old Series, FDRL.

26. Kelly to Studebaker, 26 December 1934, Education files, FERA Papers, Old Series, FDRL.

27. Kelly to Williams, 7 November 1934, Williams Papers, FDRL.

28. Ibid.

29. Ibid.

30. *Congressional Record*, 74th Cong., 1st sess., 1209.

31. Ibid.

32. U.S. Senate, *Employment for Graduates of Educational Institutions*, Letter from the Secretary of Labor, 74th Cong., 1st sess., Document 45, A35, 7–10.

33. Ibid., 1–2.

34. Ibid., 1–10.

35. FDR to Hopkins, 20 March 1935, box 96, file "Franklin D. Roosevelt, Correspondence, 1933–1940," Hopkins Papers, FDRL; U.S. Senate, *Employment for Graduates*, 7–10.

36. Among the historians who have argued that Roosevelt was reluctant to support the creation of the NYA and had to be persuaded by a persistent Eleanor Roosevelt are Tamara K. Hareven, Joseph P. Lash, and Robert A. Caro. See chapter 9.

37. Hopkins to FDR, 11 April 1935, box 13, file "NYA Early Conferences, etc.," Williams Papers, FDRL.

38. Studebaker's Community Youth Program is discussed in Rawick, "The New Deal and Youth," 178–92.

39. John W. Studebaker, radio address on NBC, 30 April 1935, "The Dilemma of Youth," in box 15, file "John Studebaker," Taussig Papers, FDRL.

40. Baker to Hopkins, 29 April 1935, box 13, file "NYA Early Conferences, etc.," Williams Papers, FDRL.

41. Ibid.

42. Perkins to Ickes, 6 May 1935, box 13, file "NYA Early Conferences, etc.," Williams Papers, FDRL.

43. Some educators wasted little time in attacking the NYA. For example, George Strayer of Columbia University Teacher's College, declared in July 1935: "The president has not only deliberately ignored the Office of Education, which is one of the cleanest and best branches of the federal service, but he has gone against the best interests of the young people involved, he has denied the competence of the school people with their years of experience and has set up a dual administration dealing with youth guidance" (*New York Times*, 3 July 1935; quoted in Rawick, "The New Deal and Youth," 192).

44. Perkins to Ickes, 6 May 1935, Williams Papers, FDRL.

45. FDR to Hopkins, 20 March 1935, box 96, file "Franklin D. Roosevelt, Correspondence, 1933–1940," Hopkins Papers, FDRL; Taussig to FDR, 9 March 1935, file "Mrs. Eleanor Roosevelt, 1935–1937," Taussig Papers, FDRL.

46. Rawick, "The New Deal and Youth," 172–84; Salmond, *A Southern Rebel*, 83.

47. Salmond, *A Southern Rebel*, 83.

48. During these months there were press accounts portraying a "beaten" Studebaker in just this way. See, for instance, *New York Times*, 16 April 1935, p. 20, col. 3; 30 June 1935, sec. 4.

49. Salmond, *A Southern Rebel*, 83.

50. U.S. Federal Security Agency, *Final Report of the NYA*, 8–22; Salmond, *A Southern Rebel*, 83–84, 127–29.

51. "National Youth Division, Copy Used While Talking with Mrs. Roosevelt," signed Aubrey Williams, 17 May 1935, in box 13, file "NYA Early Conferences, etc.," Williams Papers, FDRL.

52. The comments of Mrs. Roosevelt and Sarnoff were recorded by Williams in handwritten margin comments on his copy of the draft, "National Youth Division," ibid.

53. Memo, FDR to Hopkins, 28 May 1935, box 13, file "E," Williams Papers, FDRL; *New York Times*, 27 June 1935, p. 4, col. 3.

54. Memo, Early to McIntyre, 8 June 1935, box 13, file "E," Williams Papers, FDRL; *New York Times*, 27 June 1935, p. 4, col. 3.

55. Rosenman, *Public Papers of FDR*, 4:281–82; *New York Times*, 27 June 1935, p. 4, col. 3.

56. Ibid.

Six. Facing Failure and Fascism

1. In the last months of 1935, Williams's frustration at the delay in starting work projects was evident in nearly every speech he gave. See *New York Times*, 17 October 1935, p. 25, col. 8; 10 November 1935, p. 1, col. 7; Salmond, *A Southern Rebel*, 123–30.

2. Ibid.; "Biographical Sketches of Members of the NYA National, State and Field Staffs," box 26, file "Meeting of the NAC, NYA," April 1936, Hopkins Papers, FDRL.

3. U.S. Federal Security Agency, *Final Report of the NYA*, 233.

4. Aubrey Williams insisted after 1934 that any federal job with youth on its payroll must receive the funds necessary to ensure that it have an educational component. See Williams memo, December 1934, box 13, Williams Papers, FDRL; quoted in Salmond, *A Southern Rebel*, 76–77.

5. Minutes of the Meeting of the National Advisory Committee, 15 August 1935 (hereinafter NAC, First Meeting), 1–4, box 91, file "Duplicate: Advisory Committee Meeting," Taussig Papers, FDRL.

6. Ibid., 1–4.

7. For information on the public relations aspect of the Macfadden appointment see Salmond, *A Southern Rebel*, 122; and Roosevelt to McIntyre, 9 July 1935, box 18, OF 444-d, FDRL. Earhart, however, spoke up for women's interests at the meeting. "It is so easy to . . . forget women's needs," she told the NAC members. "I am not interested in any planning which does not consider girls as important and worthy of benefits as boys" (NAC, First Meeting, 26).

8. NAC, First Meeting, 1–4.

9. Ibid., 20, 21, 27.

10. Ibid., 28–29.

11. Ibid., 30–31.

12. Williams despaired that only a small fraction of the applicants seeking NYA employment between June and October 1935 could be placed in agency positions. See Salmond, *A Southern Rebel*, 123–24.

13. In October and November, Williams spoke on two separate occasions of five million to eight million youths "unoccupied" in America. Eleanor Roosevelt often lectured Williams during these months that the NYA was not creating enough projects for enough young people. See *New York Times*, 17 October 1935, 25; 10 November 1935, p. 1, col. 7; Salmond, *A Southern Rebel*, 137–39.

14. NAC, First Meeting, 4–5.

15. Ibid., 8–9.

16. Ibid., 8–9.

17. "President Spurs Youth Relief Work," *New York Times*, 21 August 1935, p. 15, col. 4; Howard Braucher, "The National Recreation Movement and the Fed-

eral Government," *Recreation* 29 (December 1935): 440; Braucher, "Do We Really Care?" *Recreation* 29 (November 1935): 377.

18. Roosevelt to NYA state directors, 20 August 1934, quoted in *New York Times*, 21 August 1935, p. 15, col. 4.

19. For Strayer's criticisms see *New York Times*, 25 July 1935, p. 17, col. 1; "Dangers in the National Youth Program," *School Review* 43 (September 1935): 481–85.

20. FDR Library, *Complete Presidential Press Conferences*, 6:205–7.

21. "NYA Chief Gloomy on Youth Program," *New York Times*, 17 October 1935, p. 25, col. 8; Transcript of Taussig's speech to the American Federation of Labor (no date); Taussig to ER, 17 October 1935, box 1359, file "TA–TH 1935," ER Papers, FDRL.

22. *New York Times*, 17 October 1935, p. 25, col. 8.

23. Sutton and New York State director Fairfield Osborne, Jr., attacked the lack of discretion in the early NYA program. See Salmond, *A Southern Rebel*, 123–24; Weston to Taussig, 19 October 1935, box 17, file "S. Burns Weston, 1934–1935," Taussig Papers, FDRL.

24. Salmond, *A Southern Rebel*, 7, 11; *New York Times*, 19 January 1936, sec. 7.

25. In January 1936 Williams wrote, "I believe we must broaden our school system until we reach some arrangement whereby we can make education meet more nearly the needs of life" (*New York Times*, ibid.).

26. This analysis is contained in the "preliminary draft of recommendations to the President," 10 March 1937, drafted months after Taussig's ideas had won over the committee, in box 14, file "Roosevelt, President Franklin D.," Taussig Papers, FDRL. See also Taussig's St. Louis speech, 26 February 1936, file "Miscellaneous 1936–1937," box 20, OF 444-d, FDRL.

27. Speaking at New York's town hall on 27 February 1936, Brown termed the NYA a "temporary agency" (*New York Times*, 28 February 1936, p. 1, col. 2).

28. Taussig's St. Louis speech, 26 February 1936, box 20, OF 444-d, FDRL.

29. Ibid. On the same trip Taussig warned that with the new communication technologies, "a lie travels infinitely faster today than it did a hundred years ago." He proposed the adoption of high school courses to build a defense against the effects on young minds of propaganda (*New York Times*, 27 February 1936, p. 20, col. 4). The idea of Alaska as a place to resettle refugees would, in a few years, occur to federal officials and private organizations anxious to assist Jewish refugees fleeing occupied Europe. Unsuccessfully, some groups sought congressional permission to place refugees in the Matanuska Valley (a proposal FDR briefly thought of supporting). The notion of Alaska as a haven for the unwanted proved in every such case to be nothing more than a chimera. See Henry Feingold, *The Politics of Rescue: The Roosevelt Administration and the Holocaust* (New Brunswick: Rutgers University Press, 1970), 94–97.

30. "Report Regarding Activities of the NYA in Ohio," 28 May 1936, box 75, NYA Papers, NA.

31. After the First Lady wired her husband, "You are going to make an appointment to see Charles Taussig and you are going to ask Myron Taylor to serve on the NYA Advisory Board," Roosevelt penned a note to his aide, Edwin "Pa" Watson: "Pa: Will you arrange an appointment with Taussig this week?" Memo, ER to FDR, undated but included with 1936 White House correspondence with Taussig, file "Charles Taussig," President's Personal File (hereinafter PPF) 1644, FDRL.

32. "Minutes of the Meeting of the National Advisory Committee, April 28–29, 1936," box 27, Taussig Papers, FDRL (hereinafter NAC Second Meeting). Roosevelt's alteration of the original draft of the NYA is dated 20 May 1935 and can be found in a memo from FDR to Harry Hopkins, 28 May 1935, file "E," box 13, Aubrey Williams Papers, FDRL. The American Council on Education created the American Youth Commission in October 1935 and gave it $500,000 to investigate the effectiveness of other youth-serving organizations and make recommendations for their improvement. While some commission members served on the NYA National Advisory Committee, others, drawn from the conservative educational associations, opposed federal involvement in education. The projected survey was ultimately undertaken by the AYC in Maryland, and its results were released in May 1938. The Maryland survey found that "the gap which now exists between school and employment is reaching ominous proportions," with 40–45 percent of out-of-school youths unable to find work a year after leaving school. The average delay for young people dropping out at sixteen or younger was three and one-half years. The survey recommended more vocational training and community planning for youth. See Howard M. Bell, *Youth Tell Their Story* (Washington, D.C.: American Council on Education, 1938), foreword; M. M. Chambers, *Youth-Serving Organizations* (Washington, D.C.: American Council on Education, 1941), 72–73.

33. NAC, Second Meeting, 97, 7–18.

34. Ibid.

35. Ibid.

36. Ibid., draft in "Records of the NAC," NYA Papers, NA. Puerto Rico's problems in the 1930s were the result of poverty and depression, magnified by Roosevelt's failure to realize his sincere desire for Puerto Rican reform. Taussig's interest in the island is partly explained by the unveiling in 1934 of the New Deal–supported Chardon plan. Although the New Deal in 1934 provided relief to 35 percent of the island's population, the Chardon plan was aimed at attacking "the central disease of the society rather than playing around with its symptoms," as had the relief projects. Much of the island's sugar business was to be publicly operated, with workers and owners sharing the profits equally, supplemented by a system of subsistence homesteads. The effort failed, in part because the territorial governor,

Blanton Winship (a former military man appointed by the president), opposed the efforts of Ernest Greuning, the Interior Department's director of territories and island possessions. Winship regarded the plan as an attempt by Greuning to impose a program on his territorial administration. Meanwhile, three cabinet departments (War, Interior, and Agriculture) shared hopelessly divided lines of authority on the island. By 1935, when Taussig met with both Greuning and Winship, the Chardon plan was thoroughly stalled, politically vocal youths were again raising the cry of U.S. perfidy, and the New Deal appeared to have lost control of the Puerto Rican situation. See Thomas Mathews, *Puerto Rican Politics and the New Deal* (Gainesville: University of Florida Press, 1960), 211–14, 230–31; Gordon K. Lewis, *Puerto Rico: Freedom and Power in the Caribbean* (New York: MR Press, 1963), 125–26, 129–32.

37. NAC, Second Meeting, draft in "Records of the NAC," NYA Papers, 149–54, NA.

38. Ibid.

39. Taussig to FDR, 7 May 1936, PPF box 1644, file "Charles W. Taussig," FDRL.

40. Aubrey Williams, "Youth-Aid Program Expands," *New York Times*, 5 July 1936, sec. 4.

41. FDR to Williams, 26 June 1936, PPF box 3647, file "National Youth Administration," FDRL.

42. Weston to Brown, 11 June 1936, box 115, file "Admn. S. Burns Weston, May–June, 1936," NYA Papers, NA.

43. *New York Times*, 5 July 1936, sec. 4.

Seven. Resettling to Rescue

1. James MacGregor Burns, *The Crosswinds of Freedom*, vol. 3, *The American Experiment* (New York: Alfred A. Knopf, 1989), 214; Lindley and Lindley, *A New Deal for Youth*, 86–108.

2. Salmond, *A Southern Rebel*, 133–35, 141–51; Robert G. Divine, *The Reluctant Belligerent: American Entry into World War II* (New York: Alfred A. Knopf, 1965, 1979), 59–67; Robert Dallek, *Franklin D. Roosevelt and American Foreign Policy, 1932–1945* (New York: Oxford University Press, 1979), 148; Weiss, *Farewell to the Party of Lincoln*, 143–53; B. Joyce Ross, "Mary McLeod Bethune and the National Youth Administration: A Case Study of Power Relationships in the Black Cabinet of Franklin D. Roosevelt," *Journal of Negro History* 60 (January 1975): 1–28.

3. Nor were rural youths the only group considered to be in need of integration.

In the following months the NYA provided places in the resident centers for other groups considered untutored in the tenets of democracy and the American pattern of living: prison parolees, the handicapped, and "refugees from fascism" (Austrian youths fleeing the post-*Anschluss* regime). U.S. Federal Security Agency, *Final Report of the NYA*, 13, 90, 127–31; Department of Commerce, *Historical Statistics of the United States*, 10; Bell, *Youth Tell Their Story*, foreword.

4. See chapters 3 and 6 for some background to the women's program.

5. U.S. Federal Security Agency, *Final Report of the NYA*, 179; See "Report on Educational Camps for Unemployed Young Women, 1936," box 2, "Camps," NYA Papers, NA (hereinafter "Camp Report, 1936"). Susan Wladaver-Morgan, "Young Women and the New Deal: Camps and Resident Centers, 1933–1943" (Ph.D. diss., Indiana University, 1982).

6. Women's camps assisted 8000 women; resident centers by 1940 employed 33,780 youths. U.S. Federal Security Agency, *Final Report of the NYA*, 180.

7. Wladaver-Morgan, "Young Women and the New Deal," 67.

8. Lois Scharf, "'The Forgotten Woman': Working Women, the New Deal, and Women's Organizations," in *Decades of Discontent: The Women's Movement, 1920–1940*, ed. Scharf and Joan M. Jensen (Westport, Conn.: Greenwood Press, 1983), 243–46.

9. Quoted in Wladaver-Morgan, "Young Women and the New Deal," 67–68; Marguerite Gilmore to Hilda Smith, 9 November, 12, 19 December 1935, Illinois Camp correspondence, box 321, NYA Papers, NA. Campbell's biography is contained in "Biographical Sketches of Members of the National Youth Administration Nation, Field, and State Staffs," box 26, file "Meeting of the National Advisory Committee, NYA," Harry Hopkins Papers, FDRL.

10. FERA, *Monthly Report of the Federal Emergency Relief Administration*, May 1936; "Report on Educational Camps for Unemployed Women," 28–29.

11. Wladaver-Morgan, "Young Women and the New Deal," 75–76.

12. Smith, "Educational Camps," 28–33; "Camp Report, 1936"; NYA Press Release, 15 February 1937, box 2, "Camps," NYA Papers, NA.

13. Weston to Corson, 1 August 1935, box 115, file "Admn. S. Burns Weston, July–September 1935," NYA Papers, NA; "Camp Report, 1936," 8–11.

14. "Camp Report, 1936," 8.

15. Women's Camp Program Annual Report, 12 August 1937, 46–48, box 2, "Camps," NYA Papers, NA; "Camp Report, 1936," 26; Department of Commerce, *Historical Statistics of the United States*, 12.

16. Smith, "Educational Camps," 32.

17. Ibid.; Wladaver-Morgan, "Young Women and the New Deal," 62.

18. "Camp Report, 1936," 11; a photograph of camp women listening to a reading of *Puzzled America* is in box 3007, ER Papers, FDRL.

19. Annual Report, 12 August 1937, 46–48. McKelvey's statement referring to

an NYA women's center in Glendale, Ohio, is dated 29 April 1937; box 2, "Camps," NYA Papers, NA.

20. Wladaver-Morgan, "Young Women and the New Deal," 72; Annual Report, 12 August 1937; Salmond, *The CCC*, 91.

21. Wladaver-Morgan, 76; "Supplementary Report on Educational Camps for Unemployed Women, July 1, 1937–October 1, 1937" (hereinafter "Supplementary Report"), box 2, "Camps," NYA Papers, NA; U.S. Federal Security Agency, *Final Report of the NYA*, 129–32.

22. ER, quoted in Wladaver-Morgan, "Young Women and the New Deal," 76; "Supplementary Report."

23. "Supplementary Report."

24. Wladaver-Morgan, "Young Women and the New Deal," 76.

25. Ibid.; "Supplementary Report."

26. Wladaver-Morgan, "Young Women and the New Deal," 76–77.

27. U.S. Federal Security Agency, *Final Report of the NYA*, 179–81.

28. U.S. Federal Security Agency, *Final Report of the NYA*, 179–81.

29. Ibid., 184–85.

30. Ibid., 185–87.

31. "Muskingum Conservancy Development," undated draft, box 714, file "Muskingum," David R. Williams Correspondence, NYA Papers, NA.

32. History of the NYA's involvement in the MWCD, undated memo, Future Farmers of America, at Camp Muskingum, Leesville, Ohio; "Muskingum Conservancy Development."

33. "Outline for NYA Projects in the MWCD," 11 May 1937, Technical and Personal File of David R. Williams, NYA Papers, NA.

34. Weston to Brown, 24 June 1937; "Muskingum Conservancy Development" draft; Weston to Browning, 2 February 1937; telephone conversation transcript, David Williams to Weston, 12 June 1937; Penfold, "Prospectus of Youth Activities Possible in the MWCD"; all in box 714, file "Muskingum," NYA Papers, NA; Penfold, "Prospectus," 1–4.

35. H. V. Gilson to Mark A. McCloskey, 14 October 1940, box 173, file "Region II," Resident Center Correspondence, NYA Papers, NA.

36. Johnson to Harvey, 30 January 1938, box 11, file "NYA and WPA," President's Advisory Committee on Education Papers, FDRL; the PACE, appointed on 19 September 1936, was to report on "the experience under the existing program of federal aid for vocational education, the relation of such training to general education and to prevailing economic and social conditions, and the extent of the need for an expanded program of federal aid for vocational education." See Palmer O. Johnson and Oswald L. Harvey, *The National Youth Administration* (Washington, D.C.: U.S. Government Printing Office, 1938), iii.

37. "Digest of Proceedings at National Advisory Committee Meeting, Lowrey

Hotel, St. Paul, Minnesota, October 31 and November 1, 1938," Records of the National Advisory Committee, NYA Papers, NA, 3–4.

Eight. An Agency Without Borders

1. David S. Wyman, *Paper Walls: America and the Refugee Crisis, 1938–1941* (New York: Pantheon, 1968, 1985), 27–37.

2. Ibid., 14–26; Dorothy Thompson, "Refugees: A World Problem," *Foreign Affairs* 16 (April 1938): 387.

3. Wyman, *Paper Walls*, 10–14, 43–45; Clarence E. Pickett, "Difficulties in the Placement of Refugees," *Annals of the American Academy of Political and Social Sciences* 203 (May 1939): 94–98.

4. Eric Estorick, "The Evian Conference and the Intergovernmental Committee," *Annals of the American Academy of Political and Social Sciences* 203 (May 1939): 136–41; Wyman, *Paper Walls*, 43–45.

5. Thacher Winslow to Charles W. Taussig, 29 September 1938; "Report on Refugee Youth" (undated final draft, ca. 1940), file "Refugees 1938," box 14, Taussig Papers, FDRL.

6. Wyman, *Paper Walls*, 57–62; Sumner Welles to FDR, 11 April 1938, OF 3186, FDRL; "Memorandum on White House Conference on Refugees," 13 April 1938; General Files, American Friends Service Committee Archives.

7. Wyman, *Paper Walls*, 57–62; Rosenman, *Public Papers of FDR* 8:1–3; Divine, *The Reluctant Belligerent*, 60–64.

8. *Newsweek*, 4 April 1938, 11; quoted by Wyman, *Paper Walls*, 44.

9. Erika Mann and Eric Estorick, "Private and Governmental Aid of Refugees," *Annals of the American Academy of Political and Social Sciences* 203 (May 1939): 146; Dorothy Thompson, "Escape in a Frozen World," *Survey Graphic* 28 (February 1939): 93–96; International Student Service, Information Circular, 1938–39, no. 1 "Relief for Austrian Students," October 1938, book 148, Morgenthau Diaries, FDRL. For Roosevelt's aid to refugees, see Richard Breitman and Alan M. Kraut, *American Refugee Policy and European Jewry, 1933–1945* (Bloomington: Indiana University Press, 1987), 222–35.

10. "Report on Refugee Youth" (undated final draft, ca. 1940), file "Refugees 1939–1941," box 14, Taussig Papers, FDRL; Wyman, *Paper Walls*, 168–69.

11. Mann and Estorick, "Private and Governmental Aid of Refugees," 146; de Sola Pool to Taussig, 5 May 1938; Taussig to de Sola Pool, 14 May 1938, file "Refugees 1938," box 14, Taussig Papers, FDRL.

12. de Sola Pool to Taussig, 5 May 1938, file "Refugees 1938," box 14, Taussig Papers, FDRL.

13. Taussig to de Sola Pool, 14 May 1938; "Report on Refugee Youth" (undated final draft, ca. 1940), file "Refugees 1939–1941"; de Sola Pool to Taussig, 16 May 1938, file "Refugees 1938"; both in box 14, Taussig Papers, FDRL.

14. Karl D. Hesley to Richard R. Brown, 26 May 1938; S. Burns Weston to Brown, 3 June 1938, file "Refugees 1938"; both in box 14, Taussig Papers, FDRL.

15. "Report on Refugee Youth" (undated preliminary draft, ca. 1940), file "National Advisory Committee," box 6, Taussig Papers, FDRL.

16. Thacher Winslow to Taussig, 29 September 1938, file "Refugees 1938," box 14, Taussig Papers, FDRL; Wyman, *Paper Walls*, 26.

17. Winslow to Taussig, 29 September 1938, file "Refugees 1938," box 14, Taussig Papers, FDRL; Winslow, *Youth: A World Problem*, 30–45.

18. Winslow to Taussig, 29 September 1938, file "Refugees 1938," box 14, Taussig Papers, FDRL.

19. *New York Times*, 9 September 1938, p. 1, col. 4; Winslow to Taussig, 28 September 1938, file "Refugees 1938," box 14, Taussig Papers, FDRL.

20. "Report on Refugee Youth" (undated final draft, ca. 1940), file "Refugees 1939–1941," box 14, Taussig Papers, FDRL.

21. Taussig to de Sola Pool, 4 October 1938, file "Refugees 1938," box 14, Taussig Papers, FDRL; *New York Times*, 18 November 1938, p. 2, col. 2.

22. U.S. Federal Security Agency, *Final Report of the NYA*, 131.

23. Ibid.

24. Leo Erber, Ernest Gertler, Stephen Loeb, and Theodore Advokat to "Mr. Goldman," 22 January 1939, file "Refugees 1939–1941," box 14, Taussig Papers, FDRL.

25. "Digest of Proceedings at National Advisory Committee Meeting, Lowrey Hotel, St. Paul, Minnesota, October 31 and November 1, 1938," Records of the National Advisory Committee NYA Papers, NA, 3.

26. Johnson to FDR, 12 August 1938, box 4, file "White House," Aubrey Williams Papers, FDRL.

27. U.S. Federal Security Agency, *Final Report of the NYA*, 27–28; Richard Polenberg, *Reorganizing Roosevelt's Government: The Controversy over Executive Reorganization, 1936–1939* (Cambridge: Harvard University Press, 1966), 187–88.

28. U.S. Federal Security Agency, *Final Report of the NYA*, 13–14.

29. Wayne S. Cole, *Roosevelt and the Isolationists, 1933–1945* (Lincoln: University of Nebraska Press, 1983), 424–26; Manfred Jonas, *Isolationism in America, 1935–1941* (Ithaca: Cornell University Press, 1966), 215; Robert Dallek, *Franklin D. Roosevelt and American Foreign Policy*, 252–61, 271–72.

30. U.S. Federal Security Agency, *Final Report of the NYA*, 28–29, 55.

31. Ibid., 180.

32. A 1942 report presented to the president by Taussig recommended "con-

tinuation of a youth program for reconstruction and reorientation after the war." The report, completed in March, noted that in terms of the distribution of the youth population in the country, "thirty-six states received less than their proportionate share of defense contracts when these contracts were related to youth population; twenty-two of these thirty-six states received less than half their proportionate share." The report estimated that there were fifty depressed areas in the United States, with a total population of thirteen million, receiving only 1.5 percent of the nation's defense contracts. As a result of these factors, Taussig wrote, "in these [depressed] areas youth continues to need, and to need badly, those services that the NYA has rendered in the past." See *New York Times*, 23 March 1942, p. 27, col. 1.

33. Williams added: "I am coupling with this program a re-emphasizing of all phases of work that have to do with the comprehension of meaning of democratic living in this country. . . . I am fully satisfied in my own mind that our duty in this whole thing is so very, very clear that to mistake it and to fail is to fail Democratic Government [*sic*] itself." It was "because I don't believe in the Army" that he wanted the NYA rather than some branch of the armed services to organize young people for defense work. "I know people are going to say we have sold the Youth Administration down the river but I am not worried about that." Williams to conferences of state directors, 11 November 1938, box 653, second file, NYA Records, NA; see also Salmond, *A Southern Rebel*, 142.

34. Salmond, *A Southern Rebel*, 144; U.S. Department of Commerce, *Historical Statistics of the United States*, 1:357.

35. Salmond, *A Southern Rebel*, 143–46.

36. Ibid.

37. Ibid.; "What Will Happen to Colonies?" *Newsweek*, 3 January 1944, 70–74; interview with S. Burns Weston, Keene, New York, 28 and 29 September 1982.

38. Salmond, "Aubrey Williams: Atypical New Dealer?" in *The New Deal: The National Level*, ed. John Braeman, David Brody, and Robert H. Bremner (Columbus: Ohio State University Press, 1974), 229–30.

39. Quotations are drawn from U.S. Senate, Committee on Education and Labor, *A Bill to Provide for the Termination of the National Youth Administration and Civilian Conservation Corps*, 23 March–17 April 1942, 77th Cong., 2d sess., S. 2295 (Washington, D.C.: U.S. Government Printing Office, 1942), 569–76, 642, 644.

40. Ibid., 569–76, 642, 644.

41. Ibid., 569–76, 642–44.

Nine. New Deal Youth in the American Memory

1. Those who emphasize the New Deal's deep historical roots include Leuchten-burg, *FDR and the New Deal*, 64–66, 129–33; Frank Freidel, *Franklin D. Roosevelt: Launching the New Deal*, 63–82; and Maury Klein, "The New Deal: End of a Beginning," *American History Illustrated* 8 (October 1973): 18–27, 30–32. For other perspectives see the debate condensed in Richard S. Kirkendall, ed., *The New Deal: The Historical Debate* (New York: John Wiley, 1973); and Kirkendall, "The Great Depression: Another Watershed in American History?" in *Change and Continuity in Twentieth-Century America*, ed. John Braeman, Robert H. Bremner, and Everett Walters (Columbus: Ohio State University Press, 1964), 145–89.

2. See, for instance, Paul K. Conkin, *Tomorrow a New World: The New Deal Community Program* (Ithaca: Cornell University Press, 1959); Barton J. Bernstein, "The New Deal: The Conservative Achievements of Liberal Reform," in *Towards a New Past: Dissenting Essays in American History*, ed. Barton J. Bernstein (New York: Pantheon, 1968), 263–88.

3. One such perspective, that of the New Left, is best represented by Bernstein, "The New Deal," 263–388. For a critique of the New Left position see Jerold S. Auerbach, "The New Deal, Old Deal, or Raw Deal: Some Thoughts on New Left Historiography," *Journal of Southern History* 35 (February 1969): 18–30.

4. Examples include Lindley and Lindley, *A New Deal for Youth*, 6–16; Winifred D. Wandersee, "ER and American Youth: Politics and Personality in a Bureau cratic Age," in *Without Precedent: The Life and Career of Eleanor Roosevelt*, ed. Joan Hoff-Wilson (Bloomington: Indiana University Press, 1984), 63–68; Lash, *Eleanor and Franklin*.

5. The quotation is of a statement by Ruby Black, who wrote in her 1940 biography of Eleanor Roosevelt that the First Lady had inspired the NYA in the sense of "causing something to exist and keeping it on its toes." While Eleanor Roosevelt unquestionably accomplished the latter, it is doubtful that she was indispensable to the NYA's existence. The intelligence of Eleanor Roosevelt, more than her heart, is clearer in more recent biographies. Cited by Lash, *Eleanor and Franklin*, 541.

6. For the New Deal's reluctance to engage in a sustained effort at social planning, see Leuchtenburg, *FDR and the New Deal*, 164–65.

7. For the important place that the idea of "culture" occupied in the American imagination of the 1930s, and the New Deal as well, see Warren I. Susman, "The Thirties," in *The Development of an American Culture*, ed. Stanley Coben and Lorman Ratner (Englewood Cliffs, N.J.: Prentice-Hall, 1970), 179–218; David Glassberg, "History and the Public: Legacies of the Progressive Era," *Journal of American History* 73 (March 1987): 957–80.

8. Recipients of New Deal assistance could not rely on need alone to receive

assistance, as the failure of two "compassionate" bills reveals. John A. Salmond, "The Civilian Conservation Corps and the Negro," *Journal of American History* 52 (June 1965): 75–88; Fred Greenbaum, "The Anti-Lynching Bill of 1935: The Irony of Equal Justice—under Law," *Journal of Human Relations* 15 (Third Quarter 1967): 72–85.

9. Salmond, *The CCC*, 15–29.

10. Harrison Doty, "Our Forest Army at War," *Review of Reviews* 88 (July 1933): 30–31; Roosevelt's message to Congress, 21 March 1933, in Nixon, *FDR and Conservation*, 144; "The Doughboys of 1933 Off to the Woods," *Literary Digest* 15 (29 April 1933): 22–23; "First of Army of Idle Now in Camp," *Newsweek*, 15 April 1933, 6; Roosevelt's remarks are in Harold L. Ickes, *The Secret Diary of Harold L. Ickes: The First Thousand Days, 1933–1936* (New York: Simon and Schuster, 1953), 78–80; "Conservation Army Starts Its Second Half Year," *Newsweek*, 7 October 1933, 10.

11. On 2 September 1935 Roosevelt told Roy Howard that he anticipated "a breathing spell" for further New Deal initiatives, claiming that "the basic program . . . has now reached substantial completion" (Rosenman, *Public Papers of FDR*, 4:354–57).

12. Charles P. Taft, Jr., *You and I—and Roosevelt* (New York: Farrar and Rinehart, 1936), 90; Mrs. Meyer is quoted in Edwin P. Hoyt, *The Tempering Years* (New York: Charles Scribner's Sons, 1963), 203; Lindley and Lindley, *A New Deal for Youth*, 15–16.

13. The climate of ideas in consensus America formed the milieu in which some of America's most distinguished historians approached the NYA; they tended to sketch it as a junior WPA of significance only to students of relief and New Deal politics. Hofstadter, Basil Rauch, Mary Ritter Beard, and Charles Beard all wrote of the NYA as an agency with ambitions seemingly as modest as its accomplishments. In 1939 the Beards implied that only young people in high school and college were able "to stretch out [their] education" under the NYA, and that helping 2.3 million youths attend high schools and colleges formed the sum total of its activities. Basil Rauch wrote in 1944 that the NYA's main object was "to return young people to schools and colleges and otherwise prepare them for socially constructive careers." As late as 1956, the NYA seemed to James MacGregor Burns to be an agency whose central significance was its role in helping "thousands of hard-pressed high school and college students to continue their education." See Basil Rauch, *The History of the New Deal, 1933–1938* (New York: Creative Age Press, 1944), 169; Charles Beard and Mary Beard, *America in Mid-Passage* (New York: Macmillan, 1939), 865; James MacGregor Burns, *Roosevelt: The Lion and the Fox* (New York: Harcourt, Brace, and World, 1956), 267; Daniel Bell, *The End of Ideology: On the Exhaustion of Political Ideas in the Fifties* (New York: Macmillan,

1960), 369–75; Richard Hofstadter, *The American Political Tradition and the Men Who Made It* (New York: Alfred A. Knopf, 1948), 311–47; George E. Mowry, *The Urban Nation, 1920–1960* (New York: Hill and Wang, 1965), 95, 123–28.

14. See U.S. Senate, *A Bill to Provide for the Termination of the National Youth Administration and Civilian Conservation Corps*, 569–76; Burns, *Roosevelt*, 267; Schlesinger, *The Politics of Upheaval*, 434.

15. *Congressional Record*, 79th Cong., 1st sess., 1945, 91, pt. 2: 2479.

16. See Richard A. Reiman, "Aubrey Williams: A Southern New Dealer in the Civil Rights Movement, 1945–1965," *Alabama Review* 43 (July 1990): 195–99; Salmond, *A Southern Rebel*, 201–2, 219–46.

17. Rawick was interested in radical youth movements early in his career, before undertaking his better-known research on slavery based on slave sources. His verdict on the NYA is found in his doctoral dissertation, "The New Deal and Youth," 172–90.

18. Not atypical of the postwar memoirs were the recollections of Mary McLeod Bethune, former head of the NYA's Division of Negro Affairs. In the late 1940s Bethune wrote as if all the threads of New Deal reform ran through the hands of Franklin Roosevelt and that his giant heart provided sufficient explanation for his reformist actions and intentions. When she met with Roosevelt, the president "grasped my hands," she later wrote, while "tears flowed from his eyes," and went "coursing down his cheeks." If FDR was so demonstrably moved by the determined lady who represented minority programs that he broke down in tears, Aubrey Williams (who was in the room at the time) would probably have remembered it. But at a time of liberal retreat, Bethune's memoirs contributed to the immediate needs of liberalism while adding to the historiographical personification of the NYA's origins. Mary McLeod Bethune, "My Secret Talks with FDR," *Ebony* 4 (April 1949), in *The Negro in Depression and War: Prelude to Revolution, 1930–1945*, ed. Bernard Sternsher (Chicago: Quadrangle, 1969), 57–59.

19. Eleanor Roosevelt, *This I Remember* (New York: Harper and Brothers, 1949), 162–63; Fulton Oursler, *Behold This Dreamer!* (Boston: Little, Brown, 1964), 395–400.

20. Arthur M. Schlesinger, Jr., *The Age of Roosevelt: The Coming of the New Deal* (Boston: Houghton Mifflin, 1958), 337–41; Schlesinger, *The Politics of Upheaval*, 434.

21. Undoubtedly the most energetic publicist for the NYA during the mid-1960s was the president of the United States. If, as William Leuchtenburg observed, Lyndon B. Johnson felt compelled to outperform his political mentor, FDR, it may account for the somewhat self-serving comparisons he often drew between the NYA and his own youth programs. In any case, Johnson seldom got the NYA's priorities right in his frequent retelling of the story of the New Deal and youth. What resulted were misleading contrasts between his own antipoverty programs

for youth (Job Corps and Upward Bound) and the NYA. The NYA appeared from Johnson's description as a program for the elite few, one that lifted that few to the top of the nation's leadership. Only rarely did LBJ describe the NYA as "a poverty program, a poor program, . . . in many ways similar to the program that we have today in the Job Corps, Neighborhood Youth Corps and Upward Bound." More frequently, Johnson's references to the agency were replete with the names of famous men among its alumni (Sargent Shriver and Texas governor John Connally among others). This was not wrong, but it did prevent a separation of the NYA's deeds from its designs, the two separate aspects of its significance.

To a 1967 conference of women enlisted in the War on Poverty, Johnson told a story he was to repeat a year later to student winners of a rural electrification contest: "I was on a Job Corps platform down in my state not long ago. I was speaking. As I looked down the list I saw a Governor that had been on the NYA. I saw a Congressman who had been on NYA. I saw a Chairman of the State Board of Regents who had been on NYA. So that is what happens. I see a Congressman today who was in the NYA over here. I am not going to look much more. It would take too much time from my speech." Like LBJ, some scholars have described the NYA in Nathan Miller's terms, as a "springboard for a new generation of political leaders." Miller, *FDR: An Intimate History*, 386–89; William E. Leuchtenburg, *In the Shadow of FDR: From Harry Truman to Ronald Reagan* (Ithaca: Cornell University Press, 1983), 121–61; *Public Papers of the Presidents: Lyndon B. Johnson, 1963–1964* (Washington, D.C.: U.S. Government Printing Office, 1965), vol. 1, 1963–1964, 53, 289; *Public Papers: Johnson, 1967* (Washington, D.C.: U.S. Government Printing Office, 1968), 1:515; *Public Papers: Johnson, 1968* (Washington, D.C.: U.S. Government Printing Office, 1970), 1:289, 708; Galbraith is quoted in Charles R. Morris, *A Time of Passion: America, 1960–1980* (New York: Viking Press, 1984), 91–96.

22. Morris, *A Time of Passion*, 92–93; Allan J. Matusow, *The Unraveling of America: A History of Liberalism in the 1960s* (New York: Harper and Row, 1984), 237–42.

23. Alfred Steinberg, *Mrs. R: The Life of Eleanor Roosevelt* (New York: G. P. Putnam's Sons, 1958), 268, 227–28; Lash, *Eleanor Roosevelt*, 3.

24. Tamara K. Hareven, *Eleanor Roosevelt: An American Conscience* (Chicago: Quadrangle, 1968), 71.

25. Joseph R. Kearney, *Anna Eleanor Roosevelt: The Evolution of a Reformer* (Boston: Houghton Mifflin, 1968), 25, 69.

26. Joseph P. Lash, *Eleanor and Franklin*, 537.

27. See Charles H. Trout, *Boston, the Great Depression and the New Deal* (New York: Oxford University Press, 1977), 310–16; Lyle W. Dorsett, *Franklin D. Roosevelt and the City Bosses* (Port Washington, N.Y.: Kennikat Press, 1977), 112–16; Tyack et al., *Public Schools in Hard Times*, 103–38. According to the

latter, "FDR's conservative impulse to leave institutions intact was tempered by his humanitarian desire to help the needy."

28. "New Conservation Corps a Sensible, Workable Idea," *Akron Beacon Journal*, 3 March 1983, A6; "Boost for Tomorrow's Workers Here and Now," *New York Times*, 8 December 1983.

29. Loucheim, *The Making of the New Deal*, introduction, 298–300. See note 21, above.

30. Robert A. Caro, *The Years of Lyndon Johnson: The Path to Power* (New York: Alfred A. Knopf, 1982), 341, 343–44.

31. Salmond, *A Southern Rebel*, 72–77, 81–84, 144-45.

Bibliography

Newspapers and Manuscripts

Akron Beacon Journal
Harry L. Hopkins Papers. Franklin D. Roosevelt Library, Hyde Park, New York.
New York Times
President's Official File. Franklin D. Roosevelt Library, Hyde Park, New York.
President's Personal File. Franklin D. Roosevelt Library, Hyde Park, New York.
Records of the Federal Emergency Relief Administration. Record Group 69. National Archives.
Records of the National Youth Administration. Record Group 119. National Archives.
Records of the United States Office of Education. Record Group 12. National Archives.
Eleanor Roosevelt Papers. Franklin D. Roosevelt Library, Hyde Park, New York.
Franklin D. Roosevelt Library. *Complete Presidential Conferences of Franklin D. Roosevelt*. New York: Da Capo Press, 1972.
Charles W. Taussig Papers. Franklin D. Roosevelt Library, Hyde Park, New York.
Aubrey W. Williams Papers. Franklin D. Roosevelt Library, Hyde Park, New York.

Government Documents

Congressional Record. Washington, D.C.
U.S. Bureau of the Census. *Historical Statistics of the United States: Colo-*

nial Times to the Present. Washington, D.C.: U.S. Government Printing
Office, 1975.

U.S. Bureau of Labor Statistics. *Monthly Labor Review* 38 (May 1934): 1120–23.

U.S. Children's Bureau. *Infant Mortality: Results of a Field Study in Gary, Indiana.* Bureau Publication 112. Washington, D.C.: U.S. Government Printing
Office, 1923.

———. *The Promotion of the Welfare and Hygiene of Maternity and Infancy.*
Washington, D.C.: U.S. Government Printing Office, 1930.

U.S. Congress. House of Representatives. *Hearings before the Select Committee
to Investigate the Interstate Migration of Destitute Citizens.* 29–31 July 1940.
76th Congress, 3d session, 1940.

U.S. Congress. Senate. Committee on Education and Labor. *A Bill to Provide for
the Termination of the National Youth Administration and the Civilian Conservation Corps.* 23 March–17 April 1942. 77th Congress, 2d session, 1942.
S. 2295.

———. *Employment for Graduates of Educational Institutions.* 74th Congress,
1st session, 1935. Document 45.

U.S. Department of Interior. *Effects of the Depression on Public Elementary and
Secondary Schools and upon Colleges and Universities.* Washington, D.C.:
U.S. Government Printing Office, 1938.

U.S. Department of Labor. *Baby-Saving Campaigns: A Preliminary Report on
What American Cities Are Doing to Prevent Infant Mortality.* Bureau Publication 3. Washington, D.C.: U.S. Government Printing Office, 1914.

———. Children's Bureau. *Standards of Child Welfare.* Bureau Publication 60.
Washington, D.C.: U.S. Government Printing Office, 1919.

U.S. Federal Emergency Relief Administration. *Monthly Report of the Federal Emergency Relief Administration.* Washington, D.C.: U.S. Government
Printing Office, 1933–35.

U.S. Federal Security Agency. *Final Report of the National Youth Administration.* Washington, D.C.: U.S. Government Printing Office, 1944.

U.S. Office of the Federal Register. *Public Papers of the Presidents of the
United States: Herbert Hoover.* Washington, D.C.: U.S. Government Printing
Office, 1974.

———. *Public Papers of the Presidents of the United States: John F. Kennedy.*
Washington, D.C.: U.S. Government Printing Office, 1964.

———. *Public Papers of the Presidents of the United States: Lyndon B. Johnson.*
Washington, D.C.: U.S. Government Printing Office, 1970.

Interviews and Unpublished Dissertations

Interview with S. Burns Weston, Keene, New York, 28–29 September 1982.

Rawick, George P. "The New Deal and Youth: The Civilian Conservation Corps, the National Youth Administration and the American Youth Congress." Ph.D. dissertation, University of Wisconsin, 1957.

Wladaver-Morgan, Susan. "Young Women and the New Deal: Camps and Resident Centers, 1933–1943." Ph.D. dissertation, Indiana University, 1982.

Books and Articles

Aaron, Daniel, and Robert Bendiner, comps. *The Strenuous Decade*. New York: Anchor Books, 1970.

Addams, Jane. *The Spirit of Youth and the City Streets*. New York: Macmillan, 1909.

Alderman, Lewis R. "The Emergency Education Program." *School Life* 19 (June 1934): 216–17.

"Lewis R. Alderman." *Who's Who in America*. Vol. 18: *1934–1935*. Chicago: A. N. Marquis, 1934.

Alexander, Charles C. *Nationalism in American Thought, 1930–1945*. Chicago: Rand McNally, 1969.

Alper, Benedict S., and George E. Lodgen. "Youth Without Work." *Survey* 70 (September 1943): 285–86.

Beard, Charles, and Mary Beard. *America in Mid-Passage*. New York: Macmillan, 1939.

Bell, Howard M. *Youth Tell Their Story*. Washington, D.C.: American Council on Education, 1938.

Bellush, Bernard. *The Failure of the NRA*. New York: Norton, 1975.

Bergman, Andrew. *We're in the Money: Depression America and Its Films*. New York: New York University Press, 1971.

Bernstein, Irving. *A Caring Society: The New Deal, the Worker and the Great Depression*. Boston: Houghton Mifflin, 1985.

————. *Turbulent Years: A History of the American Worker, 1933–1941*. Boston: Houghton Mifflin, 1970.

Bethune, Mary McLeod. "My Secret Talks with FDR." *Ebony* 4 (April 1949). In *The Negro in Depression and War: Prelude to Revolution, 1930–1945*, ed. Bernard Sternsher. Chicago: Quadrangle, 1969.

Blum, John M. *From the Morgenthau Diaries: Years of Crisis, 1928–1938*. Boston: Houghton Mifflin, 1959.

————. *V Was for Victory: Politics and American Culture during World War II*. New York: Harcourt, Brace, Jovanovich, 1976.

Boutwell, William Dow. "The Emergency Agencies and Education." *Congressional Digest* 2 (February 1934): 39, 64.

Braucher, Howard. "Do We Really Care?" *Recreation* 29 (November 1935): 377.

————. "The National Recreation Movement and the Federal Government." *Recreation* 29 (December 1935): 440.

Breitman, Richard, and Alan M. Kraut. *American Refugee Policy and European Jewry, 1933–1945*. Bloomington: Indiana University Press, 1987.

Bremner, Robert H., ed. *Children and Youth in America: A Documentary History, 1866–1932*. Cambridge: Harvard University Press, 1971.

Browder, Earl. *Communism in the United States*. New York: International Publishers, 1935.

————. *The People's Front*. New York: International Publishers, 1938.

Brown, Josephine C. *Public Relief, 1929–1939*. New York: Henry Holt, 1940.

Bryson, Lyman. "Education for What?" *Survey Graphic* 22 (December 1933): 619–22, 638–39.

Burner, David. *Herbert Hoover: A Public Life*. New York: Alfred A. Knopf, 1979.

————. *The Politics of Provincialism: The Democratic Party in Transition, 1918–1932*. New York: Alfred A. Knopf, 1968.

Burns, James MacGregor. *Roosevelt: The Lion and the Fox*. New York: Harcourt, Brace, and World, 1956.

Caro, Robert A. *The Years of Lyndon Johnson: The Path to Power*. New York: Alfred A. Knopf, 1982.

Carter, Dan T. *Scottsboro: A Tragedy of the American South*. Baton Rouge: Louisiana State University Press, 1969.

Chambers, Clarke A. *A Seedtime for Reform: American Social Service and Social Action*. Minneapolis: University of Minnesota Press, 1963.

Chambers, M. M. *Youth-Serving Organizations*. Washington, D.C.: American Council on Education, 1941.

Charles, Searle. *Minister of Relief: Harry Hopkins and the Great Depression*. Syracuse: Syracuse University Press, 1963.

Chase, Harry Woodburn. "The Outlook for Youth in American Life." In *Planning the Future with Youth*, ed. S. M. Keeny. New York: Association Press, 1936.

Cole, Wayne S. *Roosevelt and the Isolationists, 1933–1945*. Lincoln: University of Nebraska Press, 1983.

"Conservation Corps Army Starts Its Second Half Year." *Newsweek*, 7 October 1933.

Courtis, S. A. "A Philosophy of Reconstruction in Public Education." *The Nation's Schools* 13 (June 1934): 20–22.

Dallek, Robert. *Democrat and Diplomat: The Life of William E. Dodd*. New York: Oxford University Press, 1968.

———. *Franklin D. Roosevelt and American Foreign Policy, 1932–1945*. New York: Oxford University Press, 1979.

"Dangers in the National Youth Program." *School Review* 43 (September 1935): 481–85.

Daniels, Roger. *The Bonus March: An Episode in the Great Depression*. Westport, Conn.: Greenwood Press, 1972.

Davis, Maxine. *The Lost Generation*. New York: Macmillan, 1936.

Demos, John, and Virginia Demos. "Adolescence in Historical Perspective." *Journal of Marriage and the Family* 31 (November 1969): 632–38.

Doty, Harrison. "Our Forest Army at War." *Review of Reviews* 88 (July 1933): 30–31.

"The Doughboys of 1933 Off to the Woods." *Literary Digest* 115 (29 April 1933): 22–23.

Droze, Wilmon H. "The New Deal's Shelterbelt Project, 1934–1942." In *Essays on the New Deal*, ed. Harold M. Hollingsworth and William F. Holmes. Arlington: University of Texas Press, 1969.

Durr, Virginia F. *Outside the Magic Circle: The Autobiography of Virginia Foster Durr*. University: University of Alabama Press, 1985.

Educational Policies Commission. *The Civilian Conservation Corps, the National Youth Administration and the Public Schools*. Washington, D.C.: National Education Association, 1941.

Farley, Belmont. "The 1933 Convention in Chicago." *NEA Journal* 22 (October 1933): 173–74.

Fass, Paula S. *The Damned and the Beautiful: American Youth in the 1920s*. New York: Oxford University Press, 1977.

Federal Security Agency. *Youth on the Student Work Program*. Washington, D.C.: U.S. Government Printing Office, 1940.

Fine, Sidney. *The Automobile under the Blue Eagle: Labor, Management and the Automobile Manufacturing Code*. Ann Arbor: University of Michigan Press, 1963.

"First of Army of Idle Now in Camp." *Newsweek*, 15 April 1933.

Freidel, Frank. *Franklin D. Roosevelt: Launching the New Deal*. Boston: Little, Brown, 1973.

———. *Franklin D. Roosevelt: The Ordeal*. Boston: Little, Brown, 1954.

Graves, Frank Pierrepont. "President Roosevelt and Education." *NEA Journal* 22 (March 1933): 75–76.

Greer, Thomas H. *What Roosevelt Thought*. East Lansing: Michigan State University Press, 1958.

Hall, G. Stanley. *Adolescence: Its Psychology and Its Relations to Physiology, Anthropology, Sociology, Sex, Crime, Religion, and Education.* New York: D. Appleton, 1904.

Hareven, Tamara. *Eleanor Roosevelt: An American Conscience.* Chicago: Quadrangle, 1968.

Hofstadter, Richard. *The Age of Reform: From Bryan to FDR.* New York: Basic Books, 1977.

————. *The American Political Tradition and the Men Who Made It.* New York: Alfred A. Knopf, 1948.

Holland, Kenneth. "Work Camps for Youth." In *American Youth: An Enforced Renaissance,* ed. Thacher Winslow and Frank P. Davidson. Cambridge: Harvard University Press, 1940.

————. *Youth in European Labor Camps: A Report to the American Youth Commission.* Washington, D.C.: American Council on Education, 1939.

Hoover, Herbert. *Further Addresses upon the American Road, 1938–1940.* New York: Charles Scribner's Sons, 1940.

————. *The New Day: Campaign Speeches of Herbert Hoover.* Stanford: Stanford University Press, 1928.

Howard, Donald. *The WPA and Federal Relief Policy.* New York: Russell Sage Foundation, 1943.

Hoyt, Edwin P. *The Tempering Years.* New York: Charles Scribner's Sons, 1963.

Ickes, Harold L. *The Secret Diary of Harold L. Ickes: The First Thousand Days, 1933–1936.* New York: Simon and Schuster, 1953.

Johnson, Palmer O., and Oswald L. Harvey. *The National Youth Administration.* Washington, D.C.: U.S. Government Printing Office, 1938.

Jonas, Manfred. *Isolationism in America, 1935–1941.* Ithaca: Cornell University Press, 1966.

Judd, Charles H. "The Real Youth Problem." *School and Society* 55 (10 January 1942): 29–33.

Kazin, Alfred. *On Native Grounds: An Interpretation of Modern American Prose Literature.* New York: Raynal and Hitchcock, 1942.

Kearney, Joseph R. *Anna Eleanor Roosevelt: The Evolution of a Reformer.* Boston: Houghton Mifflin, 1968.

Kett, Joseph. *Rites of Passage: Adolescence in America, 1790 to the Present.* New York: Basic Books, 1977.

Kimball, Robert, and Alfred E. Simons. *The Gershwins.* New York: Atheneum, 1973.

Kirby, John B. *Black Americans in the Roosevelt Era: Liberalism and Race.* Knoxville: University of Tennessee Press, 1979.

Lash, Joseph P. *Eleanor and Franklin: The Story of Their Relationship.* New York: W. W. Norton, 1971.

————. *Eleanor Roosevelt: A Friend's Memoir.* Garden City, N.Y.: Double-day, 1964.

Leuchtenburg, William E. *Franklin D. Roosevelt and the New Deal, 1932–1940.* New York: Harper and Row, 1963.

————. *In the Shadow of FDR: From Harry Truman to Ronald Reagan.* Ithaca: Cornell University Press, 1983.

Lindley, Ernest K., and Betty Lindley. *A New Deal for Youth: The Story of the National Youth Administration.* New York: Viking Press, 1938.

Link, Arthur S. "What Happened to the Progressive Movement in the 1920s?" *American Historical Review* 64 (1959): 833–51.

Loucheim, Katie. *The Making of the New Deal: The Insiders Speak.* Cambridge: Harvard University Press, 1983.

Lubove, Roy. *The Professional Altruist: The Emergence of Social Work as a Career.* Cambridge: Harvard University Press, 1965.

Lynd, Robert S., and Helen M. Lynd. *Middletown: A Study in Contemporary American Culture.* New York: Harcourt, Brace, 1929.

Manchester, William. *The Glory and the Dream: A Narrative History of America, 1932–1972.* Boston: Little, Brown, 1973.

Matusow, Allan J. *The Unraveling of America: A History of Liberalism in the 1960s.* New York: Harper and Row, 1984.

Minehan, Thomas J. *Boy and Girl Tramps of America.* New York: Farrar and Rinehart, 1934.

Moehlman, Arthur B. "Looking Forward." *The Nation's Schools* 12 (August 1933): 9–10.

Morgan, Joy Elmer. "The New Deal and the Schools." *NEA Journal* 22 (November 1933): 201.

————. "The Schools and the Present Crisis." *NEA Journal* 22 (March 1933): 71.

————. "The Significance of 1933." *NEA Journal* 22 (December 1933): 239–41.

Mort, Paul R. "The National Government Must Take Part in Financing Education." *The Nation's Schools* 13 (January 1934): 21.

Mowry, George E. *The Era of Theodore Roosevelt, 1900–1912.* New York: Harper and Row, 1958.

National Education Association of the United States. *Proceedings of the Seventy-first Annual Meeting Held at Chicago, Illinois, July 1–7, 1933.* Vol. 71. Washington, D.C.: National Education Association, 1933.

Nixon, Edgar B., comp. and ed. *Franklin D. Roosevelt and Conservation.* Hyde Park, N.Y.: National Archives and Records Services, 1957.

Norton, John K. "Testing Candidates for Congress." *NEA Journal* 23 (October 1934): 177–78.

Oursler, Fulton. *Behold This Dreamer!* Boston: Little, Brown, 1964.

Parks, Gordon. *A Choice of Weapons.* New York: Harper and Row, 1965.

"Pictures by *Life* Prove Facts in 'Grapes of Wrath.'" *Life*, 19 February 1940, 10–11.

Polenberg, Richard. *Reorganizing Roosevelt's Government: The Controversy over Executive Reorganizations, 1936–1939*. Cambridge: Harvard University Press, 1966.

Pollard, James E. *The History of the Ohio State University: Its First Seventy-five Years, 1873–1948*. Columbus: Ohio State University Press, 1952.

Potter, Milton C. "The School's Role in the New Era Is Theme for Convention." *The Nation's Schools* 11 (January 1933): 52.

President's Research Committee on Social Trends. *Recent Social Trends in the United States*. New York: McGraw-Hill, 1933.

Rauch, Basil. *The History of the New Deal, 1933–1938*. New York: Creative Age Press, 1944.

Robinson, Edgar E. *The Roosevelt Leadership, 1933–1945*. Philadelphia: J. B. Lippincott, 1955.

Romasco, Albert U. *The Poverty of Abundance: Hoover, the Nation and the Depression*. New York: Oxford University Press, 1965.

Roosevelt, Eleanor. *This I Remember*. New York: Harper and Brothers, 1949.

Roosevelt, Elliott, ed. *FDR: His Personal Letters, 1928–1945*. Vol. 2. New York: Duell, Sloan, and Pierce, 1950.

Roosevelt, Franklin D. *The Press and Radio Conferences of Franklin D. Roosevelt, 1933–1945*. Franklin D. Roosevelt Library, comp. Hyde Park, N.Y.: National Historical Publications Commission, 1957.

Rosenman, Samuel I., comp. and ed. *The Public Papers and Addresses of Franklin D. Roosevelt*. New York: Random House and Harper and Brothers, 1934–45.

Salmond, John A. "Aubrey Williams: Atypical New Dealer?" In *The New Deal: The National Level*, ed. John Braeman, David Brody, and Robert H. Bremner. Columbus: Ohio State University Press, 1974.

————. *The Civilian Conservation Corps, 1933–1942: A New Deal Case Study*. Durham: Duke University Press, 1967.

————. *A Southern Rebel: The Life and Times of Aubrey Willis Williams, 1890–1965*. Chapel Hill: University of North Carolina Press, 1983.

Scharf, Lois. "The Forgotten Woman: Working Women, the New Deal and Women's Organizations." In *Decades of Discontent: The Women's Movement, 1920–1940*, ed. Scharf and Joan M. Jensen. Westport, Conn.: Greenwood Press, 1983.

Schlesinger, Arthur M., Jr. *The Age of Roosevelt: The Coming of the New Deal*. Boston: Houghton Mifflin, 1958.

————. *The Age of Roosevelt: The Politics of Upheaval*. Boston: Houghton Mifflin, 1960.

School Life. 18.9 (May 1933): 175; 19.10 (June 1934): 207; 18.10 (June 1933): 183; 22.1 (September 1936): 1–3; 22.9 (May 1937).

Sharpe, Russell T. "College and the Poor Boy." *Atlantic Monthly* 151 (June 1933): 703–5.

Sherwood, Robert. *Roosevelt and Hopkins: The Story of Their Relationship.* Boston: Houghton Mifflin, 1948.

Smith, Hilda W. "Resident Schools and Camps for Unemployed Women." Washington, D.C.: FERA mimeograph, 1934.

Sosna, Morton. *In Search of the Silent South: Southern Liberals and the Race Issue.* New York: Columbia University Press, 1977.

Stachura, Peter D. *The German Youth Movement: An Interpretative and Documentary History.* New York: St. Martin's Press, 1981.

Steinberg, Alfred. *Mrs. R.: The Life of Eleanor Roosevelt.* New York: G. P. Putnam's Sons, 1958.

Susman, Warren I. *Culture as History: The Transformation of American Society in the Twentieth Century.* New York: Pantheon Books, 1983.

Taft, Charles P. *You and I—and Roosevelt.* New York: Farrar and Rinehart, 1936.

"Charles W. Taussig." *National Cyclopedia of American Biography.* Vol. 36. New York: James T. White, 1950.

Terkel, Studs. *Hard Times: An Oral History of the Great Depression.* New York: Pantheon Books, 1970.

Tugwell, Rexford G. *The Brains Trust.* New York: Viking Press, 1968.

Tyack, David B., Robert Lowe, and Elizabeth Hansot. *Public Schools in Hard Times: The Great Depression and Recent Years.* Cambridge: Harvard University Press, 1984.

Wecter, Dixon. *The Age of the Great Depression, 1929–1941.* New York: Macmillan, 1948.

Weiss, Nancy J. *Farewell to the Party of Lincoln: Black Politics in the Age of FDR.* Princeton: Princeton University Press, 1983.

White, Graham J. *FDR and the Press.* Chicago: University of Chicago Press, 1965.

Williams, Edward A. *Federal Aid for Relief.* New York: Columbia University Press, 1939.

Winslow, Thacher. *Youth: A World Problem.* Washington, D.C.: Works Progress Administration, 1937.

Wohlforth, Robert. "Goosestepping the Jobless." *The World Tomorrow* 26 (15 February 1933): 155.

Wolfskill, George A., and John H. Hudson. *All but the People: Franklin D. Roosevelt and His Critics, 1933–1939.* New York: Macmillan, 1969.

Wyman, David S. *Paper Walls: America and the Refugee Crisis, 1938–1941*. New York: Pantheon, 1968.

"George F. Zook." *Who's Who in America*. Vol. 18: 1934–1935. Chicago: A. N. Marquis, 1934.

Index

243